LUDOBITES

ALSO BY
LUDO LEFEBVRE

CRAVE

LUDO BITES

RECIPES AND STORIES FROM THE POP-UP RESTAURANTS OF

LUDO LEFEBVRE

WITH JJ GOODE AND KRISSY LEFEBVRE

ecco

AN IMPRINT OF HARPERCOLLINS PUBLISHERS

FOR KRISSY, RÊVE, AND LUCA

HarperCollins books may be purchased for educational, business, or sales promotional use. For information please write: Special Markets Department, HarperCollins Publishers, 10 East 53rd Street, New York, NY 10022.

FIRST EDITION

Designed by Suet Yee Chong

Recipes tested and written by Rochelle Palermo

Library of Congress Cataloging-in-Publication Data has been applied for.

ISBN 978-0-06-211483-9

12 13 14 15 16 IND/QGT 10 9 8 7 6 5 4 3 2 1

 CONTENTS

ACKNOWLEDGMENTS

First and foremost we have to thank Daniel Halpern for being the coolest publisher out there. LudoBites may be a temporary restaurant with no permanent home, but you have memorialized this special moment in time in such a permanent way. You saw the vision, so . . . thank you. Thank you, Libby Edelson, for your patience with Krissy as a first-time writer, and thank you, Suet Chong, for weeding through 3,000+ blogger photos. Like LudoBites, this book has turned into a community effort.

LudoBites could not exist without our host restaurant partners, we are forever indebted to Ali Chabli (Breadbar); Susan Hancock (Royal/T); Mike Ilic (Gram & Papas); Andre Guerrero and Jan Purdy (Max); Josiah Citrin and Raphael Lunetta (Lemon Moon); and finally The Four Seasons at Hualālai Resort. Thank you!!!

JJ Goode, thank you for diving right in, picking up the pieces, and helping to shape the story. Rochelle Palermo, almost 100 recipes, your commitment and hard work is so appreciated.

Sydney Hunter, Joon Sung, Dan Moody, and Greg Bernhardt, thank you for all of your time and effort spent writing down the recipes that were in my head.

Lucy Lean, your extra set of eyes were such a tremendous help during the edit process.

Lionel and Shayla Deluy, thanks for always having your camera ready to capture any moment so beautifully.

Wesley Wong, your passion for food truly comes through in your photos; we love "doing business" with you.

Thank you, Anne Fishbein and Colin Young-Wolff, for taking such beautiful photos for *LA Weekly,* and for sharing them with us for this book.

Burton Morris, you are so creative; thank you for being such a great friend and capturing me perfectly in the LudoBites "Coq." Everyone knows the LudoBites rooster.

Peter Stougaard, each time you found the perfect creative expression for our announcements, even if we gave you twelve hours notice, merci beaucoup.

Jo Stougaard, LudoBitches, really?? Where would we be without you? Thanks for the timers on closing night of 2.0, always bringing extra wine to share with those waiting, and simply for being all about positively delicious.

Jill Bernheimer, your wine lists, even when they were illegal, completed the Ludo-Bites experience; thank you and, of course, thank you for the wine glass sponsorship.

Norbert Wabnig, who would have thought a bread, cheese, and food party would have turned into such an event; thank you and The Cheese Store of Beverly Hills for being there for the original and for all of your continued support over the years.

Will Chi, your FoodDigger dinners really were the spark that started the engine. Thank you so much for all of your unconditional support over the years, because yes, it was a fucking bakery!!!!

INTRODUCTION

It's 3 P.M. on a hot September afternoon and the Closed sign has just gone up at Gram & Papa's, a breakfast-and-lunch spot owned by my friend Mike Ilic in the heart of downtown Los Angeles's fashion district. There are still a few customers—a business guy powering through a turkey burger and, over by the window, two women with poached tuna salads who have been talking about their boyfriends since I came in an hour ago. All of a sudden, the griddle hisses and froths as one of the Gram & Papa's cooks pours on water and scrubs away the burger grease in full view of the last diners. The cleanup can't wait: a transformation is about to happen. Before the lunching women can gather their purses, a new restaurant—my restaurant—will inhabit this space, as if by magic.

Already my cooks, squeezed into a back prep area, are hard at work, cutting Cantal cheese into batons, frying chicken skin, roasting a pig's head. Wearing black T-shirts with a chef's-knife-wielding rooster on the front and the words "Just Make It Happen" on the back, my crew is eager to take over the kitchen and do some serious cooking, as soon as the guys in army-green Gram & Papa's T-shirts clear out the plastic forks and wipe the mayonnaise smears from the glass partitions. Soon my fresh waitstaff, also in black, will arrive to fold white cloth napkins, light votive candles, and set out the silverware. My wife, Krissy, has that don't-bother-me look as she answers an e-mail plea on her laptop from a big-shot begging for a last-minute table—three months ago, most of the restaurant's seats were snapped up in a thirty-second burst of Internet insanity on OpenTable.

In less than three hours, I've got 110 people coming for dinner, and I still haven't decided what to do with the oxtail broth bubbling away on the stove. Plus the brioche still needs something. Maybe four-spice powder?

"Grace! Where's the four-spice?"

"Upstairs, chef!"

"I need it, Grace . . . *now*!"

"Oui, chef. Right away, chef!"

Welcome to LudoBites.

I am a chef with a restaurant that has no permanent address, and thus no permanent place to keep the four-spice powder. In order to cook my food, I rely on the kindness of friends or friendly strangers who have a kitchen and dining room to spare. I usually appear for two or three months at a time, always at night.

I like to think of myself as a painter doing exhibitions in different locations. Each new dish I create is another piece of my art, often inspired by the place where I'm cooking. My latest exhibition is LudoBites 007, and tonight Gram & Papa's is my restaurant. But tomorrow it will belong again to Mike and the sandwich-eating lunch crowd, with barely a sign that I was ever there. That is how the pop-up game is played.

Some people call me the king of pop-ups. Jonathan Gold, the Pulitzer-Prize-winning restaurant critic at the *L.A. Times,* compared me to a roaming DJ and wrote that what I'm doing is revolutionary. In his *New York Times* review of my cooking, Sam Sifton said, "Every plate is a fully realized piece of art." LudoBites has been called a phenomenon, a revolution in dining. I love the way that sounds, but all I know for sure is that LudoBites was an accident.

I was just barely a teenager when I traveled from my home in Auxerre, France, in Burgundy, to the village of Saint-Père-sous-Vézelay. I was there to work, without pay, at L'Espérance, the three-Michelin-star restaurant run by Marc Meneau. From there, I moved 200 miles south to work for Pierre Gagnaire, and then to Paris to work for Alain Passard at L'Arpège and for Guy Martin at Le Grand Véfour, all of them demanding chefs with small armies of highly trained, meticulous cooks bustling in kitchens with walk-ins bigger than my first apartment. The chefs treated me like the lowly cook I was, rebuking me for my long hair and for showing up to work in a T-shirt. Chef Gagnaire took a shine to me, but he still had me doing prep work for two years before trusting me at the stove. Like all French chefs that came before me, I gradually learned from seemingly eternal repetition and starting at the bottom as a kid.

In 1996, I came to the United States eager to prove myself as the chef de partie at L'Orangerie, L.A.'s most famed French restaurant. Within a few short months, the chef left unexpectedly, and to my surprise I was promoted to executive chef. After six and a half years at L'Orangerie, the owner of the legendary Bastide restaurant asked me to come cook provocative avant-garde food. I eagerly took him up on the challenge, believing that because I enjoyed creating this elaborate, aggressive cuisine, it was what I was meant to cook.

Six weeks after Bastide received a Mobil five-star rating in 2005, its owner, Joe

Pytka, decided to close for a couple of months to redesign the space. It was an odd decision. After being there for a year and a half, I finally felt like we had an amazing team in the kitchen. And people were finally starting to *get* my avant-garde food, which, let me tell you, was nothing like L.A. had ever seen.

Most of the time, my job at Bastide was like a fantasy. Joe treated me well and was extremely generous. I had a great salary, an incredible kitchen, and a huge staff. For my birthday, for Christ's sake, he bought me a $15,000 Ducati motorcycle. When the restaurant was temporarily closed, Joe and I ate our way through Europe, flying on his private jet to five countries in seven days. On the way over there, we spent just enough time in New York City to eat a lavish lunch at Jean Georges before boarding the plane to make our reservation at Heston Blumenthal's the Fat Duck, outside of London, the next day. Then we were off to San Sebastián, in Spanish Basque country, for a day of incredible *pintxos*, the Basque version of tapas, and dinner at Mugaritz, to eat the food of Andoni Aduriz, who'd come from elBulli. Next we hit Venice, where we ate at, among other restaurants, Harry's Bar, where the bow-tied, white-jacketed waiters brought out plates and plates of simple, delicious food. Now, keep in mind that this trip was barely even planned in advance. Joe's assistant called me three days before we left, asking if I had a passport. "Sure, why?" I asked. Because, she said, we're all going to Europe to do some research.

Our dream trip had ended on a strange, sour note. To make a long story short, we stopped in Bangor, Maine, to refuel on our way back to L.A. There, customs officers searched the jet and found my prescription meds (I hate flying). Because I'd only found out about the trip days before we left, I took medication we had at home that had been prescribed to Krissy. Having what appeared to be drugs that weren't prescribed to you, I found out, is a no-no, especially when you're a foreigner. I was interrogated, stripsearched, and threatened with jail and deportation. In the end, everything worked out, but when I look back on it, I see that as a foreshadowing of what was to come.

When we returned to L.A., Joe and I passionately discussed what the new menu would look like once the restaurant reopened. But he was taking a long time to decide what he wanted, his ideas were changing by the week, and the redesign was taking forever. Worst of all, I wasn't cooking. Next thing I knew, almost nine months had gone by. I was going insane. I had to move on. I was desperate to cook. Reluctantly, I left Bastide, hoping to open my own restaurant.

Krissy and I embarked on a mission to open a restaurant, my restaurant. I was finished with mercurial restaurant owners, over-the-top opulence, and stratospheric checks to match. No one eats fine china and fancy curtains anyway, so why should they pay for them? Why not just serve great food in a more casual environment? Easier said than done.

We spent about a year looking. We checked out at least fifty spaces. Just four were promising. After a month or so of meeting with business owners and landlords, we had whittled those four down to, well, zero.

I was losing my mind. Imagining more negotiating and disappointment sure to come wasn't the half of it. I'm a chef. I *have to cook.* During this miserable year, I started helping my friend Ali Chabli develop items for his menu at Breadbar, a fantastic bakery and café in West Hollywood. One day, we had a thought: His place closed every day at 5 p.m. What if I took over the space at night? Just until I found a space for my own restaurant, of course. So I did just that. I whipped up an assortment of simple small plates and condiments and supplemented it with nice cheeses and charcuterie. Before I knew it, my casual menu had evolved into an elaborate Chef's Tasting Menu for $85 per person.

Unintentionally, I had started what is now known as a pop-up restaurant, but at the time, it wasn't anything but a stopgap measure. And it remained a stopgap measure until all of a sudden, it wasn't. It gradually consumed me and Krissy: the pop-up was alternately a gift, a curse, a drug.

Some days I loved life as a pop-up chef, and some days I wanted to drown myself in a vat of veal stock. The kitchens were never up to snuff, not even close. I had to work with fickle burners, defective ovens, and deep fryers that looked like they hadn't been cleaned in decades. I had to seize my storage space, piling my jars of smoked salt, va-douvan spice, and piment d'Espelette next to ketchup bottles, canned corn, and bagged white bread. I had to store my foie gras, octopus, and oxtail stock in refrigerators whose interiors looked like the aftermath of an explosion in a Kraft Foods factory.

Then there was my staff. I'd once commanded brigades of cooks who had toiled for years in the same sorts of kitchens in which I'd worked. These guys could butcher a duck in the time it takes to change a lightbulb. They burned through heaps of carrots and celery and onion, reducing the vegetables to neat little cubes at the speed of light.

At LudoBites, on the other hand, keeping top-notch staff for our irregular stints was next to impossible. So, early on, I actually scoured the dining rooms for customers who might want to help out in the kitchen. I employed eager novices, culinary students, certified nutcases, and Fred Savage (aka Kevin Arnold from *The Wonder Years*). I en-listed an eight-year-old boy to prep green beans. Sometimes staff left without a word, minutes before service began. Some quit ceremoniously, hurling curses (which I slung right back). Only after many LudoBites incarnations did I have a small team of incredible professional cooks and promising, hardworking apprentices in place.

Yet despite the shortcomings of the equipment and staff, my sky-high standards re-mained. Every night of service was a grueling challenge. There were times when I felt like packing up my knives and going home. There were a few nights when I actually did storm out of the restaurant, thinking, Fuck it, LudoBites is closed—for good. Yet the challenges were exhilarating too.

After seven LudoBites, I am a different chef. My ragtag staff and kitchens built for grilling turkey burgers forced my hand. I had to simplify my food—there was no other way. But the food still had to engage, to provoke. It still had to be *my* food. In fact, this was the first time I was truly cooking for myself, not for some overlord, or someone else's restaurant concept. So I had to discover a new way to cook and, with it, who I really was as a chef.

I realized I'd long been guilty of making overcomplicated dishes and confusing froufrou with fine food. Just because some of my mentors succeeded at elaborate dishes with seven, eight, nine components per plate didn't mean I had to do the same. Sometimes we chefs are scared to attempt a perfect plate of simply prepared fish and vegetables: your food is naked, and you can't hide flaws under swirls of sauces, melting mountains of foam, and crowns of tuiles. Trust me, you need balls to cook simple food.

Of course, that's not to say I would settle for serving chicken cutlets and green salads. I iced cheese cupcakes with fluffy chicken liver Chantilly cream. I tweaked Greek salad by turning the feta into a silky mousse. I reimagined my favorite Parisian sandwich—baguette, butter, ham, radish—as a soup capped with a foamy head of Guinness. I stopped serving cheese and charcuterie plates, the makings of which anyone with a credit card can buy for themselves. Instead, I folded Époisses into risotto, hid Fourme d'Ambert inside a tart, and stacked batons of Cantal cheese and white chocolate.

As a young chef, I had made the mistake of settling for good, not great, ingredients and then spending my time dressing them up. Now, forced to do without high-tech gadgets and a huge staff, I found myself spending more time seeking out the very best, though not necessarily the most expensive, ingredients and showcasing them, not my ego.

But I was no longer a chef with an inexhaustible budget. I could no longer FedEx fish from around the world, or splurge on luxurious cuts of meat whenever I wanted. So I looked to the same great producers, but bought less expensive seafood and cuts of meat, like mussels and squid, flank steaks and oxtail. Of course, my menus were still full of foie gras. I grew up on it—it's like butter for me.

Before LudoBites, my cooking was very French. After all, I was born in France and trained under some intense French chefs. Yet LudoBites opened my eyes to new flavors and new ways of cooking. So rather than searing a slab of foie gras, I steamed it, wrapped it in cabbage, and spooned on kimchi consommé. I pickled it. I made it into a terrine, then crammed slices of it between squid ink–spiked bread along with ham and cheese for a madcap twist on the croque-monsieur.

I still made tartares, but now they were adorned with Asian pears, fish sauce, and peanuts. I seasoned rack of lamb with bonito flakes to give it an umami-powered lift. I became obsessed with Japanese and Korean flavors, with miso and somen noodles, with kimchi and kalbi. Ginger became my garlic—I was tempted to put it in everything. L.A. had also infected me with a love for Latin flavors and dishes. Nearly every menu I wrote included ceviche. I still cooked John Dory in a *nage*, the classic French fish-poaching liquid, but I spiked it with jalapeños. My Frenchness was still part of my food—from the flavor memories I evoked to create it to the techniques I used to produce it—but the food was no longer very French. It wasn't wholly American either. It expanded on my own definitions of each cuisine and reinvigorated my love for both.

My cuisine became *à la minute*: I was no longer planning menus weeks or even months in advance but instead cooking in the moment. I might go to the market with a set of dishes in mind, then scrap them all once I got there. If I found stunning fennel bulbs instead of gorgeous tomatoes, it was bye-bye tomato salad, hello fennel marmalade. I often changed course just before the guests arrived, even midservice, halting prep, starting from scratch, and serving customers dishes that I had never made before. Ideas flitted through my head, transforming themselves from one minute to the next. I was as excited as a kid. I was having fun.

My notion of what made a perfect dish shifted. When I was younger, flavor drove my cooking and technique was more a means to show off. Today, flavor and technique work in concert. Flavor is the spark; it's how the game of invention begins. I might be inspired by a classic combination (say, celery root and truffles) or exhilarated by one that at first blush seems mad (say, celery root and sea urchin). Then once I have the flavors in mind, technique takes hold, and my objective is to find the best way to cook, to find a method that's ideally suited to whatever ingredients I mean to highlight. Flavor is the creative impulse, technique is the craft, and only together do they result in inspired food.

To that end, I drew from my past. Decades ago, Alain Passard taught me to cook slowly, to cook gently. And he taught me to cook with all five senses, to see that a roasted chicken was done, to smell that it was done, to hear that it was done. Only through years of experience can you reach this culinary state of understanding. So when I wanted to find a new way to cook rib-eye steaks, I channeled his advice and my culinary heritage. I didn't sear the steaks. I submerged them in gently bubbling lard and after four hours of steady cooking, served them in velvety slices. I treated squid similarly, abandoning the typical quick sauté for gentle cooking over low heat.

Executing the ideal technique wasn't always possible, especially with the staff I had.

My focus on technique led me to return to my roots as a cook, and when I did, customers loved it. I've served eggs every which way at LudoBites. I took pleasure in introducing customers to eggs precisely poached in their shells to 63°C, 64°C, or 65°C in an immersion circulator, a modern miracle of cookery that achieves whites and yolks with nearly the same lovely texture, but the response from my customers was never as enthusiastic as when I served scrambled eggs. Yes, scrambled eggs—done perfectly using the classic implements of cooking: whisk, pan, flame. This is much more difficult than plugging in the immersion circulator. It takes patience, practice, instinct, and getting it right requires more than a recipe or instructions. On the first night I put scrambled eggs on the menu, I looked on as my staff, even guys who had been cooking for fifteen years, made pan after disastrous pan of eggs: undercooked, overcooked, or just plain wrong texture. But gradually, the eggs improved. And once they got it, they got it. I was incredibly proud and told them they should be too. The realization that simple food is in fact the hardest food to do well inspired me as a young cook. I wanted it to inspire my cooks as well.

I was able to cook the way I did at LudoBites because I was finally my own boss. Success was mine to achieve or to surrender, and I did things my way. But perhaps the most significant change in my cooking philosophy came from the different type of interaction with customers that LudoBites fostered. Rather than toiling out of sight, behind a kitchen wall, I often cooked in full view of the people I was serving. Sometimes I was close enough to hand the plates to the diners, and to chat about the dish, about food, about life.

And whereas chefs like Alain Passard would pick through the scraps and bones left on plates as they returned from the dining room to the kitchen, dissecting them for signs that they had been cooked less than perfectly, I went online for my answers. I found out what my customers thought of virtually every dish I put out as I scrolled through photo-heavy reports of their every bite. I heard from everyone, from the well-traveled to the naive, all of them eager and opinionated. The feedback wasn't always good, of course, but a certain intimacy developed. I got to know my customers. I met their mothers, I invited them into my kitchen for cooking lessons, and I wound up learning from them too.

Once upon a time, my most important audience had been professional restaurant critics. Their approval was all-important. I also cooked to satisfy my ego. I'd serve dishes that screamed *Look what I can do!* Indeed, when the press came calling now, I was proud, of course, but a little embarrassed too, because I was cooking in a tiny bakery or café, not in a gleaming kitchen like the ones at Bastide and L'Orangerie. Then I got over

myself. I began to realize that LudoBites was successful because I wasn't taking myself as seriously as I had at the other restaurants. And my customer base had changed. The dining room at LudoBites wasn't filled with only rich gray-haired white men in suits and the occasional young couple celebrating an anniversary. My customers were as eclectic as L.A. itself.

There was a sort of synergy at work between my customers and me. They put up with brawls for reservations, shaky service, cramped tables, and sketchy neighborhoods. The food, not the lack of linens, was everything, although we even occasionally ran out of ingredients and had to create new dishes on the spot. Can you imagine Bastide running out of food? Can you imagine shelling out more than 400 euros per person for dinner at L'Arpège only to be told you had to ignore half of the menu? But at LudoBites, there was a sense of community, even of shared sacrifice if necessary. We were all in it together, part of the same exciting and unique experience. The customers gave me the freedom to cook what I wanted to cook, approaching each one of my creations with enthusiasm, if not unconditional love, and sympathy when I couldn't provide all the trappings of a proper restaurant. In return, they paid bargain-basement prices and got to experience a moment in the ever-changing reality that was LudoBites.

My relationship with my staff and my role in the kitchen changed too. As my temporary restaurant became a seemingly permanent part of my life, I decided to invest in my staff in a new way. I went from being a tyrant focused only on my food to a teacher eager to influence a new generation of cooks. We're at a critical moment in kitchen culture. So many young cooks have confidence that surpasses their abilities that it makes me laugh. Graduates of this culinary school or that come to my kitchen with designs on cooking on the line and dreaming up dishes for my menu, when they can't properly butcher a chicken, make stock, or scramble fucking eggs—but they're ready to run a restaurant, maybe even be on TV. Then there are those young cooks who learn to cook duck sous-vide before they learn how to roast one properly. We're in danger of forgetting how to cook without gadgets. Teaching was my way of reclaiming what it means to be a cook and a chef, of imparting to my staff wisdom that I had occasionally ignored myself.

Don't get me wrong, the result of cooking sous-vide can be fantastic, and I do still cook sous-vide occasionally. But to me, it's not quite cooking—it's button pressing. Worst of all, the more I'd focused on cooking with gadgets, the less fragrant my kitchen had become and the quieter it got. I missed the aromas of roasting meats, the *tsh, tsh, tsh* of the whisk, all the smells, sounds, and sights that make a kitchen such a wonderful place to work. But this kind of cooking asks a lot of you. It's difficult to do well. Just ask my staff.

This book is the story of LudoBites. There are seven chapters, because, there have been seven LudoBites so far. Each chapter is meant to capture one particular moment in time, one halting step in the evolution of LudoBites and the recipes inspired by that moment. Some of them, requiring multiple steps and time and patience, will challenge a home cook. But many are easy enough for an exciting weeknight dinner. For instance, steamed striped bass with butter braised vegetables and aioli is insanely easy and incredibly delicious. And once you make it, you'll forever have a technique to take with you on future kitchen adventures. Anyone can reproduce my Époisses risotto, whether you choose to add all the embellishments or not, to serve it as a luxurious cheese course or as dinner with a salad of well-dressed greens. My hope is that you enjoy reading the stories and cooking the recipes, and that you'll join me at the next LudoBites, whenever and wherever it may be.

In an effort to truly capture the "moments" of LudoBites, we used mostly blogger photos in the book, so this is my story told through the lens of the bloggers

KITCHEN 🥕 ROSTER

LUDO

FRANKIE

ROGELIO (breadbar employee)

JULIE (customer-intern)

SUSAN (customer-intern)

THE CHEESE STORE OF BEVERLY HILLS
DREAM TEAM (Thursday nights only)

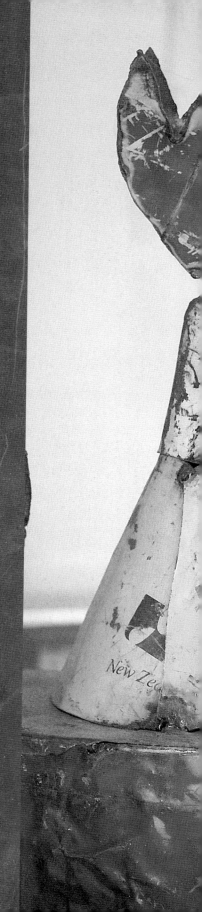

"What did you expect? I'm cooking in a fucking bakery."

That was my response to a customer who'd just told me that my food was good but not as good as it was at Bastide, my previous gig. I almost had to laugh at my situation. I had spent most of my career in the two- and three-Michelin-star kitchens of France, where I worked surrounded by dozens of cooks, an army of us toiling to create incredible, elaborate dishes, to execute the genius of a visionary chef. In the States, too, I had been lucky enough to preside over similar brigades of diligent, highly trained cooks. To ask was to get, to want was to have.

But, fine dining be damned, I was now cooking three to four nights a week for three months in a fucking bakery. With four burners and a shared prep kitchen. My reputation was at stake, and I was walking a tightrope, knowing full well that I might end up plunging to my professional death.

Krissy came up with the name and the first LudoBites was born. This clearly wasn't L'Orangerie or Bastide and we hoped the name would reflect that. After all, it was just me and one sous chef in a borrowed space. But it was still my food. You might not be getting a whole portion of the fine-dining experience—the lovably wobbly tables and bar stools made sure of that—but you were certainly getting a nice "bite."

Theoretically, it should have worked seamlessly. The bakery would close on time. We'd enter the small but tidy kitchen and start our show. In reality, we arrived in a kitchen that looked like a war zone, with stacks of dirty dishes everywhere. And every night, we had to transform Breadbar from a simple café, with long narrow tables, stools, paper napkins, and a glass case filled with bread, into a dining room.

On our first night, six people showed up, all friends. But the next night, we had twelve customers. And so it went, our audience slowly building as word got out. Soon we had a dozen people crowded around an eight-person table. We had customers I recognized from my days at Bastide and L'Orangerie, who'd bring $300 bottles of wine, while at the next table, a group of young women might break out bottles of Santa Margherita. It felt like a quirky dinner party, which was exactly what we wanted.

So what if the space was bare-bones and the service sucked? At Breadbar, customers ordered sandwiches and salads, so, of course, the staff wasn't used to explaining dishes, or doing silverware changes and all the other stuff that's Service 101 at a proper restaurant. It got so bad that Krissy stepped in. In another life, she had opened five Hooters restaurants (seriously), so she gave the staff a tutorial based on her old service manual. And at first, the food I turned out was dead simple. It had to be: I had just one of my cooks with me (my buddy Frankie, from Bastide) and some Breadbar employees, who were lovely people but didn't have anything that approached the training of my old brigade.

Since the bread was the best in L.A., I decided to gather the best ingredients to accompany it. I collaborated with The Cheese Store of Beverly Hills and served its

amazing cheese. I rounded up meat and produce from my favorite purveyors, like pork and poulardes from Four Story Hill Farm, in northeastern Pennsylvania, and peaches and persimmons from Peacock Family Farms, a few hours north of L.A. I'd let these ingredients speak for themselves and give the farms shout-outs on the back of the menu, something that a few years later became all the rage. At first the menu wasn't a list of composed dishes, but rather elements that customers could mix and match: cured meats and fish, cheeses, condiments like house-made harissa and grapefruit confit, and simple vegetable preparations like a salad of multicolored carrots grown by my favorite carrot farmer.

Soon I got restless, so I started amping up the menu's ambitions. Now I was serving foie gras miso soup and scallops with curry, yogurt, and spinach. I'd gotten so many requests from old Bastide customers that I launched omakase (chef's choice) dinners, multicourse meals for $85. I was cooking with the same techniques I used at

Bastide and with ingredients from the same producers. The only difference was that instead of pricey turbot, I used inexpensive skate. Oh, and I was cooking it in a fucking bakery.

The response was incredible. Nobody minded the shaky service. Nobody cared if they had to sit near the bathroom or next to strangers. I even got to play my favorite French rap music. Tables became communal and overcrowded. One night, it rained and we must have violated every fire code by hauling in the outdoor tables and cramming them into the dining room. Again, it didn't matter, not to my new customers or even to my old ones from Bastide. LudoBites was all about the food.

Well, not just the food. There was also a less tangible magic at work. Strangely, the most sought-after tables became the ones right in front of the glass sneeze guard, behind which I stood night after night, plating and inspecting dishes. It was like performance art where my guests became part of the act. I am sure the boom in food television helped spur this desire for front-row seating, but it was something more here. I was no more than three feet from the diners at the sneeze guard tables. There was a chef's table at Bastide but there was a wall and a small window through which guests watched us plate our food, which is really our "art." Here I felt like an artist who was able to create in a completely unexpected setting and the audience falling in love with both at the same time. Standing behind the glass sneeze guard, night after night, made me realize that the setting can outsize the expectations. When dining at three-star Michelin restaurants in Europe you expect the perfect linens, the perfect ice cubes, the perfect everything, but what if you could have that same meal in your backyard? There is no pressure to analyze or interpret, you just experience it. What a pleasure.

A cool sort of intimacy took shape. I was happy, cooking in plain sight of my customers and joking with them as I composed plates of rib-eye steak poached in lard and guacamole made from broccoli instead of avocado. I'd often hand the food directly to them. This interaction redefined for me what a restaurant is. We had created a place where you went to eat, to share, to live life. That's why LudoBites was overflowing with customers. That's why cars would slow down as they drove past, drivers craning their necks and wondering, What's going on in there? Even my harshest critic ever, the rarely enthusiastic *L.A. Times* restaurant critic S. Irene Virbila got into it, writing: "The whole thing has an impromptu, clandestine feeling and the young staff is stoked. They've been tasting dishes that, well, only Ludo could have dreamed up. And like his cooking at Bastide, some are downright delicious. But he's sure to surprise you. And intrigue you. . . . It's fun. It's BYOB—and make it a good one, something that can follow in any direction Ludo's imagination takes him. I promise, you won't be bored."

JOE PYTKA

Joe Pytka, the owner of Bastide and my boss for several years, is about seven feet tall. His hairline starts at the top of his head and his long, scraggly, yellowish hair reaches his shoulders. I don't think Joe would disagree with me if I said he could pass for a homeless man. But Joe is incredibly successful, an august director, cinematographer, and a legend in the advertising industry for his memorable commercials. He's an insatiable gourmand, and I swear he can talk knowledgeably about anything from high art to pop culture. He's also famously difficult to work with, but he always treated me well while pushing me hard to be my best. He's a major reason I am where I am today.

I first met Joe while I was cooking at L'Orangerie. My boss there was—how do you say?—a fucking asshole. So Joe comes to the restaurant with a friend dressed in his standard faded highwater Levi's, crumpled black jacket and T-shirt, looking like a hobo. When my boss sees him, he immediately decides to sit him at the worst table, where he hid anyone he didn't think reflected well on the restaurant. But Joe does what he always does and orders the best bottle of wine on the menu. The owner starts to panic—the bottle costs about $5,000 and he figures there's no way this bum can afford it. So he starts racing around, telling the managers that he's certain this guy won't pay for the wine, that he'll skip out on the bill. Finally, he runs out to the valet and demands to know what kind of car this guy arrived in, expecting some rusty jalopy. The valet takes a look and tells him, "It's a Ferrari."

This is how it goes when you're out to eat with Joe. On our last-minute culinary tour of Europe, we ate at the Michelin-starred Alain Senderens in Paris. Joe ordered a 1947 Cheval Blanc. Well, 1947 was probably the legendary wine house's best year, and Joe had drunk this wine many times before. It was priced on the list at around 12,000 euros. The sommelier made him repeat the order, just to be sure this wasn't a slip of the tongue or a funny joke from this American vagrant. Finally the sommelier brought the bottle to the table and opened it with great ceremony. What passed next were among the most excruciating thirty minutes of my life. Joe took a taste, then turned to the sommelier and asked, "Did you try this?" The flavor was gone. The sommelier started tripping over himself to explain: "It just needs to open up," etc. But Joe was right, as usual. He demanded to see the chef and the head sommelier but was told that it was their night off. The sommelier desperately offered to charge him only half price for the bottle. Ultimately, Joe didn't pay for the Cheval Blanc. We did, however, drink a similarly expensive bottle and it was delicious.

For this playful starter, I reimagined guacamole, with broccoli puree standing in for creamy avocado. Otherwise, I stay faithful to the Mexican staple, mixing in fresh jalapeño chiles, cilantro, and lime juice and serving it alongside homemade tortilla chips. I've even had success with, well, "peamole," in which fresh English peas stand in for the broccoli. This dish occasionally takes customers by surprise, and it makes them rethink their notions of what goes with what.

brocamole

SERVES 4

1½ pounds broccoli
⅔ cup grapeseed oil
½ cup lightly packed fresh cilantro
    leaves, chopped
⅓ cup diced red onion
¼ cup diced seeded tomato

1 large jalapeño chile, minced
    (about 3 tablespoons)
Juice of 2 limes (about ¼ cup)
Fleur de sel
Baked Tortilla Chips (recipe follows)

Bring a large pot of water to a boil over high heat. Meanwhile, trim the stalks from the broccoli florets (reserve the stalks for another use, if desired). Add the broccoli to the boiling water and cook for about 2 minutes, or until crisp-tender. Drain the broccoli and transfer to a large bowl of ice water to cool.

Transfer the broccoli to a colander and set aside to drain well. Squeeze the broccoli to remove any excess water.

Combine the broccoli and oil in a food processor and process to a thick puree. Transfer to a medium bowl and stir in the cilantro, red onion, tomato, chile, and lime juice. Season to taste with fleur de sel and serve with the tortilla chips.

baked tortilla chips

SERVES 4

4 corn tortillas
1 tablespoon olive oil

Sea salt

Preheat the oven to 350°F.

Brush the tortillas with the oil and cut each tortilla into 4 pieces. Arrange the tortilla pieces on a heavy baking sheet and sprinkle with salt. Bake until crisp and golden, about 20 minutes. Serve warm.

Beets and goat cheese salad has become a menu cliché for a reason: the two ingredients go so well together, the tangy cheese the perfect contrast to sweet, earthy beets. With a little tweaking—beets as deep-pink soup rather than chunks, and goat cheese morphed into sorbet—the combination seems fresh all over again.

beet gazpacho, goat cheese sorbet

SERVES 6

GAZPACHO

1 pound beets, scrubbed

1 plum tomato, halved, seeded, and diced

½ small green bell pepper, cored, seeded, and diced

2½ ounces whole-grain bread, crust trimmed and cut into cubes

⅓ cup shelled raw pistachios

1 cup extra-virgin olive oil

½ cup water

¼ cup aged balsamic vinegar (at least 8 years old)

3 tablespoons Dijon mustard

Fleur de sel and freshly ground black pepper

ACCOMPANIMENTS

Goat Cheese Sorbet (recipe follows)

About 2 teaspoons aged balsamic vinegar (at least 8 years old)

12 fresh viola flowers, optional

TO MAKE THE GAZPACHO

Put the beets in a large pot and add enough cold water to cover them. Bring to a boil over high heat, then reduce the heat and simmer just until a skewer glides easily through the center of a beet, about 30 minutes. Drain and set the beets aside until they are cool enough to handle.

Peel the beets and cut each one into 4 pieces.

Combine the beets, tomato, bell pepper, bread, pistachios, oil, water, vinegar, and mustard in a large bowl. Cover and refrigerate overnight.

Working in batches if necessary, transfer the beet mixture to a blender and puree until smooth. (I use my Vitamix for this.) Season the gazpacho to taste with fleur de sel and pepper.

TO SERVE
Pour 1 cup of the gazpacho into each bowl. Top each with a quenelle of goat cheese sorbet, then garnish with a drizzle of balsamic vinegar and 2 flowers.

goat cheese sorbet   MAKES ABOUT 1½ CUPS

1 cup goat's milk
4 ounces soft fresh goat cheese

¼ teaspoon kosher salt
Freshly ground black pepper

Combine the milk, cheese, and salt in a heavy small saucepan over medium-high heat, and using an immersion blender, puree the mixture until it is smooth and hot. Season to taste with pepper.

Transfer to a bowl, cover, and refrigerate until very cold.

About 30 minutes before serving, transfer the chilled goat cheese mixture to an ice cream maker and freeze according to the manufacturer's instructions until it is smooth, homogenized, and icy, like a sorbet. Serve immediately.

QUENELLES

The term quenelle can either refer to a French dish made of fish or meat in the form of a dumpling or as I use the term in the kitchen, a plating technique that has become the skill by which I judge all my kitchen help.

Quenelles can be formed either using one spoon or two spoons. The two spoon technique is the "old school" method and reserved these days for only the most delicate of plating, such as with caviar.

I use the one spoon quenelle to serve ice cream and mousses. And task all of my students to master the perfect football oval shape before they complete their time in my kitchen.

To make the perfect one spoon quenelle, it must be done in one movement. Think of a clock, starting scooping at 15 minutes and you should have the perfect oval by the time you reach 45 minutes. The key is temperature of ingredients. Your spoon should first sit in VERY hot water for about 10 seconds and you should allow your ice creams and mousses to temper for a few minutes so to have a creamy texture versus hard texture.

But if you ask me, it is all about the perfect spoon, you must have a spoon with finesse, preferably French. I usually scour French antique stores when I go home, because you know, they just don't make spoons like they used to.

Good miso soup is a brilliant thing. I especially love when you come across the little cubes of tofu that grace some versions. Ah, I thought, but what if instead of tofu, the cubes were foie gras! So I added cubes of raw duck liver to the bowl and poured on the hot broth. The tasty fat leaches into the dashi—a home-cook-friendly broth you make in minutes, not a long-simmered French stock—infusing it with even more flavor. English peas and fava beans make great springtime additions; during the winter, I look to radishes and turnips.

foie gras miso soup

SERVES 4

¼ cup fresh English peas
¼ cup shelled fava beans, outer skin removed
2 ounces enoki mushrooms, ends trimmed
¼ cup very thinly sliced red onion
1½ tablespoons very thinly sliced fresh peppermint leaves

½ sheet nori, cut into very fine strips
16 Four (2-ounce) cubes Grade A foie gras
Fleur de sel and freshly ground black pepper
8 teaspoons light yellow miso
5 cups Dashi (recipe follows)
Chive blossoms for garnish

Blanch the peas and fava beans in a saucepan of boiling salted water just until tender, about 2 minutes. Drain and transfer to a bowl of ice water to cool; drain well.

Divide the peas, beans, mushrooms, red onion, peppermint, and nori among four small soup bowls. Score both sides of the foie gras cubes in a crosshatch pattern and set the cubes in the bowls. Sprinkle the foie gras with fleur de sel and pepper. Smear 2 teaspoons of the miso on one edge of each bowl.

Put the dashi in a heavy small saucepan, cover, and bring to a simmer over high heat. Pour the simmering broth into the bowl, covering the foie gras and vegetables. Garnish with chive blossoms and serve immediately.

dashi

MAKES ABOUT 7 CUPS

8 cups water
Two 6-by-4-inch pieces kombu

4 cups packed bonito flakes (about
1½ ounces)

Combine the water and kombu in a medium saucepan and let stand for 15 minutes.

Bring the water to a simmer over high heat, then remove the saucepan from the heat and remove and discard the kombu. Add the bonito flakes, cover, and steep for 20 minutes.

Strain the dashi through a fine-mesh sieve into a bowl.

When I invited a customer named Julie Lee into my kitchen, the idea was that she would lend a hand in exchange for learning from me, the "big-time" chef. Instead, I ended up learning from her. I mentioned that I wanted to give beef tartare an Eastern inflection, and she started rhapsodizing about Asian pears. Next thing you know, she and I came up with this peanut vinaigrette with herbs, sesame oil, lime juice, fish sauce, and crisp cubes of the aromatic fruit. It was fantastic! By the end of her time there, she'd also taught me how to properly soak rice paper to make summer rolls. It just drove home one of my favorite aspects of LudoBites: I might be the driving force behind it, but I was only one of many contributors to its magic.

beef tartare, asian pear, peanut vinaigrette

SERVES 6

PEANUT VINAIGRETTE
1 Asian pear, peeled, cored, and cut into ⅓-inch dice
⅓ cup raw roasted peanuts, chopped
¼ cup toasted sesame oil
Juice of 1 large lime (about 3 tablespoons)
1 ounce fresh ginger, peeled and grated on a Microplane
2 tablespoons crushed palm sugar
2 tablespoons fish sauce (preferably Three Crabs brand)
2 sprigs fresh cilantro, leaves removed and coarsely chopped
4 red shiso leaves, very thinly sliced

Kosher salt and freshly ground black pepper to taste

CROUTONS
3 tablespoons Clarified Butter, melted (recipe follows)
1 baguette

BEEF TARTARE
1 pound boneless beef eye of round (preferably Wagyu)
6 quail eggs

Stir all the ingredients in a medium bowl just to blend, not to emulsify.

Preheat the oven to 400°F.

Cut the baguette on a very sharp diagonal into slices that are about ¼ inch thick and 2 to 3 inches long; you need 18 slices (reserve the remaining baguette for another use). Arrange the slices in a single layer on a rimmed baking sheet and brush with the clarified butter. Bake until golden brown, about 12 minutes. Remove from the oven.

Remove any excess fat and sinew from the beef and cut the beef into ⅓-inch cubes. Keep the beef well chilled at all times.

Spoon the beef into the center of six dinner plates. Crack 1 egg, separate the white and yolk, and carefully place the egg yolk atop one portion of the beef. Repeat with the remaining eggs and beef (reserve the egg whites for another use, if desired). Divide the vinaigrette among six small ramekins and serve it alongside the beef tartare with the croutons.

clarified butter

MAKES ABOUT ¾ CUP

1 cup (8 ounces) unsalted butter

Cook the butter in a heavy small saucepan over medium heat until melted and beginning to simmer (do not stir). Remove from the heat. Spoon off the foam from atop the butter. Carefully pour the clarified butter into a small bowl, leaving the liquid whey and milk solids behind. Cool the clarified butter. Cover tightly and refrigerate.

Do ahead
The clarified butter can be prepared up to 1 week ahead. Keep tightly covered and refrigerated.

A throwback to my days at L'Arpège, where I first learned to make avocado mousse. Sometimes we'd top it with caviar to add a burst of saltiness or with passion fruit seeds, which look a bit like fish eggs, to provide little sweet-tart explosions. Together with barely cooked prawns—sweet ones from Santa Barbara, if you can manage it—the mousse is really special, a lovely composition of colors and textures.

prawns, avocado mousse, passion fruit

SERVES 4

AVOCADO MOUSSE

2 ripe avocados, halved, peeled, and pitted
2 tablespoons fresh lemon juice
⅓ cup heavy cream
Kosher salt and freshly ground white pepper

PRAWNS

12 live prawns (5–7 per pound) or jumbo shrimp
2 tablespoons almond oil
12 shaved slices Parmigiano-Reggiano
1 lemon
3 passion fruits, halved, pulp and seeds scooped out
Fleur de sel

TO MAKE THE MOUSSE

Puree the avocados with the lemon juice in a food processor until very smooth and creamy. Add the cream and pulse twice. Scrape the bowl and pulse again just to blend; do not overmix the mousse, or it will lose its smooth, creamy appearance. Season to taste with salt and white pepper. Transfer to a container, cover, and refrigerate for up to 3 hours.

TO PREPARE THE PRAWNS

Bring a large pot of lightly salted water to a boil over high heat. Remove the pot from the heat, add the prawns, and let stand for 2 minutes. Drain and transfer the prawns to a large bowl of ice water to cool completely.

Drain the prawns, peel, and devein.

Spoon 3 nice thick lines of avocado mousse onto each of four plates. Place 1 prawn on each line of mousse. Drizzle a little almond oil over each prawn, then top with the slices of Parmigiano-Reggiano. Grate some lemon zest over the prawns. Spoon the passion fruit pulp over and around the prawns, sprinkle with fleur de sel, and serve.

For me, this is Christmas in a bowl, evoking many happy memories of the holiday. Not a sunny L.A. Christmas, but a snowy scene, a cabin in the woods. Rice velouté, essentially a risotto cooked past al dente and pureed with milk, serves as the snowy white expanse. I hide a five-minute egg in the rich soup. To conjure up the woods, I pair button mushrooms and pine needles, so effective a combination that I swear it feels like you're tasting the forest floor—in a good way. When I first made this dish, I plucked the needles straight from the ornament-laden tree in my living room and infused them into oil, the lovely emerald green a pop of color against the stark soup.

white rice velouté, egg, mushrooms, christmas tree oil

SERVES 8

RICE VELOUTÉ
1 tablespoon duck fat
1 shallot, diced
½ cup Arborio rice
2 tablespoons dry white wine, such as Chardonnay
2¼ cups whole milk, or more if needed
1 cup Chicken Stock (page 39)
2 tablespoons mascarpone cheese
Kosher salt and freshly ground white pepper

MUSHROOM SOUBISE
3 tablespoons clarified butter
12 ounces white button mushrooms, cleaned and very thinly sliced

Kosher salt and freshly ground white pepper
2 tablespoons unsalted butter
2 onions (about 1 pound total), sliced
1 cup heavy cream

EGGS MOLLET
10 large organic eggs (see Note)

About 2 teaspoons Christmas Tree Oil (recipe follows)

Melt the duck fat in a heavy large saucepan over medium heat. Add the shallot and sweat until tender but not browned at all, about 2 minutes. Add the rice and sauté for 2 minutes. Add the wine, then add the milk and chicken stock, bring to a simmer, stirring frequently, until the rice is very tender, about 25 minutes (don't be afraid of overcooking the rice; it should be very soft). If the mixture becomes too thick, add more milk to give it a creamy consistency.

Stir the mascarpone into the velouté and season to taste with salt and white pepper. Transfer to a blender and blend until very smooth. The velouté should be thick enough to coat the back of a spoon; if it is too thick, add more milk to adjust the consistency. Transfer to a saucepan and set aside.

TO MAKE THE SOUBISE

Heat the clarified butter in a large cast-iron skillet over medium-high heat. Add the mushrooms and sauté until crisp and a nice golden brown color, about 10 minutes. Season to taste with salt and white pepper.

Transfer the mushrooms to a cutting board and let cool slightly, then coarsely chop them.

Melt the 2 tablespoons of butter in a heavy large saucepan over low heat. Add the onions and cook, stirring often, until they are translucent but have not taken on any color, about 15 minutes.

Reduce the heat to low, add the cream, and cook until the onions are very tender and the mixture has thickened slightly, about 40 minutes.

Transfer the onion mixture to a blender and blend until smooth. Season to taste with salt and pepper.

Return the soubise to the saucepan, stir in the mushrooms and rewarm over medium heat. Check the seasoning, then set aside, covered to keep warm.

TO PREPARE THE EGGS

Bring a medium saucepan of water to a boil over high heat. Reduce the heat to medium, gently lower the eggs into the simmering water, and cook for 5 minutes (see

Note). Using a slotted spoon, transfer the eggs to a bowl of ice water just until cool enough to peel—no longer than 2 minutes, or the eggs will be too cool when you serve them. Remove the eggs from the water and carefully peel them (some of the shells may be a bit tricky).

TO SERVE

Reheat the rice velouté. Spoon about ⅓ cup of the mushroom soubise into the center of each of eight small soup bowls. Place an egg on the soubise in each bowl. Spoon about ¼ cup of the velouté over each egg to cover, drizzle each with about ¼ teaspoon of the Christmas tree oil, and serve immediately.

Note: Don't hesitate to cook an extra egg or two so you can crack one open to check that the yolk is cooked properly—that's what I always do. The yolk should be creamy and warm.

christmas tree oil

MAKES ½ CUP

½ cup grapeseed oil
¼ cup coarsely chopped pine needles

Combine the oil and pine needles in a blender and blend until the oil becomes green. Transfer to a container, cover, and let infuse overnight in the refrigerator.

Strain the oil through a fine-mesh sieve; discard the solids. Store the oil in a glass jar in the refrigerator up to 2 weeks; bring to room temperature before using.

I grew up in Burgundy, which is famous for its snails (escargots), and they were slinking around almost everywhere I turned. When I was ten I was famous (at least in my family) for my ability to gobble them . . . the way most kids eat M&Ms. Who could blame me, when they were baked with garlic, parsley, lemon, and a lot of butter—a magical assemblage of flavors? I evoke them here in oatmeal cooked like risotto, then mixed with bright-green parsley puree, served with simply sautéed, lovably chewy snails and a frothy, featherlight garlic sauce.

green oatmeal, sautéed snails, green garlic bubbles

SERVES 6

GREEN GARLIC BUBBLES
1 cup whole milk
3 green onions, very thinly sliced
2 garlic cloves, chopped
2 tablespoons freshly grated
    Parmigiano-Reggiano
Kosher salt and freshly ground
    white pepper
1 teaspoon soy lecithin

GREEN OATMEAL
2 tablespoons unsalted butter
1 shallot, finely chopped
1 garlic clove, minced
½ cup steel-cut oats

2 cups whole milk
¾ cup Chicken Stock (page 39)
¼ cup Parsley Puree (recipe follows)
Grated zest of 1 small lemon
Kosher salt and freshly ground white
    pepper

ESCARGOTS
48 escargots (snails)
Kosher salt and freshly ground black
    pepper
3 tablespoons clarified butter

Pink and white garlic flowers for
    garnish (optional)

TO MAKE THE GREEN GARLIC SAUCE

Combine the milk, green onions, and garlic in a heavy small saucepan and bring to a boil over medium heat, then reduce the heat and simmer gently, until the green onions and garlic are very tender, about 15 minutes.

Add the Parmigiano-Reggiano to the garlic mixture, transfer to a blender, and blend until smooth. Strain through a fine-mesh sieve into a small saucepan and discard the solids. Season the sauce to taste with salt and pepper. Set aside.

TO MAKE THE OATMEAL

Melt the butter in a heavy medium saucepan over medium heat. Add the shallot and garlic and sauté until translucent but not browned at all, about 2 minutes. Stir in the oatmeal, then add the milk and chicken stock and bring to a simmer over medium-high heat. Reduce the heat to low, cover, and simmer very gently, stirring often, until the mixture has thickened into a creamy porridge, about 45 minutes. Stir in the parsley puree and lemon zest and season to taste with salt and white pepper.

TO PREPARE THE ESCARGOTS

Lightly season the escargots with salt and pepper. Heat a 12-inch cast-iron skillet over high heat. Add the clarified butter. Once the butter is sizzling hot, add the escargots in one layer and sauté until they feel crisp to the touch all over, about 3 minutes. Transfer the escargots to a baking sheet lined with paper towels to absorb the excess butter.

TO SERVE

Bring the garlic sauce just to a simmer. Add the lecithin and mix with an immersion blender until bubbles form. Remove from the heat.

Spoon the oatmeal into six small soup plates. Place 8 escargots atop the oatmeal in each plate. Using a large spoon, scoop the bubbles from the garlic sauce and spoon them over the escargots to cover. Garnish with the garlic flowers, if desired, and serve immediately.

parsley puree

MAKES A SCANT 1 CUP

2 large bunches fresh flat-leaf
parsley, leaves only (about 4 cups
packed)

3 ice cubes

Blanch the parsley in a large pot of boiling salted water until the leaves are very soft but still green, about 3 minutes. Drain and transfer to a large bowl of ice water to cool, then drain again.

Transfer the parsley to a food processor and puree with the ice cubes until smooth.

chicken stock

MAKES ABOUT 10 CUPS

4 pounds chicken bones, necks,
and feet
1 carrot, chopped
1 onion, chopped

1 leek, chopped
5 fresh bay leaves
2 large fresh flat-leaf parsley sprigs
3 quarts cold water

Rinse the chicken bones, necks, and feet in cold water. Place the chicken pieces in a heavy large stock pot. Add the carrot, onion, leek, bay leaves, and parsley. Add the cold water. Bring to a boil over medium-high heat. Reduce the heat to medium-low and simmer gently for 3 to 4 hours, skimming the stock every 15 minutes to remove the fat and foam that accumulate at the top.

Strain the stock through a fine-meshed strainer. Refrigerate the stock until cold. Remove the fat from the top of the stock. Cover and keep refrigerated 2 days before using.

People are always asking about this sandwich, perhaps because the jet-black bread (squid ink provides the color, my mentor Pierre Gagnaire provided the inspiration) looks so cool. Or it could be that it's impossible to resist a croque-monsieur made with fine cheese and good ham, let alone one that also includes a decidedly untraditional slab of foie gras terrine. At LudoBites, we made the bread, terrine, and jam ourselves, but if you end up buying these components (any good bread, a butcher's terrine, your favorite jam), you'll still get great results.

Etorki is a sheep's-milk cheese from Spain's Basque country; Idiazábal is a smoked sheep cheese from the same region.

black foie gras croque-monsieur, amaretto cherry jam

SERVES 6

3 medium zucchini, cut lengthwise into
⅓-inch-thick slices
About 6 tablespoons Clarified Butter
(page 31), melted
Kosher salt and freshly ground black
pepper
Twelve ½-inch-thick slices Black Squid
Ink Bread (recipe follows)
6 ounces Etorki cheese, thinly sliced

6 thin slices serrano ham or prosciutto
di Parma
Six ½-inch-thick slices Foie Gras Terrine
(recipe follows)
3 ounces Idiazábal cheese, thinly sliced
1 sheet edible gold leaf (optional)
½ cup Amaretto-Cherry Jam (recipe
follows)

Heat a large grill pan over medium-high heat. Brush the zucchini slices on both sides with 1 tablespoon of the clarified butter and sprinkle with salt and pepper. In batches, grill the zucchini for 2 minutes on each side, or until it is just tender and grill marks have appeared. Set aside.

Brush one side of each slice of bread with some of the clarified butter. Place 6 slices buttered side down on the work surface. Top each with one-sixth of the Etorki cheese, then arrange 3 slices of the grilled zucchini, side by side, atop the cheese. Place a slice of ham, a slice of terrine, and one-sixth of the Idiazábal cheese atop each sandwich. Top the sandwiches with the remaining bread, buttered side up.

Heat the remaining clarified butter on a large nonstick flat griddle over medium heat. Grill the sandwiches for 3 to 5 minutes on each side, or until the cheeses melt, the foie gras softens and is warmed through, and the sandwiches are crisp on the outside. Cut the sandwiches in half, top with the gold leaf, if desired, and serve each with a spoonful of cherry jam.

foie gras terrine

2 lobes (about 2 pounds total) Grade A foie gras
About 1 tablespoon fleur de sel
About 1 teaspoon freshly ground white pepper

Grated zest of 1 small lemon (use a Microplane)

Preheat the oven to 200°F. Let the foie gras come to room temperature (if it is cold and hard, you won't be able to devein it without it crumbling apart). Gently separate the 2 sections of each lobe. Using a spoon or clean fingers, remove the red veins that run down the length of the lobes. Season the lobes on all sides with the fleur de sel, white pepper, and lemon zest.

Gently place the foie gras lobes on top of each other in a 3-cup (6-by-4-by-3½-inch) enameled cast-iron terrine mold. Reposition the lobes as necessary to form a more even layer, but don't press on them. The foie gras may extend above the edges of the terrine, but it will melt down into the mold as it cooks. Cover with

aluminum foil and set the terrine in a large baking pan. Place the pan in the oven and pour enough cold water into the baking pan to come halfway up the sides of the terrine. Bake until the center of the terrine is warm, not hot, checking every 15 minutes, about 1 hour and 45 minutes total. To see if the terrine is done, insert the tip of a small knife into the center of the foie gras and leave it there for about 10 seconds, then press the knife to your lip—it should be warm, but not hot.

Remove the terrine from the water bath and set it on a rimmed baking sheet. If your terrine mold has a press, use it to gently press the foie gras. If you don't have a press, cut a rectangular piece of cardboard the size of the top of the terrine and wrap it in foil, set it on top of the warm foie gras, lay some weights (such as 8-ounce soda cans) on top, and gently press down on the terrine. Refrigerate the terrine overnight on the baking sheet.

Remove the weights from atop the terrine. Spoon off all the fat that has accumulated on top of the foie gras and transfer it to a small saucepan. Set it over low heat to melt the fat; do not allow the fat to boil. Strain the warm fat and let cool to lukewarm.

Wipe the terrine mold clean. Use a small offset spatula to flatten the top of the foie gras, scraping some of the foie from the higher side onto the lower side so that the foie gras is even, if necessary. Pour enough of the reserved fat into the terrine to create a ½-inch-thick layer over the foie gras. (Reserve any remaining fat to use for cooking meat or potatoes.) Refrigerate the terrine until the fat is cold and firm.

Dip the terrine mold into a large bowl of hot water for 1 minute. Then dip a thin sharp knife into hot water, wipe it dry, and run it along the sides of the terrine to loosen it. Invert the terrine onto a cutting board and gently tap the mold to release the foie gras.

To serve, dip a large sharp knife into hot water, then cut the terrine into ½-inch-thick slices, rewarming the knife between cuts.

The terrine can be stored about 2 weeks before cutting, for about one week and after cutting.

black squid ink bread

MAKES 1 LOAF

⅓ cup warm water (105° to 110°F)
2 tablespoons active dry yeast
3¾ cups all-purpose flour, plus
    more for dusting
1 tablespoon granulated sugar
2 teaspoons kosher salt

1¼ cups whole milk
3 tablespoons squid ink
3 tablespoons unsalted butter, melted
    and still warm
1 large egg, beaten to blend

Stir the warm water and yeast together in a small bowl. Let stand until the yeast dissolves, about 10 minutes.

Combine the flour, sugar, and salt in the bowl of a stand mixer fitted with the dough hook, and stir to blend. Whisk the milk and squid ink in a small bowl to blend, add to the flour mixture, along with the yeast mixture, and mix to form a soft dough. Gradually mix in the melted butter and mix at medium speed until the dough is smooth and elastic, about 2 minutes. The dough should feel slightly tacky.

Using floured hands, transfer the dough to a lightly floured work surface and form it into a ball. Lightly oil a bowl and put the dough in the bowl. Cover and refrigerate until the dough doubles in volume, about 1 hour.

Oil a 12-by-4-by-3-inch loaf pan. Punch down the dough and shape it into a 10-inch rectangular loaf. Place the loaf in the prepared pan. Cover with a towel and let rise in a warm, draft-free area until almost doubled in volume, about 30 minutes.

Preheat the oven to 375°F. Lightly brush the top of the bread with some of the egg. Bake until an instant-read thermometer inserted into the center of the loaf registers 200°F, about 45 minutes. Cool the bread in the pan for 5 minutes, then transfer the loaf to a cooling rack and cool completely.

amaretto cherry jam   MAKES ABOUT 1½ CUPS

1 pound dark cherries, pitted
About ¼ cup granulated sugar

2 to 3 tablespoons amaretto

Combine the cherries and 3 tablespoons of the sugar in a heavy medium saucepan, cover, and cook over medium heat, stirring occasionally, until the cherries begin to exude their juice, about 5 minutes. Reduce the heat to low, partially cover, and simmer gently, stirring occasionally, until the cherries are very tender and the juice has reduced to a light syrup, about 30 minutes.

Remove from the heat and stir in 2 tablespoons of amaretto. Taste and adjust the flavors of the jam, adding more sugar and another tablespoon of amaretto if desired. Serve at room temperature.

The jam can be stored in refrigerator for up to 2 weeks.

Jonathan Gold is a much better writer than I am, so I will let him give the summary of this dish. He described it as one of the Top 10 Dishes of 2007 in the *L.A. Weekly*: "I remember the udon, cooked softer than any Japanese chef would dare, seasoned with the French-style Sri Lankan curry blend called *vadouvan*, that with its citrus-peel tang and burnt-onion sweetness tasted almost exactly like a bowl of the thick Iranian soup *asht*—a four-culture carom shot that landed exactly on point."

lobster udon vadouvan

SERVES 6

LOBSTERS

⅔ cup distilled white vinegar
2 tablespoons kosher salt, plus more to taste
3 live Maine lobsters (about 1½ pounds each)
2 tablespoons clarified butter
3 tablespoons salted butter
Freshly ground white pepper

BROTH

3 tablespoons acacia honey
2 shallots, very thinly sliced
2 tablespoons rice vinegar
1 tablespoon sherry vinegar
2 cups plus 2 tablespoons water, preferably purified
2 tablespoons cornstarch
2 lemons, peeled and suprêmed (page 49)

2 oranges, peeled and suprêmed
2 pink grapefruits, peeled and suprêmed
Kosher salt and freshly ground white pepper

VADOUVAN BUTTER

6 tablespoons unsalted butter
6 tablespoons Vadouvan (recipe follows)
Fleur de sel and freshly ground white pepper

6 heads baby bok choy
6 ounces dried udon noodles
2 ounces enoki mushrooms, ends trimmed
6 baby carrots, very thinly sliced lengthwise, preferably rainbow carrots

Combine 8 quarts water, vinegar, and salt in a large pot and bring to a boil over high heat. Add 1 lobster and immediately turn off the heat. Let the lobster cook gently in the hot water for 3 minutes. The lobster will be medium-rare at this point (the meat will be sautéed later). Remove the lobster from the hot water and put it in a large bowl of ice water to cool. Repeat with the remaining 2 lobsters, returning the water to a boil before adding each one.

Remove the tail, claw, and knuckle meat, keeping the tails and claw meat intact. Discard the shells. Cover the lobster meat and refrigerate until ready to serve.

TO MAKE THE BROTH

Bring the honey to a boil in a heavy large saucepan over medium-high heat. Stir in the shallots, then deglaze with the vinegars. Stir in 2 cups water, and slowly bring to a boil.

Meanwhile, mix the cornstarch in a small bowl with the remaining 2 tablespoons water until a smooth, thick paste forms. Whisk the cornstarch mixture into the boiling water and continue whisking for 1 minute to blend it well. Then add the citrus segments and simmer gently for 25 minutes, or until the broth reduces to a nice light sauce and the citrus segments break apart. Season to taste with salt and white pepper. Remove from the heat and keep warm.

TO MAKE THE VADOUVAN BUTTER

Melt the butter in a heavy small saucepan over medium-low heat. Add the vadouvan, and fleur de sel and white pepper to taste. Remove the pan from the heat and let infuse for 10 minutes.

TO COOK THE BOK CHOY AND NOODLES

Blanch the bok choy in a large pot of boiling salted water just until crisp-tender, about 1 minute. Using tongs, transfer the bok choy to a plate and set aside. Return the water to a boil, add the noodles, and cook, stirring often, until al dente, about 4 minutes. Drain and set aside.

Heat the clarified butter in a large nonstick sauté pan over medium-high heat. Add the lobster meat and sauté for 2 minutes on each side. Add the salted butter and cook, basting the lobster pieces with the melted butter, until the meat is just cooked through, about 1 minute. Using tongs, transfer the lobster meat to a baking sheet lined with paper towels to absorb any excess butter. Season the lobster with salt and white pepper.

TO SERVE

Reheat the broth over medium-high heat. Add the bok choy, noodles, mushrooms, and carrots and simmer for 2 minutes. Season the broth to taste with salt and white pepper.

Divide the broth, vegetables, and noodles among six wide soup plates. Top with the lobster and drizzle the vadouvan butter all over. Serve immediately.

vadouvan

MAKES ABOUT 2 CUPS

2 pounds onions, cut into 1-inch
    pieces
2 pounds shallots, halved
12 garlic cloves

¼ cup grapeseed oil
1 teaspoon fenugreek seeds
1 tablespoon thinly sliced fresh
    curry leaves (optional)

1 tablespoon ground cumin

1 teaspoon ground cardamom

1 teaspoon brown mustard seeds

¾ teaspoon turmeric

½ teaspoon freshly grated nutmeg

½ teaspoon red pepper flakes

¼ teaspoon ground cloves

1 tablespoon kosher salt

½ teaspoon freshly ground white pepper

Working in 3 batches, pulse the onions in a food processor until coarsely chopped; transfer the onions to a bowl. Repeat with the shallots and then the garlic.

Heat the oil in a deep heavy 12-inch nonstick skillet over high heat until it shimmers. Add the onions, shallots, and garlic and sauté until golden and browned in spots, 25 to 30 minutes.

Meanwhile, position a rack in the center of the oven and preheat the oven to 350°F. Line a heavy large rimmed baking sheet with parchment paper.

Grind the fenugreek seeds in a spice grinder, clean coffee grinder, or mortar and pestle. Stir the fenugreek into the onion mixture, along with the remaining ingredients.

Transfer the onion mixture to the prepared baking sheet and spread it out evenly in a thin layer. Bake, stirring occasionally with a skewer to separate the onions, until they are well browned and barely moist, about 1 hour. Let cool.

The vadouvan may be stored in a dark dry place for up to 1 month.

CITRUS SUPRÊME

Citrus "suprême" is a cutting technique that removes the peel, pith, and membrane, leaving the most flavorful parts of the fruit and the pretty little pieces for plating and presentation. It is quite simple.

Using a small sharp knife, cut the top and bottom parts of the fruit. Place one of the cut sides down. Cut the peel and pith away from the fruit following the contour of the fruit. Holding the fruit in the palm of your hand, carefully cut along both sides of the membrane of each segment and lift the V-shaped suprêmes from the fruit. .

When you have beautiful fillets of wild striped bass, an East Coast fish that has become an obsession of mine, you don't have to do much to them. I employ my secret weapon, seasoning the fish with the incredible French-Basque chile powder called piment d'Espelette and serve it with a marmalade inspired by the South of France, where fish and fennel often collide.

wild striped bass, fennel marmalade, piment d'espelette

SERVES 4

FENNEL MARMALADE
3 fennel bulbs (about 2½ pounds total)
2 ½ cups dry red wine, such as Pinot Noir
¼ cup clover honey
¼ cup red wine vinegar
Kosher salt and freshly ground white pepper

STRIPED BASS
Four 6-ounce wild striped bass fillets with skin
Kosher salt and freshly ground white pepper
2 teaspoons piment d'Espelette
2 tablespoons olive oil
8 teaspoons mustard oil
2 green onions, very thinly sliced

TO MAKE THE FENNEL MARMALADE

Cut each fennel bulb lengthwise in half and cut out the cores. Cut the fennel lengthwise into ⅛-inch-thick slices.

Place the fennel slices in a heavy large saucepan and add the red wine, honey, vinegar, and a pinch each of salt and white pepper. Bring the mixture to a boil over medium-high heat, then reduce the heat to medium and cook, uncovered, stirring occasionally until the liquid has evaporated, the fennel is very tender, and the marmalade has begun to caramelize on the bottom and sides of the pan, about 1 hour. Season to taste with salt and white pepper.

Season the fish with salt, white pepper, and the piment d'Espelette. Place the fish skin side down in a large nonstick sauté pan. Drizzle the olive oil around the fish, set the pan over medium heat, and cook for 9 minutes. Turn the fish over and cook for 3 minutes longer until the center is almost opaque and before the fish begins to flake.

TO SERVE

Spoon the hot fennel marmalade into the center of four plates. Set the fish atop the marmalade. Drizzle 1 teaspoon of the mustard oil over each fillet, sprinkle with the green onions, and serve.

Alain Passard at L'Arpège taught me the virtues of cooking gently, and here I apply his wisdom to a cut of meat that is often grilled or otherwise treated to aggressive heat. By poaching the steaks ever so slowly in lard, you achieve meat so tender it melts in your mouth. The technique yields the same results as sous-vide, so forget cooking in a bag. As for the other components, the dish is a study in synergy: Potato and pear makes a great pairing. Pear goes well with blue cheese. And blue cheese is a very American (and very tasty) partner for beef.

Note: Make sure to get high-quality lard. You'll find it at good butcher shops and some farmers' markets. Ideally, the lard will have a golden tinge, not a snowy white color.

rib eye, potato-pear gratin, blue cheese sabayon

SERVES 8

RIB EYE

One 5¼-pound boneless rib-eye roast, trimmed of the chain, excess fat, and silverskin
7 pounds high-quality lard
Kosher salt and freshly ground black pepper
Fleur de sel

SHALLOT OIL

1 cup canola oil, plus more for deep-frying
8 ounces shallots, sliced ¼ inch thick

BLUE CHEESE SABAYON

1 gelatin sheet
6 large egg yolks
3 tablespoons water
3 ounces Roquefort cheese
½ cup heavy cream
Kosher salt and freshly ground white pepper

Potato-Pear Gratin (recipe follows)

Let the beef stand at room temperature for 1 hour.

Heat the lard to 240°F in a large pot over medium heat (use a deep-fry thermometer to regulate the temperature of the lard).

Using butcher's twine, tie the beef into a compact shape to help ensure even cooking. Season the beef generously with kosher salt and pepper. Submerge the beef in the hot lard and cook, turning occasionally, until an instant-read meat thermometer inserted into the center of the meat registers 110°F, about 1 hour. Remove the beef from the lard, put it on a baking sheet, and let it rest for 25 minutes.

TO MAKE THE SHALLOT OIL

Add enough oil to a heavy medium saucepan to fill it halfway, and heat the oil over medium heat to 300°F (use a deep-fry thermometer to regulate the temperature of the oil). Working in batches, fry the shallots until dark golden brown, about 4 minutes per batch. Using a spider or a wide-meshed spoon, transfer the shallots to a baking sheet lined with paper towels to drain.

Put the fried shallots and the 1 cup oil in a blender and blend vigorously for 45 seconds.

MEANWHILE, TO MAKE THE SABAYON

Soak the gelatin in a bowl of cold water until it softens, about 5 minutes.

Whisk the yolks and the 3 tablespoons water in a heatproof bowl set over a saucepan of simmering water until the mixture has quadrupled in volume, about 3 minutes. Reduce the heat to low and continue to whisk until the mixture is glossy and forms thick ribbons when the whisk is lifted from the bowl, about 3 minutes. Remove the softened gelatin from the water and add to the sabayon. Add the cheese and whisk vigorously to blend.

Set a medium bowl over a large bowl of ice water. Transfer the sabayon to the bowl and gently stir with a silicone spatula until cold and thickened but not set.

Whip the cream in another large bowl until thick and fluffy, then gently fold the whipped cream into the sabayon. Season the sabayon to taste with salt and white pepper. Cover and refrigerate.

TO SERVE

Cut the rib eye into thin slices and arrange on eight plates. Spoon the shallot oil on top of the beef, then sprinkle the beef with fleur de sel and pepper. Spoon the potato gratin alongside the beef, spoon the sabayon over the beef, and serve.

potato-pear gratin   SERVES 8

1 tablespoon unsalted butter, at room
  temperature
4 large russet (baking) potatoes
  (about 2¾ pounds)
1 tablespoon fresh lemon juice
4 Anjou pears
2 cups heavy cream

4 garlic cloves, minced
2 fresh thyme sprigs
Kosher salt and freshly ground
  black pepper
½ cup freshly grated Parmigiano-
  Reggiano

Position one rack in the center of the oven and another in the top third and preheat the oven to 375°F. Coat the inside of a 3-quart casserole dish with the butter. Fill two large bowls with cold water.

Peel the potatoes, then cut them on a mandoline, or with a sharp knife, into about ⅛-inch-thick slices. Reserve the potato slices in one bowl of cold water.

Add the lemon juice to the second bowl of cold water. Cut the pears in half, peel them, core them, then cut them on the mandoline into ⅛-inch-thick slices; reserve them in the cold lemon water. (Holding the potatoes and pears in water will prevent them from browning, but if you work quickly enough, you can skip this step and assemble the gratin straightaway.)

Combine the cream, garlic, and thyme in a heavy medium saucepan and bring just to a simmer over medium heat.

Drain the potato and pear slices, place them on paper towels, and pat them dry with kitchen towels. Cover the bottom of the prepared casserole dish with a layer of about one-fourth of the potato slices, then top with a layer of about one-third of the pear slices. Continue alternating the layers, forming 4 layers of potatoes and 3 of pears.

Remove the thyme from the hot cream and season the cream to taste with salt and pepper. Pour the cream over the potato-pear layers. Cover the dish with aluminum foil and bake on the center rack of the oven for 40 minutes.

Remove the foil and sprinkle the Parmigiano-Reggiano over the top of the gratin. Place the casserole dish on the top oven rack and bake until the gratin is golden brown on top, about 25 minutes. Let cool for 10 minutes before serving. The cream can also be made ahead and refrigerated. Reheat when ready to serve.

There is some management needed here. While the beef cooks, the gratin can be made and put in the oven. While the beef and the potatoes cook, the shallot oil and the sabayon can be made. Sabayon oil can be made in advance too.

Cooks in Spain understand the harmony of chocolate and olive oil. Inspired by this happy union, I underline their similarly silky textures by making a chocolate mousse and drizzling on orange-infused olive oil. For a sneaky surprise, the mousse packs the hot kick of chile powder. The heat takes a few seconds to register, adding to the fun.

spicy chocolate mousse, orange oil

SERVES 10

CHOCOLATE MOUSSE
½ cup whole milk
2 tablespoons piment d'Espelette
10 ounces bittersweet chocolate
   (70% cacao), chopped
4 large eggs, separated
6 tablespoons unsalted butter,
   melted

1⅓ cups confectioners' sugar
1⅓ cups heavy cream

ORANGE OLIVE OIL
¼ cup extra-virgin olive oil
Grated zest of 2 oranges (use a
   Microplane)

TO MAKE THE CHOCOLATE MOUSSE

Combine the milk and piment d'Espelette in a small saucepan, cover, and bring to a simmer over medium heat. Remove from the heat and set aside for 30 minutes to infuse.

Stir the chocolate in a large heatproof bowl set over a saucepan of simmering water until melted and smooth. Strain the milk mixture through a fine-mesh sieve into the melted chocolate and stir to blend. Set the chocolate mixture aside until cool to the touch, about 15 minutes.

Using an electric hand mixer, beat the egg yolks, melted butter, and ⅔ cup of the confectioners' sugar in a medium bowl until light and airy. In the bowl of a stand mixer fitted with the whisk attachment, beat the egg whites with the remaining ⅔ cup confectioners' sugar until soft peaks form. (You may also use the hand mixer with clean beaters.)

Using a large rubber spatula, fold the egg yolk mixture into the cooled chocolate mixture. Gently fold in half of the egg whites to lighten the chocolate mixture, then fold in the remaining egg whites.

Beat the cream in the mixer bowl until soft peaks form. Fold the whipped cream into the chocolate mixture, making sure not to overmix the mousse, so it retains a light, airy texture. Cover and refrigerate until cold, at least 3 hours, and up to 1 day.

TO MAKE THE ORANGE OIL

Combine the oil and orange zest in a food processor and blend for 1 minute. Transfer the oil to a container and store in the refrigerator; bring to room temperature before using. This could be made in advance.

TO SERVE

Spoon the mousse into wide shallow bowls. Drizzle the oil over and around the mousse.

I gave the classic rum-soaked French cake an L.A. makeover, with a nod to the city's vibrant Mexican population and to one of my favorite spirits. I added fleur de sel to the whipped cream, and the salty-sweet pleasure won't be lost on anyone fond of margaritas.

tequila babas, salty chantilly

SERVES 8

BABAS

Nonstick cooking spray

2 tablespoons warm whole milk
  (105° to 110°F)

2 teaspoons active dry yeast

¾ cup all-purpose flour

2 teaspoons granulated sugar

¼ teaspoon fine sea salt

1 large egg

4 tablespoons unsalted butter,
  at room temperature

TEQUILA SYRUP

2 cups water

1¼ cups granulated sugar

½ cup añejo tequila

ALOE VERA GELÉE

4 gelatin sheet

1 cup aloe vera juice

2 tablespoons water, preferably
  filtered

¼ cup granulated sugar

MOUSSELINE:

¼ cup heavy cream

½ cup Pastry Cream (recipe follows)

SALTED CHANTILLY

½ cup heavy cream

¼ teaspoon fleur de sel

TO MAKE THE BABAS

Set eight 1½-ounce savarin molds (about 3 inches in diameter) on a baking sheet and spray the molds with nonstick cooking spray.

Stir the warm milk and yeast in a small bowl to blend. Let stand until the yeast dissolves, about 10 minutes.

Using an electric mixer, blend the flour, sugar, and salt in a large bowl. Add the yeast mixture and egg and mix well. Gradually beat in the butter. The dough will be very sticky. Transfer to a pastry bag fitted with a plain tip and pipe the dough into the prepared savarin molds, dividing it equally. Cover with plastic wrap and let rise in a warm, draft-free area until the dough doubles in volume, about 30 minutes.

Position a rack in the center of the oven and preheat the oven to 375°F.

Uncover the molds and bake until the babas are golden brown and a skewer inserted near the center of a baba comes out clean, about 15 minutes. Invert the babas onto a cooling rack, remove the molds, and cool completely.

TO MAKE THE SYRUP

Combine the water and sugar in a large wide saucepan and bring to a boil over high heat, stirring to dissolve the sugar. Add the tequila and return the syrup to a boil, then remove the pan from the heat.

Working in batches, submerge the babas in the hot syrup just until soaked through, about 45 seconds per side, turning them with a wide slotted spoon, then transfer the babas to a cooling rack set over a baking sheet to drain. Cool completely.

TO MAKE THE GELÉE

Soak the gelatin in a bowl of cold water until it softens, about 5 minutes. Then squeeze out any excess liquid.

Combine the aloe vera juice, water, and sugar in a small saucepan and bring to a boil over high heat, stirring with a whisk to dissolve the sugar. Remove the softened gelatin from the water and whisk it into the aloe mixture until it dissolves. Transfer the gelée to a 6-by-4-inch baking dish or a rectangular or other small square container so you have a ½-inch-thick layer of gelée. Make in advance and refrigerate until cold and set.

TO PREPARE THE MOUSSELINE

Beat the heavy cream in a medium bowl until thick and fluffy. Fold in the pastry cream. Set aside.

Beat the cream and fleur de sel in a medium bowl until thick.

Cut the gelée into eighteen ¾-inch cubes.

Place a baba in the center of each of eight plates. Spoon about 2 tablespoons of the pastry cream mixture into the center of each baba. Arrange 3 cubes of gelée around each baba. Spoon the Chantilly onto one side of the plates and serve immediately.

pastry cream

MAKES ABOUT 2 CUPS

2 cups whole milk
1 vanilla bean, split lengthwise
½ cup granulated sugar

6 large egg yolks
¼ cup cornstarch
2 tablespoons unsalted butter

Put the milk in a heavy small saucepan. Scrape the seeds from the vanilla bean and add them to the milk, along with the pod. Bring the milk to a simmer.

Meanwhile, using an electric mixer, beat the sugar and egg yolks in a large bowl until light and fluffy, about 2 minutes. Mix in the cornstarch. Gradually mix in the hot milk mixture. Return the mixture to the saucepan and whisk over medium-low heat until the pastry cream thickens and bubbles begin to break on the surface, about 8 minutes. Remove from the heat, remove the vanilla pod, and whisk in the butter. Transfer to a small bowl and press plastic wrap directly onto the surface of the cream. Refrigerate until cold, at least 3 hours, and up to 2 days.

KITCHEN  ROSTER

LUDO

ARNOLD (sous chef)

ALEX (garde manger)

MIGUEL (fired)

LILLI (breadbar employee—quit)

STEVE (breadbar employee—quit)

ELI (Twitter sous chef of the day)

ERIN (Twitter intern)

CHRISTINE (Twitter "girl")

JOSIE (blogger intern)

JULIE (Twitter, then hired)

TU (customer—intern)

TEHRA (customer hired)

ELODIE (customer—intern)

JOANNA (friend of Elodie, in town for wedding,
worked for two weeks)

CHRIS (borrowed from Hatfield's)

PHILLIPE (quit)

SOHROB (eight-year-old)

OH AND THAT GUY WHO GOT ARRESTED (lasted two days)

SANSEI TIM (Ludo's karate instructor—intern)

"I'm sorry, we're closed tonight. The chef's in a bad mood."

It was just two days after we'd opened. Customers had been complaining about the new menu format (a set menu with three choices for appetizers and three for main dishes rather than à la carte small plates). My meat delivery was late and the wrong fish order had showed up. *Merde!* I thought. If I ran my restaurant the way these assholes run their companies, I'd be sleeping on the street. Enough. Everything was fucked, the food couldn't be perfect, so I decided to close for the night. And then I uttered that fateful sentence to a customer who called asking about that night's menu.

I wasn't happy, and neither was Krissy when I called her to tell her I was shutting it all down just a few hours before service began. Poor Krissy. She had picked up her phone while she was at the animal hospital. The vet had just told her that our dog had a brain tumor. LudoBites 2.0 was off to a great start.

How do you follow up a miracle? In the strange days after the first LudoBites ended, we fielded call after call from people who wanted to partner together on restaurants from L.A. to Shanghai. Ali from Breadbar wanted to open a sandwich shop with me. And I still hadn't relinquished my dream of opening a brick-and-mortar restaurant of my own. The only thing that never crossed my mind was doing another LudoBites.

Don't get me wrong, our first LudoBites was great—a bit of magic we conjured up in a borrowed kitchen with a borrowed restaurant crew. But it had been a one time thing, done by the seat of our pants, something that I never imagined would happen again. No one does pop-up restaurants for a living. It was a fun interlude between, you know, *real* jobs.

Shanghai was tempting, a chance to really delve into the Asian flavors I'd begun to toy with at LudoBites, but they wanted a full-time commitment for three years. No, thank you. Ali couldn't commit, so the sandwich idea drifted away. And we still couldn't find a good deal for our own restaurant. Maybe this is why I placed what seemed like the safest bet: a group known for its high-volume nightclubs and restaurants offered me a job opening at a huge Mediterranean-themed restaurant at a new hotel in Las Vegas. The position would be something totally new for me. I was used to serving maybe a hundred customers per night. These guys built their business model on serving nearly a thousand. It also meant money and stability, something I desperately wanted. Best of all, Krissy and I would be close enough that she could come see me every weekend.

At first, I was excited. To me, Mediterranean food means color and spice. It's hot deserts. It's blue sea. Its a vacation. I was inspired by what Jean-Georges Vongerichten did with Asian flavors at Spice Market and envisioned something in the same vein with Mediterranean spices. Some of the partners had been to dinner at my house, eaten my food, and said they liked my ideas. The next time they ate my food, though, at a menu tasting it was a fucking disaster. They didn't like a thing—not my beet gazpacho (they said they didn't like cold soup), not the brandade (one guy thought the salt cod was scrambled eggs), not even the heirloom tomatoes with feta mousse, one of the most popular items at LudoBites. After that catastrophic night, they gave me a list of dishes they *did* want on their "Mediterranean" menu: sliders, quesadillas, and . . . a knish, all to be enjoyed in a dining room shared with half-naked women washing each other in bathtubs. They actually brought in a chef from New York to show me how to make the knish. I was traumatized. I've spent a lot of time in the Mediterranean, and I've never once seen a slider, a quesadilla, or a fucking knish. This was not what I'd signed up for. And yet, even in the middle of that bad dream, I learned some invaluable business skills. I was overseeing a kitchen staff of more than eighty cooks in a restaurant that had opened with almost 500 employees. At LudoBites, I was lucky to get one sous chef; here I had six sous chefs plus a whole crew of trained cooks—and not one of them spoke French. We were doing 700 to 800 covers a night and in the process I learned things about food costs that no French chef ever taught me. I have to admit that I picked up some valuable lessons about managing people and budgets. I also learned how to say "no" a lot more.

Ultimately, they let me put some of my dishes on the menu. I had fun playing with the different oils, salts, and raw fish I'd used for my Ludo's *crudo* plate. I was thrilled with the individual paellas I created, and the lobster, potato, and truffle pizza was pretty awesome, if I do say so myself. *Gourmet* magazine called it a must. But Vegas and I just weren't meant to be and the request to put a one pound meatball on the menu was the straw that broke, shall we say, my culinary back.

It was the most miserable moment of my career. I learned the hard way that money can't buy happiness. I was losing my drive to cook. And for the first time in my life, I started to doubt myself.

But just before I left Vegas, I got a lucky break. *Top Chef Masters* called. I knew there was no way I'd still be in Vegas by the time the show aired, but I didn't have another restaurant to attach my name to. I'd be competing against guys with well-known restaurants, like Wylie Dufresne and Rick Bayless. Krissy understood that we needed to build on the publicity the show would provide. So I couldn't just be "Ludo Lefebvre, once chef at a restaurant in Vegas but now nowhere in particular." I decided to say I was the chef at LudoBites. Of course, this meant that by the time the first show aired, we had to be in business. LudoBites had to come back.

We had to move fast. Ali from Breadbar told me that I was welcome to return and use the space, but he said he couldn't handle front of the house this time, it was just too stressful for him. I certainly understood. I realized LudoBites could no longer just be a party for friends and anyone who happened to stop in. LudoBites had to grow up. I would have to run the whole show myself and hire all my own people. And there's no way I could handle that without a partner. This is when Krissy came in and turned LudoBites the Party into LudoBites the Business.

It was terrifying. First of all, I didn't know if L.A. would welcome me back after my stint in Vegas or give me the cold shoulder. I would've understood the scorn for someone who appeared to have turned his back on the city for Vegas-sized money. Then there was Krissy, writing check after check, setting up our own supplier accounts, buying liability insurance, starting a payroll system—all before we knew whether or not we'd have a single customer. I felt like an athlete who hadn't been in the game for a while. It had been a year and a half since I'd done the kind of cooking I loved, the kind that kept me up nights, giddy with excitement. My spirit was broken, and I needed some inspiration. I needed to go to Paris.

France was where I'd fallen in love with cooking and where I'd been lucky enough to work under some of the country's finest chefs, but this time, I was seeking a different kind of inspiration. I wasn't interested in fine dining, I wanted to eat food from the new generation of chefs who had carved out their own definition of freedom.

Paris is the center of the "bistronomie" movement, which started back in the 1990s when Yves Camdeborde gave up his position at a Michelin two-star restaurant—a rare thing when I was a young chef in France unless you were heading to another Michelin-starred restaurant—to open his own place, devoted to simple, good food in a cozy but plain space. Now there are many such places, like Châteaubriand in the 11th arrondissement, a little bistro where the bearded staff wear jeans, T-shirts, and sneakers to work, and where the chef, Inaki Aizpitarte, spends little money on the ambiance so he can splurge on the food—the best ingredients, the best technique. Or places like Le Baratin in Belleville, where Raquel Carena, an Argentinean woman in her sixties, runs the kitchen by herself and serves elegant, perfectly seasoned, and, best of all, simple food.

I just loved it. I thought, Aha! Amazing food doesn't necessarily mean froufrou food. Instead of blowing a million dollars on decor, as I see chefs do again and again in the States. In Paris, you find an empty bistro and repaint the walls. That's it. No fancy chandelier. No expensive silverware. No Riedel wineglasses. I thought, maybe LudoBites wasn't just a phase, a stopgap, a way to pass the time until I could open a proper restaurant. I'm a cook. I love to feed people, to make them happy. Give me a sea of fancy induction burners, a dinky grill, or a hot plate—it doesn't matter, I just need to cook.

But after I'd informed the woman on the phone that we were closing due to my bad mood—she hung up before I had the chance to tell her I was half-joking—she took to Twitter: "UMMM . . . just called ludobites for tonights menu and they say, 'the chef is in a bad mood and doesnt want to cook tonight. we're CLOSED' WTF?!" Next thing you know, the whole thing blows up on the popular website EaterLA, and our PR person, Rachel, calls Krissy, who was still having a grand old time at the animal hospital, to try to do damage control. Rachel suggested we issue a statement. Then Krissy made an important decision. "You know what?" she said. "Ludo works for himself and doesn't need to explain anything to anybody. If he's in a bad mood, I don't want him cooking for me." Rachel just laughed: "I love it!"

So our manager called every customer with reservations to apologize, and we closed for the night. That was a real breakthrough for me. For the first time, I truly understood that LudoBites was *my* restaurant. Krissy and I no longer had our comfortable salaries. We were living paycheck to uncertain paycheck. But I was able to cook my food, my way. I loved it. We started fresh the next day. We had a new menu, the chef had had a good night's sleep, and, best of all, no one seemed to hold it against us. Bloggers even defended us. When we opened for our third night of service, we were busier than we'd expected.

So busy, in fact, that we were running out of food. So, of course, that was when

Mr. Pulitzer, Jonathan Gold, showed up. He'd made a reservation under a different name, and he had a tendency to eat on the late side (especially if the Lakers were playing). When Krissy told me who had just walked in, I flipped. *You have to be fucking kidding!* We had virtually no food left. I told her that we couldn't serve him. We'd been open for mere days, with no "friends-and-family" nights or other practice runs in the weeks before. *Please, someone make this guy disappear!* Krissy convinced me that I had to serve him something. She sat him and then broke the news: "Mr. Gold, we won't even give you the menu, because it's no longer relevant, but we'll serve you what we can." I took a deep breath and got to work.

I had fried chicken on the brain that night. I was planning to try a new dish the next evening, Basque vegetables topped with panfried chicken. I'd been experimenting, but the dish wasn't ready for prime time. Still, I didn't have a lot of options. So while Krissy served Jonathan one of the last portions of foie gras miso soup, I started frying a batch of chicken, and like the good French boy I am, I used duck fat.

Less than a week later, Jonathan's First Bite column began: "On the third night of LudoBites, the restaurant ran out of food." I winced, steeling myself for a verbal thumping. It never came. Instead, he called the miso soup a tour de force. My risky improvisation? He said the fried chicken "could have made a New Orleans grandmother weep with happiness." Reading that made me want to do the same.

Our next step was to hunt down the person we'd started to call Twitter Girl. We found her blog, which had a photo of her. So we printed it out and posted it in the kitchen, along with a note: "WANTED! If you see this girl, please let us know, quick." This is something many restaurants do, but with photos of big-time magazine and newspaper critics. But for us, she had become a Very Important Person. Then, one night, there she was. Although we didn't let on that we recognized her that night (we did make an extra effort to ensure that she'd have nothing to complain about), when she came back again, I confronted her. She was so embarrassed. But by the end of our chat, we were both laughing. Now we're friends. Krissy and I even went to her wedding.

And thanks to her, two Luddites like Krissy and me discovered the power of Twitter. We joined to investigate Twitter Girl, but soon we were having fun tweeting about our daily triumphs and trials ("Has anybody seen my fish order? I think it's stuck on the 405") and even using Twitter to recruit cooks. We were so excited when I reached the 100-follower mark; today, @ChefLudo has more than 20,000. Twitter became an indispensable tool for developing the community that LudoBites has become.

That's not to say the three months of LudoBites 2.0 were easy. There was my disastrous appearance on *Top Chef Masters*. I was eliminated early, all because of a quesadilla! I almost had to laugh at the irony: in Vegas, I'd been serving two hundred quesadillas per night. In another respect, though, the show was a wonderful thing. I was reenergized by just being around other chefs again, around people who cared so much about food. And when it aired it got people buzzing about LudoBites.

There were the extremely emotional forty-eight hours after a blogger wrote a post disparaging my preparation of foie gras and criticizing my beef tartare for being too rare—if beef tartare isn't *raw*, then it isn't tartare. Krissy saw the post and went nuts. She mounted a defense of our food in the blog's comment section, taking the blogger to task for not explaining that she was unfamiliar with the foods she was passing judgment on, but she also applauded her for trying new things and invited her back to dine with us, and Ludo would personally explain the dishes. Krissy and I were sure we had done the right thing by responding, but all hell broke loose. Other commenters claimed that Krissy had bullied this woman and made her cry. The blogger herself was so upset that she took her post down, but another blogger told her to put it back up. Much of the L.A. blogger community got involved in the drama, and accusations were flying. The Web, we learned, could be a scary place.

Ultimately, the whole blogger blowup was a valuable learning experience for us. We did not have investors if LudoBites failed, not only did we not get paychecks, but we would lose all of our investment. To have someone criticize my food was one thing—I get it, a chef can never please everyone. But if that criticism was unfounded and unfair? That was dangerous. It was just too much.

To make matters worse, a few days later, Krissy informed me that I'd be cooking for a table of twelve bloggers. A guy I met at LudoBites 1.0, named Will Chi, had started a site called FoodDigger, which hosted meals for bloggers at restaurants. Krissy decided to organize it for the night of my *Top Chef Masters* episode, bringing in a TV to make it a viewing party. After my recent experience, I was not exactly thrilled to be cooking for a bunch of people who could eviscerate me with a few deft keyboard strokes. The day of the dinner, I told Krissy, fuck it, I wasn't doing it. No way. But ultimately I changed my mind, even after Krissy told me that Ms. I Don't Like Ludo's Foie Gras would be in attendance. Before the meal I told them, more or less, that I was cooking for them against my will.

But then my anger was redirected, at the TV. Because there I was on-screen, with subtitles at the bottom. I mean, I know I have a thick accent, but come on! Not just that, the show seemed to be edited with the exclusive purpose of making me look like an insane person. I was screaming at the TV and next thing I knew, the bloggers were laughing—and I was too. Long story short, everyone had a great time, and Krissy and I made a bunch of new friends. Ms. Foie Gras even ate her namesake dish twice that night and liked it. Since that night, she has become a great and trusted friend and supporter of LudoBites.

And how weird it was to sit back and watch these bloggers snap photos of every dish and jot down notes after what seemed like every bite. Restaurants used to worry about professional restaurant critics. Suddenly everyone was a critic. It was scary, but incredible too. Our customers were part of our lives in a new way. We were all part of the same community. The members of the new media establishment were embracing us, a new kind of restaurant, not with blind adoration but with the sort of complex love you find in families. Krissy and I now say this all the time, but bloggers *made* LudoBites. They came, they ate, and they wrote and wrote and wrote.

From the day the *Top Chef Masters* episode aired, every single seat in our restaurant was full. And I was dealing with more staff disasters than ever. There were the no-shows, and there were the no-shows with amazing excuses, like the cook who told me he was going to be late because he'd been arrested. (He never showed up.) There was the blogger who won our "Be Ludo's Sous Chef for a Night" contest on Twitter (our sly way of borrowing a set of hands for the kitchen) and proceeded to drop two gallons of black-truffle-infused oxtail stock on the floor an hour before service. Then there was the six-foot-five Russian server. I had about eight plates of food ready at the pass, waiting to be taken to Table 20. I called to him to take these plates, and take them now. "No," he said. "I'm busy." The correct answer to my request, if you're wondering, is "*Oui,* chef." After all, I'm the fucking boss. But what did he do? He stared at me, like a statue, for what seemed like fifteen minutes. Finally, he said, "Why don't you take the food yourself?" I couldn't believe it. So I'm standing there screaming at this guy who could have deboned me like a quail with his bare hands. (At the same time, I'm thinking, Wow, you actually said that to your boss—God Bless America!) I fired him then and there, at 7:30 P.M. on an incredibly busy Friday night. That was just two hours after I'd fired a line cook. The staff was getting smaller by the hour. At one point, we were so desperate that we had an eight-year-old in the kitchen, trimming green beans.

But eventually we found some wonderful workers, like the cadre of astoundingly diligent Mexican bussers, dishwashers, and cooks who'd bust their asses at LudoBites each night, after having worked another job all day. And the two women we hired directly from the packed tables in the dining room. One minute they were slurping white asparagus velouté with their families or friends; the next thing you know, they had a job making that very same velouté the next night.

The antagonism between our customers and us, which had defined our early nights, had transformed into affection. On our last night, one of our new friends, Jo Stougaard, the blogger behind My Last Bite, brought in a big red *Top Chef* timer to help us turn tables. The timer would go off after two hours, but nobody wanted to leave. We gave away a lot of Champagne to customers who had to wait an hour or more for their tables, but they were incredibly patient. That night, I knew we'd got the magic back. We were a big community, a big family: our staff and our customers, detractors and fans alike. We were all there to experience a new sort of dining. No longer did I worry about not having a big fancy kitchen or a troupe of veteran cooks. I had my freedom, and that was all I needed.

I've never understood why anyone would order a plate of charcuterie at a restaurant. All those cured meats are good, sure, but unless the chef is making them himself, you might as well go to the store and buy them. You want something from the mind of the chef. That's what I was thinking when I developed this dish, a playful reinterpretation of those plates of coppa, *jamón iberico,* or *saucisson sec.* Spanish chorizo becomes a chilled creamy soup, the classic cornichon accompaniment becomes a sorbet, and cubes of summer melon provide texture and sweetness. It may sound odd, but trust me, to taste it is to love it. Jonathan Gold named it a Top 10 dish for 2009, saying: "A cool cream-flavored funky, smoky Spanish chorizo, bathing cubes of juicy ripe melon and splinters of ice—ice that expressed the essence of cornichons and pickled onions, with a texture as jagged as its taste. A soup that is worth the wait."

chorizo soup, melon, cornichon sorbet

SERVES 6

SOUP

1½ pounds hot Spanish chorizo (preferably Palacios brand), casing removed and the meat very thinly sliced

3¼ cups half-and-half

½ cup heavy cream

Freshly ground white pepper

CORNICHON SORBET

1 cup drained cornichons

1 cup sliced yellow onions

1 cup Simple Syrup (page 300)

2 tablespoons water, preferably flat mineral water

GARNISHES

¾ cup of ¼-inch diced cantaloupe

¾ cup of ¼-inch diced honeydew melon

Combine the chorizo, half-and-half, and heavy cream in a heavy large saucepan and bring to a near-simmer over medium heat. Reduce the heat to low, cover, and simmer gently for 30 minutes (do not allow the soup to boil).

Strain the soup into a high-powered blender, discard the chorizo. Blend the soup until smooth and creamy. Season to taste with pepper. Pour into a bowl, cover, and refrigerate until cold (the soup will thicken as it chills).

MEANWHILE, TO MAKE THE SORBET

Combine the cornichons and onions in a food processor and process until finely chopped. Transfer to a bowl and whisk in the sugar syrup and water. Refrigerate until cold.

About 20 minutes before serving, transfer the cornichon mixture to an ice cream machine and freeze according to the manufacturer's instructions.

TO SERVE

Pour the cold soup into small bowls. Top each with a quenelle of cornichon sorbet and garnish with the diced melons. Serve immediately.

Sometimes chefs have to give customers what they want. And boy, do people love tuna tartare. Yet I wanted to do something different, something fun. I started toying with colors, playing with the tuna's beautiful red hue and adding yet more shades of purples and reds in the form of beets, balsamic vinegar, and berries. It's not your typical tuna tartare.

raw tuna, red beets, watermelon

SERVES 4

RED BEET BATH
1 cup fresh red beet juice
2 tablespoons balsamic vinegar
2 tablespoons reduced-sodium soy sauce

BERRIES
16 fresh red raspberries
16 fresh golden raspberries
8 fresh blackberries
⅓ cup extra-virgin olive oil
Pinch of wasabi paste

TUNA
About 12 ounces sushi-grade ahi tuna,
    cut into sixteen ¾-inch cubes
¼ cup toasted sesame seeds
Eight ¾-inch cubes seeded watermelon
3 tablespoons toasted sesame oil
8 fresh mint leaves

TO MAKE THE RED BEET SAUCE
Whisk the beet juice, balsamic, and soy sauce in a small bowl to blend. Transfer the mixture to a whipped cream dispenser and load it with 2 nitrous oxide cartridges. Refrigerate until cold.

TO PREPARE THE BERRIES
Combine the berries, olive oil, and wasabi paste in a medium bowl and mash to a puree with a fork.

Roll the pieces of tuna in the sesame seeds.

Shake the container of beet sauce vigorously for 30 seconds, then pipe the sauce into the center of four shallow soup plates. Place 4 pieces of the tuna, 2 spoonfuls of the berry puree, and 2 cubes of watermelon in each bowl. Drizzle the sesame oil over, garnish with the mint leaves, and serve immediately.

As a mayonnaise-loving Frenchman, I am in great debt to the Italian cook who invented tonnato sauce, essentially a mayo made from canned tuna packed in olive oil. But rather than pairing it with thinly sliced cooked veal tenderloin, as you'd find at a restaurant in Piemonte, I decided to make a veal tartare, melt-in-your-mouth cubes of raw veal tossed with plump, briny raw oysters and a drizzle of almond oil. It may sound unusual, but I promise that this elegant take on surf-and-turf will be a huge hit at your table.

veal tartare, oysters, tonnato-style

SERVES 4

TONNATO SAUCE

One 5-ounce can white tuna packed
    in olive oil, drained
1 large egg
3 tablespoons white wine vinegar
1½ tablespoons Dijon mustard
1 tablespoon drained capers
½ cup extra-virgin olive oil
⅓ cup grapeseed oil
Kosher salt and freshly ground
    white pepper

VEAL TARTARE

8 ounces veal tenderloin, cut into
    ⅓-inch dice
8 Kumamoto oysters, shucked

3 tablespoons almond oil
Fleur de sel and freshly ground
    white pepper to taste

GARNISHES

1 avocado, halved, peeled, pitted,
    and diced
8 fresh almonds, peeled, or unsalted
    raw almonds
8 fresh purple basil leaves
1 lemon

Combine the tuna, egg, vinegar, mustard, and capers in a food processor and process to blend. With the machine running, gradually add the olive oil and grapeseed oil, processing until smooth.

Press the sauce through a fine-mesh sieve into a bowl; discard the solids. Season the sauce to taste with salt and white pepper. Transfer the sauce to a whipped cream dispenser and load it with 2 nitrous oxide cartridges. Refrigerate until cold.

Toss all the ingredients together in a medium bowl. Refrigerate until chilled.

Shake the container of tonnato sauce vigorously for 30 seconds, then pipe the sauce into the center of four shallow soup plates. Spoon the veal tartare on top. Arrange the diced avocado around the tartare, top with the almonds and basil leaves, and grate lemon zest over each serving. Serve immediately.

This is a dish that taught me a lesson. I first cooked it in homage to something Krissy and I ate at Paris's opulent Le Grand Véfour. The brilliant chef, Guy Martin, paired braised oxtail, black truffle, and potatoes to tremendous effect in a sort of shepherd's pie for kings, not sheepherders. My rendition was decidedly less elaborate, and instead of potatoes, I used polenta spiked with plenty of butter and Cantal cheese. Customers freaked out. It was all they could talk about. I still get requests for the dish. At first, I couldn't understand it. It's a simple dish: Braise oxtails, reduce the cooking liquid, and cook some polenta. You could easily make it at home. I wondered, Don't people want more from me as a chef? Shouldn't I do something more, perhaps add a lovely Parmesan tuile, at the very least? Then I realized, it's not all about me, it's not about satisfying *my* need to show customers how clever I can be. People love simple food that tastes really good. My main job? Make sure it does.

oxtail, creamy cantal polenta, black truffle

SERVES 6

OXTAIL

One 3¾-pound oxtail, cut into 2 or 3 pieces
2 onions, coarsely chopped
2 carrots, peeled and coarsely chopped
2 celery stalks, coarsely chopped
1 leek, coarsely chopped
1 bouquet garni—a sprig each of parsley, thyme, and rosemary, plus 1 bay leaf tied together with twine
About 14 cups cold water

Kosher salt and freshly ground white pepper

BLACK TRUFFLE SAUCE

1 cup black (winter) truffle juice (preferably La Truffière brand)
2 tablespoons unsalted butter, at room temperature
1 black (winter) truffle (preferably La Truffière brand), very finely chopped

Kosher salt and freshly ground white
    pepper

Creamy Cantal Polenta (recipe follows),
    just made
2 tablespoons chive flowers for garnish

TO PREPARE THE OXTAILS

Combine the oxtail pieces, onions, carrots, celery, leek, and bouquet garni in a heavy
large pot. Add enough cold water to cover, bring to a simmer over medium heat, and
simmer very gently for about 3 hours, until the meat is falling off the bone.

Strain the cooking liquid into a heavy medium saucepan (you should have about 8
cups broth); reserve the oxtails. Simmer the broth over medium-high heat until it is
reduced to 4 cups, about 40 minutes.

Meanwhile, using your fingers, remove the oxtail meat from the bones and remove
and discard the cartilage and bones. Set the meat aside.

Transfer 2 cups of the reduced broth to a small saucepan and set it aside for the
truffle sauce. Add the oxtail meat to the remaining broth and simmer gently for 30
minutes, or until most of the liquid has evaporated but there's still enough to coat the
meat. Season with salt and white pepper and keep warm.

MEANWHILE, TO MAKE THE SAUCE

Simmer the reserved broth until reduced to 1 cup, about 20 minutes. Add the truffle
juice and simmer until the liquid is reduced by half, about 20 minutes.

Gradually add the butter to the sauce, whisking to blend. Whisk in the truffle and
season to taste with salt and white pepper.

TO SERVE

Using a slotted spoon, remove the oxtail meat from the cooking liquid and divide
it among six small soup bowls. Spoon a generous amount of the truffle sauce over
the meat. Cover with the hot polenta. Garnish with the chive flowers and serve immediately.

creamy cantal polenta

SERVES 6

1¾ cups Chicken Stock (page 39)
1¼ cups whole milk
¾ cup water
1 teaspoon finely chopped garlic
¾ cup polenta

¾ cup shredded Cantal cheese
4 tablespoons unsalted butter, at
    room temperature
Kosher salt and freshly ground black
    pepper

Combine the chicken stock, milk, water, and garlic in a heavy medium saucepan and bring to a boil over medium-high heat. Whisking constantly, gradually sprinkle in the polenta. Reduce the heat to low, partially cover, and simmer, whisking often, for 20 minutes, or until the polenta is thick and creamy. Stir in the cheese and butter and season to taste with salt and pepper.

I used to look on in wonder as Pierre Gagnaire, one of my culinary mentors, created a velouté that tasted vividly of white asparagus using just the scraps left over after peeling and prepping the vegetable for another dish. Now I make a similar creamy soup whenever I can lay hands on the beautiful fat spears from Europe with their eggshell color and pleasant, slight bitterness. I hide a scoop of mozzarella ice cream in the soup, and then I dollop on glossy orange orbs of salmon roe, add a tangle of lightly dressed fennel, and sprinkle on black olive powder—which only sounds as if it's difficult to make.

white asparagus velouté, mozzarella ice cream, fennel, black olive

SERVES 8

VELOUTÉ
2 tablespoons unsalted butter
4 shallots, very thinly sliced
1 pound large white asparagus, peeled and cut into fine dice
2 teaspoons granulated sugar
2 cups heavy cream
½ cup water
Kosher salt and freshly ground white pepper

BLACK OLIVE POWDER
16 Moroccan oil-cured black olives, pitted

FENNEL SALAD
1 fennel bulb, trimmed
1½ tablespoons extra-virgin olive oil
1 teaspoon finely grated lemon zest
1½ tablespoons fresh lemon juice
Kosher salt and freshly ground white pepper

ACCOMPANIMENTS
Mozzarella Ice Cream (recipe follows)
¼ cup salmon roe

TO MAKE THE VELOUTÉ

Melt the butter in a heavy large saucepan over medium heat. Add the shallots and sauté for 3 minutes, or until tender but not browned. Stir in the asparagus and sugar, pour in the cream, and add enough cold water to cover the asparagus. Bring to a simmer and simmer gently for 15 to 20 minutes, until the asparagus is very tender.

Working in batches if necessary, transfer the soup to a blender and puree until very smooth. Season the velouté to taste with salt and white pepper, and let cool; then cover and refrigerate until cold. Store for 2 to 3 days.

TO MAKE THE OLIVE POWDER

Preheat the oven to 300°F.

Put the olives in a small baking pan and bake until dry, about 35 minutes. Set the olives aside to cool.

Transfer the dried-out olives to a spice grinder or clean coffee grinder and grind to a powder. Set aside.

TO MAKE THE FENNEL SALAD

Using a mandoline, cut the fennel crosswise into very thin slices. Toss the fennel with the olive oil, lemon zest, and lemon juice in a medium bowl. Season to taste with salt and white pepper.

TO SERVE

Pour the velouté into four shallow soup bowls. Place a large quenelle of mozzarella ice cream in the center of each bowl, mound the fennel salad on top, sprinkle with the black olive powder, and garnish with the salmon roe. Serve immediately.

mozzarella ice cream   MAKES ABOUT 3 CUPS

1 gelatin sheet
¾ cup heavy cream
½ cup whole milk
8 ounces buffalo mozzarella,
    drained, tough outer skin
    removed, diced

Kosher salt and freshly
    ground white pepper

Soak the gelatin in a bowl of cold water until it softens, about 5 minutes.

Combine the heavy cream and milk in a heavy small saucepan and bring to a very gentle simmer over medium heat. Reduce the heat to low, add the diced mozzarella, and whisk to blend; do not allow the mixture to simmer. Remove the softened gelatin from the water and whisk it into the mozzarella mixture until it dissolves. Season to taste with salt and white pepper. Transfer to a bowl and let cool, then refrigerate until cold.

About 45 minutes before serving, transfer the mozzarella mixture to an ice cream machine and freeze according to the manufacturer's instructions. Serve immediately.

ICE CREAMS AND MOUSSES

In the restaurant, I always use a Paco-Jet for making ice creams and mousses. The Paco-Jet allows me to produce an ice cream or mousse in small batches and "spin" it right before plating to perfectly smooth ice cream or mousse. This reduces waste and helps control food cost while producing the freshest product. The ice cream and mousse recipes in this book have been tested in a traditional home ice cream maker. In some places, we have said you can make it in advance and freeze for the sake of time management. If you do make it in advance and freeze, please note that what comes out of the freezer will be noticeably harder than what went in, so it is vital that you allow the ice cream to sit and temper for 3 to 5 minutes after removing it from the freezer. This will give you the best chance to mimic the texture of the freshly churned product. If you have the time, you will achieve the best result by making your ice creams and mousses on the same day as the rest of the recipe and churning them immediately before serving.

I'm a big fan of Greek salad: the sweetness of the tomatoes and red onion, the invigorating saltiness of the olives and feta, and the sharpness of vinegar. But whenever I take a bite, I can't help but wish the feta had a nicer texture. For this salad, I didn't change the flavor profile, and I didn't change the composition. I just rehabilitated the feta with a simple technique: Simmer briefly with cream, add gelatin, blend, and refrigerate. The next day, you'll have a fantastic mousse with the flavor of feta and the luscious texture of burrata.

greek salad, feta mousse

SERVES 6

FETA MOUSSE

2 tablespoons cold water
¾ teaspoon unflavored powdered gelatin
8 ounces Greek feta cheese, crumbled
½ cup heavy cream
Freshly ground white pepper

SALAD

2¼ pounds assorted heirloom tomatoes (about 6), diced
Fleur de sel and freshly ground black pepper
5 tablespoons extra-virgin olive oil
1 cup Niçoise olives, pitted and halved
½ small red onion, thinly sliced
1 tablespoon chopped fresh oregano

TO MAKE THE FETA MOUSSE

Put the cold water in a small bowl, sprinkle the gelatin over it, and let stand for 5 minutes, or until the gelatin softens.

Meanwhile, combine the feta cheese and cream in a heavy small saucepan, bring to a simmer over medium heat, and simmer for 1 minute, or just until the cheese is almost completely melted. Remove from the heat and stir in the softened gelatin until it dissolves.

Transfer the mixture to a blender and puree until smooth and a bit foamy. Season to taste with white pepper. Transfer the mousse to a bowl and press a sheet of plastic wrap directly onto the surface. Refrigerate for 30 minutes, or until set. (The mousse can be prepared up to 2 days ahead.)

About 20 minutes before serving, remove the mousse from the refrigerator and let stand until it returns to room temperature.

TO SERVE THE SALAD

Whisk the mousse to loosen it. Arrange the tomatoes on each plate and season them lightly with fleur de sel and pepper. Top with a quenelle (or scoop) of mousse. Drizzle the oil over the tomatoes and mousse, garnish with the olives, red onion, and oregano, and serve.

LudoBites 2.0 became a sort of bistro serving food from around the world. I had great fun exploring the flavors of Spain, Greece, Italy, Japan, and, as in this dish, India. I zoomed in on a combination I adore: curry, with its aromatic and lively mixture of spices, and the tangy, cooling yogurt that often comes with it. I made an emulsion of curry and yogurt and drizzled it on top of seared scallops and briefly sautéed spinach. And, just like that, you can close your eyes and pretend you're in India.

scallops, baby spinach, curried yogurt sauce

SERVES 4

YOGURT SAUCE

2 tablespoons clarified butter

2 sweet onions, such as Vidalia or Maui, thinly sliced

1 tablespoon grated peeled fresh ginger

2 garlic cloves, minced

¼ cup Madras curry powder

2 fresh curry leaves

One 32-ounce container plain whole-milk yogurt

2 tablespoons light brown sugar

Fleur de sel

2 tablespoons unsalted butter, cut into pieces

SCALLOPS AND SPINACH

20 large sea scallops, tough tendons removed

Kosher salt and freshly ground black pepper

2 tablespoons clarified butter

1 tablespoon unsalted butter

10 ounces baby spinach, cleaned and dried

Fleur de sel

TO MAKE THE YOGURT SAUCE

Melt the clarified butter in a heavy large saucepan over medium heat. Add the onions, ginger, garlic, curry powder, and curry leaves and cook, stirring, for 10 minutes, or until the onions soften but do not brown.

Stir in the yogurt and brown sugar, season to taste with fleur de sel, and cook over medium-low heat, stirring occasionally, for 20 minutes, or until the onions are very tender and the sauce has reduced slightly.

Strain the yogurt mixture through a fine-mesh sieve into a bowl, pressing on the solids; discard the solids. Blend the strained sauce in a blender until smooth. Blend in the butter. Season to taste with fleur de sel. Set aside.

MEANWHILE, TO PREPARE THE SCALLOPS AND SPINACH

Season the scallops with salt and pepper. Heat a large nonstick sauté pan over high heat until hot. Add 1 tablespoon of the clarified butter. Add half of the scallops and cook for 1 to 2 minutes on each side, or until golden brown on both sides and almost opaque in the center. Transfer to a plate and tent with foil to keep warm. Repeat with the remaining 1 tablespoon clarified butter and scallops. Wipe out the pan.

Melt the 1 tablespoon butter in the sauté pan over medium-high heat. Add the spinach and sauté for 3 minutes, or just until it wilts. Season to taste with fleur de sel.

TO SERVE

Mound the sautéed spinach in the center of four plates. Surround the spinach with the scallops. Drizzle the yogurt sauce over the spinach and scallops and serve immediately.

If I could have any pasta dish in the world, it would be a well-made *cacio e pepe:* high-quality pasta, Pecorino cheese, and a lot of black pepper—maybe a little butter (hey, I'm French, after all). That's it. So simple, so incredible. But I wanted to add some excitement, a little surprise for my customers. So instead of pasta, I swap in celery root cut into spaghetti-like strands. I fell head over heels for celery root when I was cooking at L'Arpège under Alain Passard. He'd cook the whole gnarly, bulbous root in a salt crust for three hours, then crack the crust, peel the celery root, and slice it. From there, with nothing more than butter, black pepper, and a little whole-grain mustard, he turned one of the most homely vegetables into a showstopping dish.

"spaghetti" cacio e pepe   SERVES 6

2 large celery root bulbs (about 1 pound each), peeled and cut into long julienne (about 6 cups)
6 tablespoons unsalted butter
2 tablespoons extra-virgin olive oil
2 cups freshly grated Pecorino Romano (8 ounces)

2 tablespoons black peppercorns, coarsely ground, plus more to taste
12 fresh sage leaves
6 large eggs
Kosher salt

Blanch the celery root in a large pot of boiling salted water just until al dente, about 1 minute. Drain, reserving 4 cups of the cooking water. Add the celery root to a large bowl of ice water to cool completely, then drain well.

Bring 3 cups of the reserved root cooking water to a simmer in a large saucepan and simmer until reduced by half, about 10 minutes. Whisk in the butter and olive oil, and simmer for 5 minutes.

Meanwhile, bring the remaining 1 cup cooking water to a boil in a large sauté pan over high heat. Add the celery root and cook, stirring occasionally, for 2 minutes to rewarm it. Drain.

Stir the celery root into the sauce and bring to a boil. Reduce the heat to low and add the cheese and pepper, stirring and tossing until the cheese melts and the sauce coats the celery root. Season to taste with salt and more pepper.

TO SERVE

Divide the "spaghetti" among six shallow bowls. Crack 1 egg, separate the yolk and the white, and place the yolk on top of a serving of spaghetti. Repeat with the remaining eggs. (Reserve the egg whites for another use, if desired.) Garnish with the sage and serve.

A perfectly cooked duck breast has moist meat and cracker-crisp skin. Achieving both can be difficult, especially when you have a staff limited in both size and skill, so I came up with a way to make it work: cook the skin and breast separately. If you remove the skin, you can roast it in the oven until it's really crisp and wonderful while you give the breast its own ideal treatment—cooking it gently in butter to medium-rare on the stovetop. Sweetness and acidity are good friends to duck's richness, so I whip up a sweet, tangy sauce made with tamarind and orange, along with an (almost) classic version of leeks vinaigrette.

duck, crispy skin, leek salad, tamarind

SERVES 4

DUCK
Four 6-ounce boneless duck breasts
2 tablespoons grapeseed oil
Kosher salt and freshly ground black pepper
2 tablespoons clarified butter

ORANGE SAUCE
2 garlic cloves
1 cup orange juice
3 tablespoons tamarind paste
1 tablespoon clover honey
2 teaspoons soy sauce
½ teaspoon Chinese five-spice powder
¼ teaspoon ground dried Thai bird chile

LEEK SALAD
2 leeks (white and pale green parts only), cut lengthwise into ½-inch-wide slices
⅓ cup grapeseed oil
2 tablespoons grated peeled fresh ginger (use a Microplane)
1 tablespoon blanched chopped garlic
2 tablespoons sherry vinegar
1 teaspoon Dijon mustard
Kosher salt and freshly ground white pepper

Preheat the oven to 350°F.

Remove the skin and fat from the duck breasts. Lay the skin in a single layer on a heavy rimmed baking sheet and bake until the skin is dry and crisp, about 40 minutes.

Combine the crisp duck skin with the grapeseed oil in a blender and blend until pureed. Season to taste with salt and pepper.

TO MAKE THE SAUCE

Blanch the garlic in a small saucepan of boiling water for 2 minutes. Drain. Finely chop the garlic.

Combine the garlic and all the remaining sauce ingredients in a heavy small saucepan, bring to a simmer over medium heat, and simmer until reduced by three-fourths, about 20 minutes. Strain the sauce through a fine-mesh sieve and set aside.

TO MAKE THE LEEK SALAD

Blanch the leeks in a large saucepan of boiling salted water for 1 minute. Drain and immediately transfer to a bowl of ice water to cool; drain well and pat dry.

Whisk the oil, ginger, garlic, vinegar, and mustard in a medium bowl to blend. Season to taste with salt and white pepper. Toss the leeks with the vinaigrette to coat.

TO COOK THE DUCK

Season the duck breasts with salt and pepper. Heat the clarified butter in a heavy large sauté pan over medium-high heat. Place the duck breasts skinned sides down in the pan and cook for 3 minutes. Turn the breasts and cook for another 3 minutes. Transfer to a cutting board and let rest for 5 minutes.

TO SERVE

Cut the duck breasts lengthwise in half and place in the center of four plates. Spoon the leek salad around the duck. Spoon the sauce over the duck. Put a quenelle of duck skin puree on top of each serving and serve immediately.

This is my accidental signature dish. For most of my life, I worked in the finest French restaurants, so you'd think that customers would be begging me for my foie gras torchon or poulet en vessie, not for my fried chicken. But there we are. My muse? I can't lie: thank you, KFC, for the crispy-crunchy inspiration. Of course I created my own version, from the Asian-inspired marinade to the very French method of frying in duck fat. It got so popular that we ended up launching the Ludo Fried Chicken Truck at the inaugural L.A. Street Food Festival in 2010. People waited in a long, snaking line, and when they got to the front, some of them would proudly show us with their iPhone timers that they'd waited three hours just to place an order!

fried chicken in duck fat, piquillo ketchup

SERVES 4

CHICKEN
1 cup reduced-sodium soy sauce
⅓ cup toasted sesame oil
3 tablespoons chile oil
1 tablespoon finely chopped peeled fresh ginger
2 teaspoons finely chopped garlic
One 3- to 4-pound chicken
6 cups duck fat
About 2 cups cornstarch for dredging
1 tablespoon herbes de Provence
Kosher salt and freshly ground black pepper

PIQUILLO KETCHUP
4 cups water
2 cups raspberry vinegar
1 cup drained jarred whole piquillo peppers (preferably Del Destino brand)
½ cup granulated sugar
Kosher salt and freshly ground white pepper
1 tablespoon Tabasco sauce

TO MARINATE THE CHICKEN

Whisk the soy sauce, sesame oil, chile oil, ginger, and garlic in a large bowl to blend; set aside.

Cut the chicken into 8 pieces: 2 breasts, 2 legs, 2 thighs, and 2 wings. Add the chicken pieces to the marinade and turn to coat. Cover and refrigerate for at least 8 hours, and up to 12 hours.

Combine the water, raspberry vinegar, piquillo peppers, sugar, and salt in a large saucepan and bring to a boil over high heat, stirring often to dissolve the sugar. Reduce the heat to medium-high and simmer uncovered, stirring often, until the liquid is reduced to a syrupy consistency, about 40 minutes.

Transfer the piquillo mixture to a blender, preferably a high-powered blender such as a Vitamix, and puree until completely smooth, adding water if necessary. Blend in the Tabasco sauce. Season to taste with salt and pepper. Transfer to a container and refrigerate until cold. The ketchup can be made at least one week in advance.

Heat the duck fat to 320°F in a heavy large frying pan over medium heat. Use a thermometer to regulate the oil temperature.

Drain the chicken pieces; discard the marinade. Toss the chicken legs and thighs with the cornstarch in a large bowl to coat lightly. Add the legs and thighs to the duck fat and cook for about 12 minutes, until an instant-read thermometer registers 160°F when inserted into the center of a chicken piece. Using tongs, transfer the legs and thighs to paper towels to drain and immediately season with some of the herbes de Provence and salt and pepper.

Return the duck fat to 320°F. Toss the chicken breasts in the cornstarch to coat lightly. Fry the coated chicken breasts for 8 minutes, or until an instant-read thermometer registers 160°F when inserted into the center of a breast. Transfer the breasts to paper towels to drain and season with the remaining herbes de Provence and salt and pepper.

Serve the chicken hot, with the piquillo ketchup alongside for dipping.

A distillation of the flavors of the South of France, this dessert pairs beautiful summer apricots with fresh rosemary and almonds, a common combination that I remember from my vacations in Antibes. At LudoBites, we baked the clafoutis to order and served it warm with a chilled almond parfait. For this version, I incorporate the almond flavor in a simple whipped cream.

apricot clafoutis, rosemary sorbet, almond cream

SERVES 6 TO 8

CLAFOUTIS

2 tablespoons unsalted butter, at room temperature

1 cup plus 2 tablespoons granulated sugar

2 pounds apricots, halved and pitted

10 large eggs

4 large egg yolks

2 cups heavy cream

1½ cups all-purpose flour

ALMOND CREAM

1 cup heavy cream

¼ cup confectioners' sugar

¾ teaspoon pure almond extract

GARNISHES

2 tablespoons dried edible lavender flowers, finely ground

2 tablespoons confectioners' sugar

Rosemary Sorbet (recipe follows)

TO MAKE THE CLAFOUTIS

Preheat the oven to 350°F. Coat the inside of a 3-quart baking dish with the softened butter, then sprinkle 2 tablespoons of the sugar into the dish and gently shake it to coat it with the sugar.

Arrange the apricots in the baking dish.

Whisk the eggs, egg yolks, and the remaining 1 cup sugar in a medium bowl for about 2 minutes, until thoroughly blended. Add the cream and flour and whisk well to blend.

Pour the batter over the apricots. Bake for 50 minutes, or until the clafoutis is golden brown and crusty on top and the center is just set.

Whisk the cream, confectioners' sugar, and almond extract in a medium bowl until the cream is very thick and fluffy. Cover and refrigerate until ready to serve.

TO MAKE THE GARNISH

Sift the lavender and confectioners' sugar into a small bowl.

TO SERVE

Cut the warm clafoutis into wedges and transfer to bowls. Spoon a small scoop of rosemary sorbet and a generous dollop of almond cream alongside each portion. Sift the lavender sugar over and serve immediately.

rosemary sorbet

MAKES ABOUT 2 CUPS

1¼ cups water
2 fresh rosemary sprigs
½ cup granulated sugar
1 tablespoon Trimoline (invert sugar) or glucose

½ teaspoon Parsley Puree (page 37, for color; optional)

Combine the water and rosemary in a small saucepan and bring to a boil over high heat. Remove the pan from the heat, cover, and set aside for 1 hour to infuse.

Strain the infused water into another small saucepan and discard the rosemary sprigs. Add the sugar and Trimoline and bring to a boil over high heat, stirring until the sugar dissolves. Stir in the parsley puree. Transfer to a bowl and refrigerate until cold.

Freeze the sorbet mixture in an ice cream machine according to the manufacturer's instructions. Transfer to a freezer container and freeze until ready to serve.

I created this during the height of the cupcake boom. But it's so tasty that it still gets me excited during this Era of the Pie. Back then, the notion of foie gras or bacon in desserts produced double takes. Today I think people realize that they're both just tasty fats, whether the preparation is sweet or savory.

Most of the components for this dessert can be prepared ahead of time. And the caramelized almond dragées are simply Jordan almonds cooked briefly in a saucepan to caramelize their sugar coating.

chocolate cupcakes, foie gras chantilly, maple-bacon coulis, caramelized almond dragées, balsamic-maple syrup

SERVES 18

CUPCAKES
½ cup unsweetened cocoa powder (not Dutch-processed)
2 ounces high-quality milk chocolate, finely chopped
½ cup boiling water
½ cup buttermilk
1 cup cake flour
¾ teaspoon baking soda
½ teaspoon fleur de sel
⅔ cup packed light brown sugar
½ cup granulated sugar
½ cup grapeseed oil
2 large eggs
1 teaspoon pure vanilla extract

FOIE GRAS CHANTILLY
⅓ cup plus 1 tablespoon heavy cream
⅓ cup confectioners' sugar
1 pound foie gras, cut into 1-inch chunks, at room temperature

MAPLE-BACON COULIS
6 slices applewood-smoked bacon
Pure maple syrup (preferably Grade A dark amber), for brushing
3 tablespoons grapeseed oil

CARAMELIZED ALMOND DRAGÉES
1 cup white almond dragées (Jordan almonds)

BALSAMIC-MAPLE SYRUP
½ cup 12-year-old balsamic vinegar

½ cup pure maple syrup (preferably
Grade A dark amber)

TO MAKE THE CUPCAKES

Preheat the oven to 350°F. Line 18 standard (⅓-cup) muffin cups with paper liners.

Combine the cocoa powder and milk chocolate in a small bowl. Add the boiling water and whisk until smooth. Whisk in the buttermilk. Set aside.

Whisk the flour, baking soda, and fleur de sel in a medium bowl to blend.

Using an electric mixer, beat the brown sugar, granulated sugar, oil, eggs, and vanilla in a large bowl until well blended. Beat in the dry ingredients and the chocolate mixture.

Divide the batter among the prepared muffin cups. Bake until a tester inserted into the center of a cupcake comes out with just a few crumbs attached, about 18 minutes. Cool in the pans on a cooling rack for 10 minutes, then transfer the cupcakes to a rack to cool completely. Leave the oven on.

TO MAKE THE CHANTILLY

Bring the cream and confectioners' sugar to a simmer in a heavy small saucepan over medium-high heat. Put the foie gras in a high-powered blender (such as a Vitamix), add the hot cream mixture, and blend just until the mixture is very smooth, about 1 minute; do not overblend. Pour the foie gras cream into a large bowl and set the bowl over another large bowl of ice water. Whisk until the foie gras cream is cold, fluffy, and thick and can hold its shape when piped. Transfer the Chantilly to a pastry bag fitted with a ½-inch plain tip. (The Chantilly may be refrigerated while the bacon cooks.)

TO MAKE THE COULIS

Lay the bacon slices on a heavy rimmed baking sheet and brush them with maple syrup. Bake until the bacon is crisp, 25 to 35 minutes; then transfer to paper towels to drain and cool completely.

Combine the bacon with the grapeseed oil in a food processor and process until the bacon is very finely chopped. (The coulis can be refrigerated in an airtight container for up to 2 days; bring to room temperature before serving.)

TO MAKE THE ALMOND DRAGÉES
Line a baking sheet with a silicone baking mat or parchment paper.

Stir the almonds in a heavy medium sauté pan over medium-low heat until most of the sugar coating melts and turns amber brown, about 5 minutes. Immediately transfer the caramelized almond mixture to the lined baking sheet and let cool completely.

When it is cool, finely chop the almond mixture. (The almonds can be stored in an airtight container at room temperature for up to 2 days.)

TO MAKE THE BALSAMIC-MAPLE SYRUP
Bring the balsamic vinegar and maple syrup to a simmer in a heavy small saucepan over medium-high heat and simmer until reduced by half, about 5 minutes. Set aside to cool completely. (The syrup can be refrigerated in an airtight container for up to 2 days; bring to room temperature before serving.)

TO DECORATE THE CUPCAKES
Pipe the foie gras Chantilly onto the cupcakes. Spoon the maple-bacon coulis atop the Chantilly. Sprinkle with the chopped caramelized almonds, drizzle with the balsamic-maple syrup, and serve.

KITCHEN 🐇 ROSTER

LUDO

ARNOLD (disappearing sous chef)

CHRIS (still on loan from Hatfields)

ELODIE (hired intern from 2.0)

QUINN HATFIELD (volunteered one night after sous chef incident)

AUSTIN (Twitter—hired after sous chef incident)

TEHRA (2.0)

RACHEL (left after two nights)

FRED SAVAGE

OMAR (chef of Royal/T)

We had such a good second run at Breadbar that it was tempting to just take a short break and set up shop there again. However, we had begun to embrace the concept of the pop-up restaurant. And LudoBites wouldn't be much of a pop-up if it didn't, you know, pop up. So the search for a new location began.

Our first option was, of all places, Bastide. My old boss, Joe Pytka, had eaten at the previous LudoBites and was intrigued by our funky little business. With Bastide closed again, after burning through two more chefs, LudoBites could potentially set up shop there. It was certainly tempting. Bastide is a beautiful restaurant with a beautiful kitchen. After three months spent in the beat-up bakery kitchen of Breadbar, the allure of dumping the Pinto and jumping back in the Rolls-Royce was almost overpowering. We would pay Joe rent, hire our own staff, and be free to do what we wanted with the food. And, of course, part of me wanted to return in triumph. I was already dreaming of the menu.

In the end, we almost had a deal, but when it got to the nitty-gritty details, I started to feel like I'd time-traveled back to those days when I wasn't free to cook what I wanted to cook, to do my food my way. Returning to Bastide would have been a step backward, and I had to move forward. But where?

Then Krissy remembered that on one of the last nights of LudoBites 2.0, an architect who'd come in for dinner had mentioned an amazing space he'd built in Culver City, called Royal/T. It's an art gallery with on-premises cafe, but the owner rarely used the space at night. Then I heard the magic words: "liquor license." So Krissy and I went to see the place and meet the owner, a philanthropist and art collector named Susan Hancock. It was a wild space, with a ceiling of exposed beams, an open floor plan, and colorful art, modern installations, and sculptures everywhere. Big artists like Murakami and Nara have had shows there. Susan was wonderful, but she didn't quite know what to make of our business model. Her space is so fantastic that she typically charged $7,500 per night to rent it out for special events. She told us she'd give us a break, charging us only $3,500. (She just didn't know the slim margins of the restaurant business.) We couldn't have done it for a quarter of that price.

Krissy began to negotiate, showing Susan our sales projections and coming up with a way to make it work for all of us. Ultimately, we'd take on all of the food and basic labor costs, Susan would take in all of the money, and then she'd pay us a percentage. Just like that, LudoBites found its third home. For the month of December, we'd take over the art gallery every Wednesday through Friday night before Christmas. Susan wanted to make sure that her Royal/T brand didn't get lost, so she insisted that we use the waitstaff from her lunch and tea service. The daytime café was modeled after the *cosplay* (short for "costume play") cafés of Tokyo, which meant all the servers wore French maid's outfits. (Susan told us that in Tokyo, the servers wore the costumes but no underwear; fortunately, Royal/T wasn't entirely authentic.) The whole thing had the real cool feeling of a performance art piece.

Of course, the performance we cared about most was the one that went on in the kitchen. *Merde*, that kitchen! The 10,000-square-foot gallery space was equipped with a tiny kitchen. The line itself was pretty decent, but there was no prep area or walk-in refrigerator, just a small fridge full of the café's breakfast and lunch foods and a couple of freezers. We had to buy our own refrigerator, and because there was no space for it in the kitchen, we had to set it up near the gallery's back door—what felt like a quarter mile from the kitchen. There was also barely anywhere to prep, with no actual prep area and the café crew using the kitchen for breakfast and lunch. Our improvised solution: do dinner prep

in the glassed-in VIP room right in the center of the gallery. We bought two steel tables, had cutting boards made for the tops, hung posters all the way around so that no one could see inside, and put a sign on the door that said Closed for Installation.

What did all this mean for my food? First of all, just minutes before our hungry customers arrived each night, we'd have to haul our mise-en-place into the kitchen and start cooking. Whenever one of our cooks needed something from the fridge, he'd have to sprint all the way there and back, scorched pans or overcooked fish awaiting his return. It was brutal. Everyone was pissed off. The food was good, but this was work, not magic.

At LudoBites, I've learned that things don't get easier until they first get harder. After our first three days of service, Krissy and I had to fly to Puerto Rico for a *Top Chef Masters* reunion charity benefit. I put my sous chef (and good friend) in charge of the ordering and prep while we were gone, so we could open for service the day after we returned. This was a first for me. I hadn't yet entrusted anyone with these kinds of responsibilities at LudoBites, but he and I had known each other for a couple of years and he had been my main guy for 2.0. We'd spent so much time together over the past six months. I thought of him as a little brother. I had faith in him.

But when I got back, I found out that instead of handling prep, he'd partied hard in Vegas that weekend. He hadn't gone in to check the delivery orders. As we got closer to service, I realized that, among other things, he'd forgotten to cook the potato cakes for the fried chicken dish, one of our most popular, and the mise-en-place for the grilled duck wasn't ready either. Before the orders even started coming in, we were behind.

I took him aside and tried talking to him. Krissy reminds me that I liberally employed the f-word. After all, he was one of the leaders of the kitchen, the guy that I trusted. He hardly said a thing in response. So we got back to cooking, and I watched him walk away. I figured he'd forgotten something and was on that long slog to the refrigerator. Five minutes went by. Tickets were piling up. Maybe he was in the bathroom. Ten minutes. More tickets. Fifteen minutes. *Where the fuck is he?* We searched everywhere for him. Then Krissy came into the kitchen and announced that his car was gone.

So there we were: 7:30 P.M. All the tables were full, and the guy who was supposed to be cooking most of the entrées had vanished. At that moment, I decided to tear up all the menus and make that night's dinner a set five-course menu. It was either that or close. Krissy scrambled to print new menus and explain the situation to customers. But because we hadn't planned on serving a set menu, we didn't have enough food to feed everyone the same dishes. So there was Krissy, racing around the dining room and snatching the newly printed menus from people's hands, saying, "Sorry, that dish doesn't exist anymore." At one point, she told a guy as he sat down, "I have no idea what you are going to eat tonight, but it will cost you $39." She greeted people with 9:00 P.M. reservations by saying, "Welcome to LudoBites. You probably don't want to eat here tonight."

Thank goodness for our forgiving customers. When Krissy told that guy that she didn't know what he was going to eat, he was thrilled. "Ludo's going to cook for me, I feel like I've just hit the lottery!" She tried to preempt the wrath of a table of influential bloggers. "Go ahead," she said. "Write that tonight sucked." But the next day, we saw posts about "snatching culinary victory from the jaws of defeat." As we've said, bloggers made LudoBites, and I truly think they felt a part of our successes and stood by us during our failures (for the most part).

The next morning, Krissy called everyone who had a reservation for that night to explain that due to staffing problems there would be a set menu. The very last person on her list was a Mr. Green, and when she gave him the news, he asked, "Well, is Ludo still going to be serving his best food?" That did it. After all she'd been through the night before, her voice nearly gone from explaining the situation over and over, Krissy was spoiling for a fight. "No," she told the guy. "Actually, tonight he's going to be serving you shit." The guy laughed, a bit uncomfortably, and said, "Krissy, I'm sorry, this is Jonathan Gold." It was like a bad dream. I thought, *Merde*, this guy only shows up when I run out of food!

As a thank-you to the bloggers for their support of LudoBites 1.0 and 2.0, Krissy gave them their own photo studio at Royal/T. On our last night at Breadbar, the blogger KevinEats had told Krissy that the food was great but the lighting sucked. She was taken aback: we were running a restaurant, not a photo studio. Still, the idea stuck

with her, so she bought an inexpensive lightbox and set it up in Royal/T's VIP room. Every night, our makeshift prep kitchen morphed into a makeshift photo studio. Krissy, who always had her marketing/PR hat on, thought, If they're going to take photos anyway, why not have the food looking its best?

At first it was just funny to see customers rushing, plates in hand, from their tables to the studio. It got a little ridiculous, though, when they'd ask the servers to deliver their food straight to the lightbox. One night, there was a line of bloggers waiting to enter the studio. Sometimes I would scream at them, "Can't you just *eat* the food, guys?" OK, I admit it—the photos did look beautiful.

And I can't be mad. Bloggers have even been some of my best resources. When I wanted to learn about Mexican *mole,* Javier Cabral (online nom de guerre: The Glutster) took me to his house in East L.A., where his mother taught me how to make her incredible version of *mole zacatecano.* Next thing you know, I'm serving my fried chicken with *mole*, Cantal-cheese-spiked polenta, and a roasted ear of corn—an American classic with an Asian-inspired marinade and French

and Mexican accoutrements. This is why I love my job. I don't know everything and I'm not ashamed to admit that. It's one of the reasons I change my menu so much—I am always learning and getting excited about new things.

Yet as I served the last food of LudoBites 3.0 at Royal/T, I was exhausted. The kitchen setup caused too much stress for everyone, especially *moi*. And without an open kitchen, I felt as if I was back in the box. I couldn't see people eating as I cooked, and they couldn't see me. Part of the deal at LudoBites was that they got to see me sweating, yelling, and plating. At Royal/T, they'd ask Krissy, "Where's Ludo?" Customers even started asking if they could come into the kitchen and cook with me. If there was room, I'd have let them.

At this point our crew was pretty beat-up. In addition to our regular LudoBites nights, we were doing private parties, and we'd all been working for thirteen straight days and nights. The mood felt grim. How in the hell would we keep up this pace? We had three nights to go. Krissy and I told ourselves, Just get through these last few services. That was when Fred Savage saved the day.

After eating at LudoBites 2.0, he'd asked Krissy if he could intern in the kitchen. She couldn't believe it. Kitchen work isn't exactly fun and relaxation. But he insisted. His dream was to be a chef, though his work (and wife) wouldn't let him. So Fred entered our workforce, with very little experience but a whole lot of good energy. Here was this famous child actor, now a big-time producer and director, chopping vegetables and getting yelled at by a surly chef (sorry, Fred)—all with a freaking smile on his face. Somehow, on our last three nights, the food was working, the energy was great, and we were having fun.

To this day, I still haven't heard from my vanishing sous chef. Good riddance. But, Fred, you're welcome in my kitchen anytime.

Chefs hate waste, especially in a shoestring operation like ours. So do grandmas. Mine used to soak stale bread in milk and turn it into soup. I remember this potage well. I also have fond memories of my mother making me toast, charring the bread over an open flame until it was brittle and nearly black. I do the same to the bread for this version of my grandma's standby, so it has a pleasing bitter, smoky quality. She might not recognize the Gruyère-flavored marshmallows I use to embellish the dish, but I bet she'd like them.

bread soup, gruyère marshmallows

SERVES 6

MARSHMALLOWS
1⅔ cups whole milk
1 cup very finely grated Gruyère cheese
(the texture should be powdery)
2 tablespoons agar-agar
2 large egg whites
Pinch of kosher salt

SOUP
3 cups large cubes crustless country-style white bread

¼ cup olive oil
2 tablespoons unsalted butter
1 onion, thinly sliced
3 ounces applewood-smoked bacon, diced
2 cups Chicken Stock (page 39)
About 6 cups whole milk
3 tablespoons sherry vinegar
2 tablespoons Dijon mustard
Kosher salt and freshly ground white pepper

TO MAKE THE MARSHMALLOWS

Combine the milk, ½ cup of the Gruyère, and the agar-agar in a heavy medium saucepan and bring to a boil over high heat, stirring to dissolve the agar. Boil for 2 minutes. Strain the mixture through a fine-mesh sieve lined with cheesecloth into a bowl, and set aside to cool.

Refrigerate the marshmallow mixture until cold but not set, about 10 minutes. Whisk again to loosen it if necessary.

Line a 5-inch square baking pan with plastic wrap (if you don't have a pan of this size, use a small container so that the marshmallow mixture will be about 1 inch thick). Using an electric mixer, whip the egg whites with the salt in a large bowl until soft peaks form. Whisk in the cold Gruyère mixture. Transfer the mixture to the prepared baking pan and spread evenly, cover, and refrigerate until cold and firm, about 2 hours.

Put the remaining ½ cup Gruyère in a small bowl. Cut the marshmallow mixture into 1-inch cubes and roll in the cheese to coat. Set aside.

TO MAKE THE SOUP
Preheat the oven to 375°F.

Toss the bread cubes with the olive oil in a large bowl to coat. Spread the bread cubes on a baking sheet and bake, turning them after 15 minutes so they brown evenly, until very dark brown, about 30 minutes. Remove from the oven and set aside.

Melt the butter in a heavy large saucepan over medium heat. Add the onion and bacon and sauté until pale golden, about 12 minutes. Add the toasted bread, then stir in the chicken stock, 5 cups of the milk, the vinegar, and mustard, bring to a simmer, and cook, stirring occasionally, until the bread is soft, about 20 minutes.

Working in batches, transfer the soup to a blender, preferably a Vitamix, and blend until very smooth, adding up to 1 cup more milk to thin the soup if necessary. Season to taste with salt and white pepper.

TO SERVE
Ladle the hot soup into six soup bowls. Place 3 Gruyère marshmallows in each bowl and serve.

If you name a classic dish from Burgundy, you can bet I've experimented with it in my kitchen: in this case, *oeufs en meurette*, poached eggs in red wine broth. To lighten it all a bit, I employ red cabbage, to give the sauce a deeper color using less wine than the original, and agar-agar, to give it a rich texture without adding a ton of butter. I poach the eggs so the yolks remain creamy and serve it all with toast draped with lardo, a stand-in for the usual bacon.

egg, red cabbage, lardo

SERVES 4

SHALLOT OIL
½ cup grapeseed oil
¼ cup sliced shallots
1 small garlic clove, crushed
1 large fresh thyme sprig
Kosher salt and freshly ground black
  pepper

RED CABBAGE BROTH
1 cup dry red wine
¾ cup red wine vinegar
1 shallot, thinly sliced
2 tablespoons black peppercorns
2 fresh thyme sprigs
1 cup red cabbage juice

1 tablespoon agar-agar
Kosher salt and freshly ground black
  pepper

TOASTS
Eight ½-inch-thick slices baguette
2 tablespoons olive oil
8 very thin slices lardo
8 borage flowers

POACHED EGGS
⅓ cup distilled white vinegar
Kosher salt
4 large eggs

TO MAKE THE SHALLOT OIL
Combine the oil, shallots, garlic, and thyme in a jar. Cover and let infuse for 1 week.

Strain the oil into another container and season to taste with salt and pepper.

TO MAKE THE BROTH

Combine the red wine, vinegar, shallot, peppercorns, and thyme in a medium sauce-pan, bring to a boil over high heat, and boil until reduced to ½ cup, about 12 minutes.

Add the cabbage juice and agar-agar and bring back to a boil, whisking constantly to dissolve the agar. Reduce the heat to medium-low and whisk for 3 minutes to ensure the agar is entirely dissolved. Season to taste with salt and pepper. Strain the broth into a small saucepan and keep hot over low heat.

TO MAKE THE TOASTS

Preheat the oven to 375°F.

Brush the baguette slices with the olive oil and put them on a heavy baking sheet. Bake until the toasts are golden brown and crisp, about 5 minutes per side. Remove from the oven.

TO POACH THE EGGS

Combine 4 cups water, the vinegar, and a pinch of salt in a medium saucepan and bring to a boil over high heat, then reduce the heat so that the water barely simmers. Carefully crack the eggs into the water and poach until the whites are set but the yolks are still creamy, about 3 minutes. Using a slotted spoon, transfer the eggs to a plate lined with paper towels to drain briefly.

TO SERVE

Pour the hot broth into four soup plates. Place a poached egg in the center of each bowl. Arrange the lardo on top of the toasts and set the toasts in the soup. Drizzle some of the shallot oil over the soup and toasts, garnish with the borage flowers, and serve.

Restaurants with fine china, endless wine lists, and a legion of servers can be wonderful, but all that ceremony and spectacle is passed on to the customer in an eye-popping bill. I've worked at many restaurants like that, and it frustrated me that many people who wanted to try my food couldn't afford to. So at LudoBites 3.0, I continued serving dishes from Bastide to my new customers. This one fit right in with Royal/T's Japanese vibe. It contains all the sushi components I love, just rearranged a little. There's still lovely raw tuna, but the sushi rice becomes rice ice cream and the seaweed becomes crunchy, candied nori. Same flavors, but completely different textures and temperatures.

tuna, sushi-rice ice cream, candied nori, ginger

SERVES 8

GINGER OIL
½ cup extra-virgin olive oil
One 2-inch piece fresh ginger, peeled
   and thinly sliced

CRYSTALLIZED NORI
2 cups Simple Syrup (page 300)
1 sheet nori

GINGER EMULSION
3 tablespoons fresh ginger juice
1 tablespoon honey
About ⅔ cup canola–olive oil blend
   (30%–70%)

Kosher salt and freshly ground white
   pepper

TUNA
40 thin slices toro or Bluefin tuna
   (about 2 pounds)
8 pinches (1 teaspoon) of shichimi
   togarashi
One 3-ounce container daikon sprouts,
   trimmed
Fleur de sel

Sushi-Rice Ice Cream (recipe follows)

Combine the oil and ginger in a heavy small saucepan and heat to 212°F over medium-high heat. Remove from the heat and set aside to cool.

Transfer the ginger mixture to a container, cover, and let infuse at room temperature for 24 hours; then strain the oil and discard the ginger.

Preheat the oven to 200°F. Line a baking sheet with a silicone baking mat.

Heat the simple syrup to 180°F in a wide sauté pan. Submerge the nori in the syrup for 30 seconds (the nori sheet will shrink), then remove it from the syrup, draining well, and lay on the prepared baking sheet.

Bake the nori just until it is dry, about 10 minutes (it should not be crisp at this point). Using kitchen shears, cut the nori into strips. Arrange the nori strips on the baking sheet and bake until crisp, about 15 minutes (the nori will become crisper as it cools). Remove from the oven.

Using an immersion blender, blend the ginger juice and honey in a small deep bowl or container. With the blender running, slowly drizzle in enough oil to make a thick emulsion. Season to taste with salt and white pepper.

Lay 5 slices of the tuna on each of eight plates. Sprinkle with the togarashi and top with the daikon sprouts. Sprinkle with fleur de sel. Spoon some of the emulsion alongside each serving, and put a quenelle of sushi ice cream on top of the tuna. Drizzle some ginger oil over the plates, garnish with the crystallized nori, and serve.

sushi-rice ice cream

½ cup sushi rice (Japanese short-
   grain rice)
1 cup whole milk
2 teaspoons glucose

2 large egg yolks
¼ cup granulated sugar
About 2 tablespoons rice vinegar
Kosher salt

Rinse the rice in a sieve under cold running water until the water runs clear. Put the rice in a heavy small saucepan, add ⅔ cup cold water, cover, and bring the water to a simmer over high heat. Reduce the heat to medium-low and simmer gently until the rice is tender and the water has been absorbed, about 18 minutes. Remove from the heat.

Add enough water to the cooked rice to cover it by 3 inches, then stir to blend. Using a strainer or a mesh spoon, transfer the rice to a blender, preferably a Vitamix, and puree, adding just enough of the rice water to create a smooth, thick mixture.

Combine the milk and glucose in a heavy medium saucepan and bring to just below a simmer over medium-high heat.

Meanwhile, whisk the egg yolks and sugar in a medium bowl until thick and lemon-colored. Slowly add half of the hot milk to the egg mixture, whisking constantly. Pour the tempered egg mixture back into the remaining milk and cook over low heat, stirring constantly with a silicone spatula, until the custard thickens enough to coat the back of a spoon, about 8 minutes; do not allow it to simmer.

Strain the custard into a bowl, set the bowl over a larger bowl of ice water, and stir until cold.

Stir 1½ cups of the rice puree into the custard. Season to taste with the vinegar and salt.

Freeze the custard mixture in an ice cream maker following the manufacturer's instructions. Pack the ice cream into a freezer container and cover with plastic wrap pressed directly onto the surface of the ice cream, and then the lid. Freeze until scoopable. (The ice cream can be stored in the freezer for up to 2 weeks.)

beet gazpacho, goat cheese sorbet (photograph by William Furniss)

prawns, avocado mousse, passion fruit (photograph by William Furniss)

foie gras miso soup (photograph by Darin Dines)

black foie gras croque-monsieur, amaretto cherry jam (photograph by William Furniss)

spicy chocolate mousse, orange oil (photograph by kevineats.com)

green escargot with oatmeal (photograph by William Furniss)

raw tuna, red beets, watermelon (photograph by Tomo Kurokawa of Tomostyle)

chorizo soup, melon, cornichon sorbet (photograph by Wesley Wong/eatsmeetwes.com)

white asparagus velouté, mozzarella ice cream, fennel, black olive (photograph by kevineats.com)

greek salad, feta mousse (photograph by Eugene Lee)

oxtail, creamy cantal polenta, black truffle
(photograph by Wesley Wong/eatsmeetwes.com)

veal tartare, oysters, tonnato-style (photograph by Wesley Wong/eatsmeetwes.com)

fried chicken in duck fat, piquillo ketchup (photograph by Arnold Gatilao/Christel Okihara)

fourme d'ambert torte, red pears, honey-balsamic syrup (photograph by kevineats.com)

guacamole, exotic fruits, crystallized-ginger ice cream (photograph by weezermonkey.com)

My first few months at L'Orangerie were spent learning from the chef Gilles Épié. One of the great tricks he taught me was deep-frying foie gras in a beignet. Need I say more? This dish is as rich as it is fun, but the chutney cuts through all that richness.

foie gras beignets, apricot-saffron chutney

SERVES 8

BEIGNETS
One 16-ounce lobe foie gras
2 cups Chimay Grand Réserve or other dark beer, at room temperature
1½ tablespoons active dry yeast
1¾ cups all-purpose flour, or more if needed
Kosher salt
Canola or safflower oil for deep-frying

CHUTNEY
1 cup dried apricots, quartered
1 tablespoon clover honey
1 tablespoon rice vinegar
¼ teaspoon saffron threads
½ cup water

TO PREPARE THE FOIE GRAS BALLS

Allow the foie gras to come to room temperature. Cut twenty 8-inch squares of doubled Grade #60 cheesecloth (preferred) or doubled plastic wrap.

To clean the foie gras, pull on the large veins to remove them. Cut the foie gras into ½-inch cubes. Using a scale, divide the cubed foie gras into eight 2-ounce portions; or if you do not have a scale, cut the lobe into 8 portions of equal size. Place 1 portion in the center of a square of cheesecloth or plastic wrap. Pull the edges of the sheet up over the foie gras, gather them together, and twist together to compact the foie gras (if using plastic, be careful to avoid trapping air inside). If using cheesecloth, tie the twisted ends of the cheesecloth close to the ball of foie gras with string, or wrap a rubber band around the twisted ends to hold the cheesecloth tight against the foie gras, maintaining its shape. Refrigerate the foie gras balls for at least 4 hours.

Combine the apricots, honey, vinegar, and saffron in a heavy small saucepan, set over medium heat, cover, and cook, stirring every 10 minutes, until the apricots are very tender, about 35 minutes.

Transfer the apricot mixture to a food processor and blend until smooth. Let cool, then cover and refrigerate until cold. (This will keep for 1 week.)

TO MAKE THE TEMPURA BATTER

Stir the beer and yeast in a medium bowl to blend. Set aside until the yeast is completely dissolved, about 10 minutes.

Whisk the flour into the beer mixture to form a thin batter. Allow the batter to sit at room temperature for 45 minutes before using (the batter will thicken slightly).

TO MAKE THE BEIGNETS

Pour 3 inches of oil into a large heavy pot and heat over medium heat to 375°F. Season the batter with salt.

Unwrap 1 foie gras ball and push it onto the end of a straight metal carving fork. Dip the foie gras into the tempura batter to coat lightly, making sure the foie gras is fully covered and that at least ¼ inch of the fork is also coated. (If the batter seems too thin, whisk more flour, 1 tablespoon at a time, into it to thicken.) Dip the foie gras ball into the hot oil and keep it submerged until the batter begins to turn light golden brown, about 30 seconds. Using a wooden spatula, push the beignet off the fork (a metal implement would stick to the batter and create a hole) and continue to fry the beignet for another 30 to 40 seconds, until the batter turns a deep golden brown. Using a slotted spoon, remove the beignet from the oil and drain on paper towels. Coat and fry the remaining foie gras in the same way.

Season the hot beignets with salt and serve with the chutney.

I guess I had Japan on the mind during this LudoBites—the Japanese women servers in maid's outfits were probably to blame. I decided to lacquer cod in a sweet, sticky glaze similar to often-bastardized-but-frequently-tasty teriyaki and serve it with mashed potatoes. Well, not just mashed potatoes, but a smooth emulsion of the mash, olive oil, and garlic that gets extra flavor from cod bones. It's a little like French brandade or Basque cod pil-pil, so I guess Japan wasn't the only place on my mind.

cod teriyaki, pil-pil potatoes, pink grapefruit

SERVES 6

KAFFIR LIME OIL
½ cup grapeseed oil
½ cup fresh kaffir lime leaves

PINK GRAPEFRUIT CONDIMENT
⅔ cup fresh pink grapefruit juice
2 tablespoons granulated sugar
1 tablespoon agar-agar

PIL-PIL POTATOES
2 tablespoons olive oil
⅓ cup sliced onion
1 garlic clove, smashed
4 ounces black cod bones
⅓ cup extra-virgin olive oil
½ cup (about 4 ounces) peeled baked
    potato pulp
⅓ cup whole milk
¼ cup heavy cream
Kosher salt and freshly ground
    white pepper

COD
¼ cup clover honey
¼ cup mirin
¼ cup sake
¼ cup soy sauce
Six 6-ounce skinless cod fillets

TO MAKE THE KAFFIR LIME OIL
Combine the oil and leaves in a small saucepan and heat to 250°F. Remove the pan from the heat and let steep for 1 hour.

Strain the oil into a container; discard the leaves.

Combine the juice, sugar, and agar-agar in a heavy small saucepan and bring to a boil over high heat, whisking to dissolve the sugar and agar. Reduce the heat to medium-low and cook for 4 minutes, stirring, to ensure the agar is completely dissolved. Remove from the heat and set aside to cool completely, stirring occasionally.

TO MAKE THE POTATOES

Heat the olive oil in a small saucepan over medium-low heat. Add the onion and garlic and sauté until tender, about 3 minutes. Add the fish bones and cook until the meat on the bones is opaque and the bones begin to fall away from the meat, about 8 minutes. Stir in the extra-virgin olive oil and potato pulp, reduce the heat to low, and cook very gently for 1 hour.

Remove the pan from the heat and set aside to infuse the flavors for 2 hours.

Pass the potato mixture through a food mill into a bowl. Warm the milk and cream in a heavy small saucepan over medium-high heat. Stir enough of the milk mixture into the potato mixture to make soft mashed potatoes, then season to taste with salt and white pepper. Keep warm.

TO PREPARE THE COD

Combine the honey, mirin, sake, and soy sauce in a heavy small saucepan and bring to a boil over high heat, stirring to blend. Reduce the heat to medium and simmer until the sauce has reduced to about ⅓ cup, about 10 minutes. Remove from the heat.

Preheat the broiler. Place the fish fillets on a heavy baking sheet and brush them with the sauce. Broil the fish for 8 minutes, or until opaque on the inside, caramelized on the outside, and beginning to char in spots.

TO SERVE

Set a piece of fish in the center of each of six plates. Whisk the grapefruit condiment to loosen and blend it, then place a quenelle of it on the right side of each fillet. Spoon a line of potato pil-pil along the left side of each fillet, drizzle with some of the kaffir lime oil, and serve.

I just love this, so simple and so French: Perfectly steamed fish. Butter-braised winter vegetables like radishes and Brussels sprouts. And aioli, but made with yuzu, a Japanese citrus fruit, instead of lemon. Because it is so simple, the dish's success relies entirely on the quality of your ingredients and careful execution.

striped bass, yuzu aioli, garden vegetables

SERVES 4

YUZU AIOLI
1 large egg
1 garlic clove
¼ cup fresh yuzu juice
1 cup extra-virgin olive oil
Grated zest of 1 yuzu
Kosher salt

VEGETABLES
7 tablespoons unsalted butter
1 tablespoon minced shallot
2 bunches Easter Egg or other red radishes, stems trimmed
2 teaspoons granulated sugar
¼ cup champagne vinegar
½ cup Chicken Stock (page 39)
2 cups thinly sliced cauliflower florets, preferably a mix of white, green, and purple, blanched in boiling water until al dente
8 ounces baby Brussels sprouts, blanched until al dente, drained, and halved

1 tablespoon finely chopped fresh chives
1 tablespoon finely chopped fresh mint
Kosher salt and freshly ground white pepper

STRIPED BASS
1 lemon, cut into 8 wedges
6 large fresh mint sprigs
Four 6- to 7-ounce skinless striped bass fillets
Fleur de sel and freshly ground white pepper

GARNISH
3 tablespoons fresh chervil leaves
3 tablespoons small fresh tarragon leaves
3 tablespoons small fresh mint leaves
3 tablespoons small fresh lemon verbena leaves
3 tablespoons small fennel sprigs

Using an immersion blender, blend the egg, garlic, and yuzu juice in a medium bowl until smooth. With the blender running, slowly add the olive oil, mixing until the aioli thickens and becomes creamy. Whisk in the yuzu zest and season to taste with salt; then refrigerate.

TO PREPARE THE VEGETABLES

Melt 2 tablespoons of the butter in a heavy large saucepan over medium heat. Add the shallot and sauté until translucent, about 2 minutes. Add the radishes and sauté for 1 minute, then add the sugar and stir for 2 minutes. Add the vinegar, chicken stock, and 4 tablespoons of the butter, cover the vegetables with a round of parchment paper, and cook for 10 minutes. Remove the parchment and stir in the cauliflower, Brussels sprouts, and the remaining 1 tablespoon butter. Simmer until the liquid thickens slightly and the vegetables are crisp-tender, about 3 minutes. Stir in the chives and mint and season to taste with salt and white pepper.

MEANWHILE, TO PREPARE THE FISH

Fill a deep skillet halfway with water, add the lemon wedges and mint, and bring the water to a boil over medium heat. Set a steamer basket in the skillet. Season the fish with fleur de sel and white pepper, lay the fillets in the steamer, cover, and steam until just cooked through and opaque in the center, about 6 minutes.

TO SERVE

Lay a fish fillet in the center of each of four plates. Arrange the vegetables around the fish and spoon a generous amount of the yuzu aioli on the rim of the plate. Scatter the herbs and fennel sprigs nicely over the plates and serve immediately.

Blanquette de veau Japanese-style: I toss the tender stewed veal—cooked with dried shiitake mushrooms and kombu as well as the traditional leeks and carrots—with a tangle of udon noodles and let the stewing liquid serve as broth. Cream, miso, and sesame come together in an umami-packed condiment that I paint onto the rim of each bowl.

veal, udon, enoki mushrooms, sesame-seed miso

SERVES 8

VEAL

3 quarts water, preferably filtered

One 6-by-4-inch sheet kombu

2 onions, one sliced in half, one cut into large dice

2½ pounds boneless veal shoulder, excess fat trimmed and cut into large chunks

10 ounces thickly sliced applewood-smoked bacon, cut into large dice

4 cups dry white wine

1½ cups dried shiitake mushrooms

2 carrots, cut into large dice

1 leek, thickly sliced

¼ cup mirin

¼ cup reduced-sodium soy sauce, or more to taste

¼ cup sake

Kosher salt and freshly ground black pepper

Juice of ½ lemon

CARAMELIZED ONIONS

3 tablespoons grapeseed oil

2 onions, thinly sliced

Kosher salt

SESAME-MISO CONDIMENT

2 tablespoons fromage blanc

1 tablespoon white miso

1 tablespoon white sesame seeds, toasted

1½ teaspoons heavy cream

1 teaspoon wasabi paste

FOR SERVING

12 ounces dried udon

½ cup very thinly sliced scallions

4 ounces enoki mushrooms, stems trimmed

2 tablespoons chopped nori

TO PREPARE THE VEAL

Combine the water and kombu in a large pot and set aside to steep for 30 minutes.

Remove the kombu from the water.

Using a kitchen torch, char the halved onion.

Add the veal, bacon, white wine, shiitake mushrooms, charred onion, diced onion, carrots, and leek, and bring just to a boil over high heat. Reduce the heat to medium-low and cook very gently for 2 hours, or until the veal is tender. Remove from the heat and let the veal cool in the braising liquid.

Using a slotted spoon, transfer the veal to a bowl. Shred the meat and put it in a saucepan.

Strain the cooking liquid through a fine-mesh sieve lined with cheesecloth into a large saucepan; discard the solids. You should have about 3 quarts broth. Bring the broth to a simmer and simmer until reduced to 8 cups, about 20 minutes.

Add the mirin, soy sauce, and sake to the broth and season to taste with salt, pepper, and the lemon juice. Taste and add more soy sauce, if desired.

Spoon some of the broth over the veal to moisten; bring to a gentle simmer, then remove from the heat. Cover the veal and the remaining broth to keep them both very hot.

MEANWHILE, TO MAKE THE CARAMELIZED ONIONS

Heat the oil in a large cast-iron skillet over medium-high heat until it is very hot but not smoking. Add the onions and a large pinch of salt and sauté until the onions are pale golden brown, about 5 minutes. Reduce the heat to medium-low and cook until the onions are amber brown, stirring often, about 25 minutes. Remove from the heat.

TO MAKE THE SESAME-MISO CONDIMENT

Using a silicone spatula, stir all the ingredients in a small bowl to form a smooth, creamy paste.

TO SERVE

Cook the noodles in a large pot of boiling salted water until al dente. Drain. Divide the noodles and veal among eight large soup plates. Top with the caramelized onions, scallions, and mushrooms. Spoon the sesame-miso condiment on the edges of the plates. Ladle the hot broth over, garnish with the nori, and serve immediately.

Once you become known for fried chicken, you can't stop serving it. Requests for it came constantly from my customers. But I didn't want to keep cooking the same thing, so I turned the juicy, crispy bird into a salad, gilding it with Dijon mustard in different guises—in a honey-spiked mayonnaise, in a classic vinaigrette, and as a powder for dusting the plates. By using a high-quality mustard from Burgundy, you will be able to make a mustard powder that far exceeds any regular old powder. Make extra and keep it in your spice drawer.

dijonnaise fried chicken salad, mustard vinaigrette

SERVES 4

DRIED MUSTARD POWDER
¼ cup Dijon mustard

SEASONING SALT
2 garlic cloves, crushed
¼ cup kosher salt
½ teaspoon coarsely ground black peppercorns
¾ teaspoon minced fresh thyme
1½ teaspoons finely chopped fresh sage
¼ teaspoon freshly grated nutmeg

HONEY-MUSTARD MAYONNAISE
½ cup honey wine (hydromel)
1 large egg yolk
1½ tablespoons Dijon mustard
¼ teaspoon kosher salt
½ cup grapeseed oil

VINAIGRETTE
1 large shallot, finely chopped
2 tablespoons white wine vinegar
2 teaspoons Dijon mustard
¾ teaspoon Seasoning Salt (above)
¼ teaspoon coarsely ground black peppercorns
Pinch of cayenne pepper
5 tablespoons grapeseed oil

CHICKEN
2 boneless, skinless chicken breasts
2 boneless, skinless chicken thighs, sinew removed
½ cup buttermilk
¼ cup Dijon mustard
2 teaspoons Seasoning Salt (above)
½ teaspoon freshly ground black pepper

3 pinches of cayenne pepper

4 cups fresh bread crumbs (from day-old white bread)

Peanut oil for pan-frying

6 thin slices pancetta or bacon

4 cups torn Boston lettuce leaves

4 cups tender yellow frisée leaves

¼ cup fresh tarragon leaves

1 preserved lemon, pulp removed and discarded, peel very finely diced

Seasoning salt (above)

TO MAKE THE MUSTARD POWDER

Preheat the oven to 140°F. Line a baking sheet with a silicone baking mat.

Spread the mustard over the baking mat in a very thin layer and bake overnight.

Scrape the dried mustard into a spice grinder or clean coffee grinder and grind to a powder. Set aside.

TO MAKE THE SEASONING SALT

Rub the garlic and salt together in a small bowl with your fingertips to release the garlic oil until the salt is moist and fragrant. Strain the salt through a sieve into another small bowl; discard the garlic. Add the pepper, thyme, sage, and nutmeg to the salt, rubbing the ingredients together with your fingertips until thoroughly blended. (The salt can be stored airtight in the refrigerator for up to 2 weeks.)

TO MAKE THE HONEY-MUSTARD MAYONNAISE

Boil the honey wine in a heavy small saucepan over high heat until reduced to 2 tablespoons, about 8 minutes. Let cool completely.

Combine the reduced wine, egg yolk, mustard, and salt in a blender and blend well. With the blender running, slowly add the oil and blend until smooth and creamy. Refrigerate until ready to use.

TO MAKE THE VINAIGRETTE

Whisk the shallot, vinegar, mustard, seasoning salt, black pepper, and cayenne in a small bowl to blend. Gradually whisk in the oil.

Starting at the thinner end, cut each chicken breast on the bias into 4 pieces. Cut each chicken thigh on the bias into 4 pieces. Using a meat mallet, flatten each piece of chicken slightly.

Mix the buttermilk, mustard, 1 teaspoon of the seasoning salt, the pepper, and a pinch of the cayenne in a large bowl to blend. Add the chicken pieces and stir to coat, then cover and refrigerate for at least 1 hour or up to 1 day.

TO COOK THE CHICKEN

Mix the bread crumbs, the remaining 1 teaspoon seasoning salt, and the remaining 2 pinches cayenne in a shallow dish. Remove the chicken pieces from the marinade and coat them with the bread crumb mixture, pressing the crumbs firmly onto the chicken.

Heat ¼ inch of peanut oil in a heavy large skillet over medium-high heat until very hot but not smoking. Working in batches, fry the chicken until golden brown on both sides, about 6 minutes per batch. Drain on paper towels and keep warm in a low oven while you assemble the salad.

Meanwhile, cook the pancetta in a heavy medium skillet over medium heat until golden brown and crisp, about 8 minutes. Drain on paper towels, then crumble and keep warm.

TO MAKE THE SALAD

Toss the Boston lettuce, frisée, tarragon leaves, and preserved lemon in a large bowl with enough of the vinaigrette to coat. Season to taste with seasoning salt.

TO SERVE

Arrange the salad on four plates. Place the fried chicken pieces on top and sprinkle with the crumbled pancetta. Put a quenelle of honey mayonnaise on one edge of each plate and sprinkle the plates with some of the mustard powder. Serve immediately.

At home, a cheese course need not be more than sliced pears with hunks of beautiful blue cheese, but I like to play a little with this magnificent pairing. So I adapt a classic Pithiviers, a puff pastry tart filled with almond cream, with a béchamel finished with what might be my favorite blue cheese, Fourme d'Ambert, instead of the cream. Poached pears and balsamic syrup are sweet counterpoints to the savory torte.

fourme d'ambert torte, red pears, honey-balsamic syrup

SERVES 8

FOURME D'AMBERT BÉCHAMEL
4 tablespoons unsalted butter
½ cup all-purpose flour
1¼ cups whole milk, hot
4 ounces Fourme d'Ambert blue cheese, cut into big pieces
Kosher salt and freshly ground white pepper

RED PEARS
1 cup red beet juice
1 cup water
½ cup granulated sugar
Juice of 1 lemon

1 vanilla bean, split lengthwise
2 Anjou pears, peeled

HONEY-BALSAMIC REDUCTION
½ cup balsamic vinegar
½ cup acacia honey

TORTE
Two 10-ounce pieces Puff Pastry (recipe follows)
1 large egg yolk, beaten with 1 teaspoon water, for egg wash
2 tablespoons water
2 tablespoons granulated sugar

TO MAKE THE BÉCHAMEL
Melt the butter in a heavy medium saucepan over medium heat. Whisk in the flour and cook for 3 minutes, but do not allow the mixture to brown. Whisk in the hot milk and bring to a boil, whisking, then reduce the heat and simmer, whisking constantly,

until the sauce thickens, about 5 minutes (the sauce will be thicker than most bé-chamels). Remove from the heat and whisk in the cheese. Season to taste with salt and white pepper.

Transfer the béchamel to a container and let cool, then cover and refrigerate until cold, at least 6 hours.

TO POACH THE PEARS

Combine the beet juice, water, sugar, and lemon juice in a heavy medium saucepan. Scrape the seeds from the vanilla bean into the saucepan, then add the pod and bring the mixture to a boil over high heat, stirring to dissolve the sugar.

Add the pears, cover them with a round of parchment paper, and simmer over medium heat, rotating the pears occasionally so they cook evenly, until tender but not mushy, about 15 minutes. Transfer the pears to a baking pan to cool; discard the poaching liquid or reserve it for another use, if desired. Once the pears are cool, remove the cores and quarter the pears lengthwise.

TO MAKE THE HONEY-BALSAMIC REDUCTION

Combine the vinegar and honey in a heavy small saucepan and bring to a boil over high heat, whisking to blend. Reduce the heat to medium and simmer until the mixture is reduced to a syrup, about 10 minutes. Transfer to a bowl and set aside to cool.

TO MAKE THE TORTE

Preheat the oven to 425°F. Line a heavy large baking sheet with parchment paper.

On a lightly floured work surface, roll out each piece of puff pastry into an 11-inch square. Transfer 1 pastry square to the prepared baking sheet. Gently spoon the blue cheese béchamel over the pastry, leaving a 2-inch border around the edges.

Brush the pastry edges with some of the egg wash. Top with the second pastry square and press the edges firmly together to seal, taking care to remove any air bubbles. Using a sharp knife and the bottom of a 10-inch tart pan or a pot lid as a guide, cut the pastry into an 11-inch round. Brush the top with the egg wash. Using the knife tip, decoratively score the top of the pastry like the rays of the sun.

Bake until the pastry puffs and is golden brown on top, about 35 minutes. Reduce the heat to 350°F and continue baking until the pastry is cooked through and golden brown all over, about 30 minutes. Remove from the oven.

Meanwhile, just before the torte is done, stir the water and granulated sugar in a small saucepan over medium-high heat until the sugar dissolves and the mixture is syrupy, about 2 minutes. Remove from the heat.

TO SERVE

Brush the warm sugar syrup over the warm torte (this will make the pastry crispy when it cools).

Cut the tourte into 8 pieces and place each piece on a plate. Place a wedge of poached pear alongside each one, drizzle with some of the honey-balsamic reduction, and serve.

puff pastry

MAKES 2½ POUNDS (FOUR 10-OUNCE PIECES)

3¼ cups all-purpose flour
2 teaspoons kosher salt
8 tablespoons (1 stick) unsalted
butter, cut into 1-inch pieces and
chilled, plus 14 ounces
(3½ sticks) unsalted butter, at
room temperature

1 cup cold water, or more if needed

Combine the flour and salt in a food processor and pulse to blend. Pulse in the chilled butter pieces. With the machine running, gradually add the water through the feed tube, blending just until a soft dough forms; add more water 1 tablespoon at a time if needed.

Transfer the dough to a lightly floured work surface and knead until smooth. Roll out the dough into a 15-by-12-inch rectangle. Turn the dough if necessary so a short end is toward you, and brush away any excess flour. Spread the room-temperature butter over the bottom two-thirds of the dough. Fold the unbuttered top third over the center, then fold the remaining buttered third over it, as if you were folding a letter. Refrigerate for 45 minutes.

Return the dough to the lightly floured work surface, with a long side toward you. Roll out the dough again into a 15-by-12-inch rectangle. Brush away any excess flour. Fold the narrow ends of the dough in to meet at the center, again brushing away any excess flour. Fold the dough in half again, as if you were closing a book. Cover the dough and refrigerate for 30 minutes.

Repeat the rolling and folding of the dough 3 more times, refrigerating the dough for 30 minutes after each turn.

Cut the dough crosswise into 4 equal pieces. Wrap each piece separately in plastic wrap and refrigerate for up to 1 week.

Here I have a little fun with the crêpes suzette, cutting small rounds from the crêpes and sandwiching them with pastry cream, so they look like ravioli. I also make use of California's great citrus, spooning my take on the orange-butter sauce onto the ravioli and keeping things lighthearted by serving an orange milk shake alongside.

orange "ravioli," orange milk shake

SERVES 6

PASTRY CREAM
½ cup whole milk
1½ teaspoons finely grated orange zest
2 large eggs
½ cup granulated sugar
¼ cup all-purpose flour
1 tablespoon cornstarch

ORANGE-PEEL CONFIT
⅔ cup water
¼ cup granulated sugar
2 tablespoons glucose
3 tablespoons pomegranate syrup
Juice of 1 lemon
1 orange, peel julienned

CRÊPE RAVIOLI
½ cup plus 1 tablespoon all-purpose flour
3 large eggs
¾ cup heavy cream

¾ cup whole milk
2 tablespoons Grand Marnier
2 tablespoons olive oil, plus more for cooking the ravioli
1 tablespoon finely grated orange zest
2 oranges, suprêmed (page 49)
1 large egg, beaten, for egg wash

4 cups Simple Syrup (page 300)

ORANGE SAUCE
¼ cup Grand Marnier
¼ cup granulated sugar
¼ cup Simple Syrup (page 300)
2 tablespoons fresh orange juice
6 tablespoons cold unsalted butter, cut into pieces
1 tablespoon fresh lemon juice

ACCOMPANIMENT
Orange Milk Shake (recipe follows)

TO MAKE THE PASTRY CREAM

Combine the milk and orange zest in a heavy small saucepan and bring to a boil.

Meanwhile, using an electric mixer, beat the eggs and sugar in a small bowl until light and fluffy, about 5 minutes. Mix in the flour and cornstarch.

Gradually mix the hot milk mixture into the egg mixture. Return the mixture to the saucepan and whisk over medium-low heat until the pastry cream becomes very thick and bubbles begin to break on the surface, about 3 minutes.

Transfer the pastry cream to a small bowl and press plastic wrap directly onto the surface of the cream. Refrigerate until cold, at least 3 hours, and up to 2 days.

TO MAKE THE ORANGE-PEEL CONFIT

Combine the water, sugar, and glucose in a heavy small saucepan and bring to a boil over high heat, stirring to dissolve the sugar. Stir in the pomegranate syrup and lemon juice and return to a boil. Add the orange peel and cook over medium heat until the syrup thickens, about 8 minutes. Remove from the heat and set aside.

Whisk the flour and eggs in a large bowl to blend. Add the cream, milk, Grand Marnier, oil, and orange zest and whisk to blend. Cover the batter and refrigerate until cold, about 1 hour.

Lightly brush a 7- to 8-inch nonstick crêpe pan with oil and heat over medium heat. Pour 2 tablespoons of the crêpe batter into the pan and quickly swirl the pan to coat the bottom thinly and evenly. Cook until the edges of the crêpe are light brown, about 30 seconds. Loosen the edges gently with a rubber spatula, then, using your fingertips, carefully lift up the crêpe and turn it over. Cook until the bottom begins to brown in spots, about 20 seconds. Transfer the crêpe to a baking sheet. Repeat with the remaining batter, brushing the pan lightly with more oil if necessary before adding more batter; you should have about 20 crêpes.

Using a 3-inch round cutter, cut out 2 rounds from each crêpe. Lay half of the crêpe rounds on the work surface, then spoon 1 tablespoon of the pastry cream onto the center of each round. Place 1 orange segment on each. Brush some of the beaten egg on the edges of each round, then top each with another crêpe round and press to seal the edges. Don't worry if the edges do not seal completely—the filling should be thick enough that it won't ooze out. Keep the assembled ravioli covered until you're ready to cook them.

Heat the simple syrup in a heavy wide saucepan over medium-high heat until it is hot but not boiling; reduce the heat to medium-low if necessary. Working in batches (a total of three), gently add the ravioli to the simple syrup and cook until they are heated through, about 3 minutes.

Combine the Grand Marnier, sugar, simple syrup, and orange juice in a heavy medium saucepan and bring to a boil over high heat, stirring to dissolve the sugar. Simmer for 5 minutes, until thickened slightly. Add the butter and return the mixture to a boil, whisking to blend. Whisk in the lemon juice. Set the sauce aside, covered to keep it warm.

Using a slotted spoon, remove the ravioli from the simple syrup and place 3 ravioli on each of six plates. Spoon about 3 tablespoons of the sauce over and around the ravioli on each plate. Spoon the orange-peel confit on top of the ravioli and serve with the milk shakes.

orange milk shake   SERVES 6

2 cups fresh orange juice
2 cups Vanilla Ice Cream (page 344)

1 cup ice cubes
¾ cup whole milk

Boil the orange juice in a heavy small saucepan over medium heat until it is reduced to ½ cup. Remove from the heat and cool completely.

When ready to serve, combine the reduced orange juice, ice cream, ice, and milk, in a Vitamix and blend until smooth and creamy. Pour into six chilled small glasses and serve immediately.

Many customers are surprised to see avocado as part of a dessert course, but to me, it seems perfectly natural. The ripe fruit's creamy pastel-green flesh seems like something a master pâtissier would dream up, and it feels right at home alongside lightly sweetened cubes of tropical fruit and spicy ginger ice cream.

guacamole, exotic fruits, crystallized-ginger ice cream

SERVES 6

ICE CREAM
2¼ cups whole milk
6 large egg yolks
3 tablespoons granulated sugar
3 ounces crystallized ginger, diced

GUACAMOLE
2 ripe avocados, halved, peeled, and pitted
¼ cup Simple Syrup (page 300)
3 tablespoons extra-virgin olive oil
Juice of 1 lime
1 red jalapeño chile, seeded and very finely diced

EXOTIC FRUITS
Twelve ½-inch cubes mango
Twelve ½-inch cubes pineapple
Twelve ½-inch cubes banana
½ cup Simple Syrup (page 300)

ACCOMPANIMENTS
3 passion fruits
12 fresh cilantro leaves
12 small red shiso leaves

TO MAKE THE ICE CREAM

Bring the milk to just below a simmer in a heavy medium saucepan over medium-high heat.

Meanwhile, whisk the egg yolks and sugar in a large bowl until creamy and lemon-colored. Slowly add half of the hot milk to the egg mixture, whisking constantly.

Pour the tempered egg mixture back into the remaining milk, add the ginger, and cook over low heat, stirring constantly in figure eights with a silicone spatula, until the custard thickens enough to coat the back of a spoon, about 10 minutes; do not allow it to simmer.

Pour the custard into a bowl, set the bowl over a bowl of ice water, and stir until cold. Cover and refrigerate overnight.

Blend the custard in a blender until smooth, then strain through a fine-mesh strainer into a bowl. Freeze the custard in an ice cream maker following the manufacturer's instructions. Press the ice cream into a freezer container and cover with plastic wrap pressed directly on top of the ice cream and then with the lid. Freeze until scoopable, or for up to 1 day.

TO MAKE THE GUACAMOLE

Using a fork, mash the avocados with the syrup, olive oil, lime juice, and jalapeño in a medium bowl; some chunks should remain. Cover and refrigerate until ready to use.

TO PREPARE THE FRUITS

Toss all the fruits with the simple syrup in a medium bowl to coat. Cover and refrigerate until ready to use.

TO SERVE

Place a generous spoonful of the guacamole into each of six large bowls. Spoon the fruit mixture on top, then spoon a quenelle of ginger ice cream alongside each serving. Cut the passion fruits in half and scoop the pulp, juice, and seeds over the fruit. Garnish with the cilantro and shiso and serve immediately.

it was LudoBites the Party, then it was LudoBites the Business. Now, as Krissy likes to say, it had become LudoBites the Investment. Committing to this project meant committing to the permanence of our temporary restaurant. Mike was a huge help. He really *got* LudoBites. He also seemed to know everyone in the neighborhood. As he was making calls like crazy asking locals for chairs and tables to borrow, Krissy and I were trawling for stuff in every Goodwill and used furniture store we could find.

On move-in day, we pulled up to the space with my Chevy Tahoe packed to the brim with our newly purchased plates, silverware, glassware, ice buckets, and candleholders—everything we all take for granted when we dine out—and enough of it to serve many courses to more than 120 people per night. Somehow we had to fit all our food into a space where the walk-in fridge and freezer were already full. We were cramming two restaurants into one tiny one, and there was an unspoken ongoing battle for who got to command which corner or which bit of counter space. We'd share flour and sugar, but that was about it. We had to make sure that no one from the day operation would mess with my champagne vinegar, foie gras, or dried bonito. It felt like we were college roommates moving in together for the first time.

And, let me tell you, I made a crazy roommate. Gram & Papa's wasn't up to my sky-high standards. So that first day I was screaming, at no one in particular. I spent hours down on my hands and knees with buckets of hot water and bleach, scrubbing the floors in a doomed effort to achieve the spotless glow of a fine-dining kitchen. Mike got defensive, and I flipped. I yelled at him, "Fuck it, I'll leave right now." I had crossed a line.

I knew he was struggling to keep his restaurant open. LudoBites offered him a marketing infusion, more advertising than money could buy. He had been working incredibly hard, and he wasn't even paying himself a salary. He was thinking that maybe he'd fucked up by opening where he had, when he had. So when I threatened to leave, I could almost see his heart sink.

An hour or so later, we had a frank discussion. He apologized for the condition of things. I told him why I'd blown up, why I occasionally go into lunatic mode, why a perfectionist would have a hard time moving from borrowed restaurant to borrowed restaurant. We began to understand each

other. As Mike said, this moment "felt like hugging your brother after a fistfight." It was OK that anger bubbled up to the surface as long as mutual respect flowed underneath.

By the time we were ready to open, I was as happy with the place as I was ever going to be. It was clean. We'd hung Christmas lights in the windows and my funky paintings on the walls. The service line was adorned with clip-on lights so my cooks could see what they were plating. Of course I'd have to contend with the kitchen equipment, including a couple of beat-up ovens that had never been calibrated, a moody freezer, and maddeningly finicky burners.

I was lucky that my former sous chef at Bastide, Sydney Hunter, was available, and I eagerly hired him. He's an incredible cook, and after the sous-chef debacle of 3.0, I needed someone reliable as my number two. Two of the other cooks had decent kitchen experience. The rest did not.

Up until now, most of our kitchen staff had been borrowed hands, with a motley crew of bloggers, customers, and other rascals helping out a day here or two days there. In the newfound spirit of our commitment and investment, we decided to make some more full-time hires. Well, "hires" might be too strong a word. Because of the razor-thin margins and other economic peculiarities of LudoBites, we couldn't pay these newbies. So we looked to culinary students, who could at least get school credit for their work with us. Yet we were asking so much of these guys—eight-hour shifts would easily stretch to ten or twelve hours—that I decided to pay them in another currency. In the typical *stage*, culinary students are stuck in the basement chopping onions. And, sure, there was plenty of that at LudoBites, but I let my guys plate dishes and sometimes even cook during service. If I was going to make it work, I had to come to trust them, and I had to teach them. And I wanted to show these kids the stuff they really needed to know if they seriously wanted to do what they thought they wanted to.

There was Holly, who had taken a sabbatical from her job in marketing research to juice lemons, peel pearl onions, and attempt a perfect quenelle, those oblong orbs chefs insist on any time they serve anything ice cream–textured. As a newbie, she got to plate dishes on opening night. And she got her first mandoline-caused injury. But after shaving off layers of skin and leaking red for fifteen minutes, she wasn't freaking out about the blood, but rather about the fact that her injury was interfering with her setting up her mise-en-place. I was so proud.

And there was Jacob, a seventeen-year-old enrolled in his high school's culinary program who worked with me three nights a week. I just loved having this guy's energy in the kitchen. It was almost comical; whenever I called his name, he'd appear precisely one second later, yelling, "Yes, chef!" I swear, this guy could've been in Long

Heat the milk in a heavy medium saucepan over medium heat until hot; do not allow it to come to a simmer. Whisk in the almond flour. Cover and keep warm over low heat, stirring every 15 minutes for 3 hours to infuse.

Combine the vinegar, water, wine, sugar, and sachet in a heavy large saucepan and bring to a boil over high heat, stirring to dissolve the sugar. Remove the pan from the heat, cover, and set aside until the mixture is just warm.

Combine the grapes and capers in a glass jar and pour enough of the warm vinegar mixture over the grapes to cover them completely. Refrigerate for 2 hours.

Transfer the almond mixture to a food processor and puree until smooth. Transfer to a small bowl and cover to keep warm.

Season the scallops with salt and pepper. Heat a large nonstick sauté pan over high heat until a wisp of smoke comes off the pan. Add the butter, then the scallops, and cook for 1 minute on each side, or until golden brown on both sides but still raw in the center.

Line up 3 scallops down the center of each of four plates. Lay 3 grape halves flat on each plate, with a few capers. Lay a few slices of raw cauliflower on each plate, top with a scoop of ice cream, and garnish with an additional slice or two of cauliflower. Spoon a quenelle of almond puree alongside, drizzle with some curry oil, and serve immediately.

curry oil

½ cup grapeseed oil
4 teaspoons Madras curry powder

Heat the oil to 180°F in a small heavy saucepan over low heat. Add the curry powder and blend with an immersion blender for 1 minute.

Transfer the oil to a container, cover with plastic wrap, and poke holes into the plastic wrap. Refrigerate overnight. Stir before using.

cauliflower ice cream

½ head cauliflower (about 11 ounces), cored, separated into florets, and very thinly sliced
¼ teaspoon freshly grated nutmeg
1 teaspoon kosher salt

3¼ cups whole milk
2½ cups heavy cream
12 large egg yolks
½ cup granulated sugar

TO MAKE THE CAULIFLOWER PUREE

Put the sliced cauliflower in a heavy large saucepan and add the nutmeg and salt, then add 1½ cups of the milk and 1 cup of the cream, to just cover the cauliflower. Bring to a boil, then reduce the heat to medium-low and simmer until the cauliflower is tender but not mushy, about 8 minutes.

Drain the cauliflower in a sieve set over a bowl; reserve the cooking liquid. Puree the cauliflower in a high-powered blender on high until it is very smooth, adding some of the cooking liquid if necessary. Measure out 1 cup of the puree.

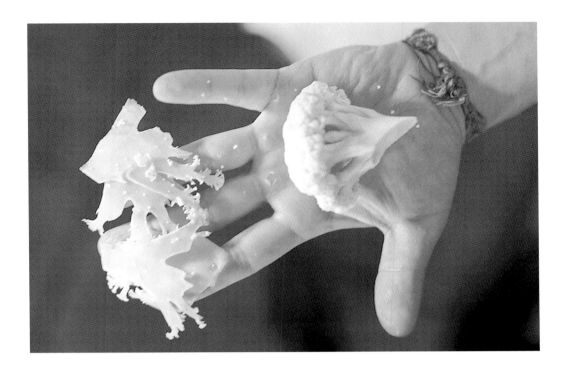

Combine the remaining 1¾ cups milk and 1½ cups cream in a heavy medium saucepan and bring just to a simmer.

Meanwhile, whisk the eggs and sugar in a medium bowl to blend. Gradually add one-half of the hot milk mixture to the egg mixture, whisking constantly. Pour the tempered egg mixture back into the remaining hot milk and, using a silicone spatula, stir the custard over medium-low heat, scraping the bottom of the saucepan and stirring in figure eights, until thickened enough to coat the back of a spoon, about 4 minutes. Strain the custard through a fine-mesh sieve into a bowl and set the bowl in a bowl of ice water. Let cool completely, stirring often.

Whisk the cauliflower puree into the custard. Refrigerate until cold.

Freeze the custard in an ice cream machine according to the manufacturer's instructions.

I could eat ceviche every day, and I could dream up a different version every day, pairing the fish, after it has "cooked" briefly in an acidic liquid and been infused with its flavor, with all manner of sauces and vegetables, varying the textures and flavors. In this take on a Mexican ceviche, the costars are the spark of pickled red onions and a stripe of sweet-tart Meyer lemon gel.

dorade ceviche, heirloom tomato, jalapeño, red onion, meyer lemon, olive oil

SERVES 4

PICKLED RED ONION
1 small red onion, cut into thin julienne
1 cup red wine vinegar
¼ cup water
2 teaspoons granulated sugar
2 teaspoons kosher salt

MEYER LEMON GEL
¾ cup fresh Meyer lemon juice, strained
1½ tablespoons agar-agar

CEVICHE
Two 7-ounce skinless dorade fillets
About 1 cup fresh lime juice

ACCOMPANIMENTS
1 heirloom tomato, cored, halved
    lengthwise, and cut into ¼-inch-thick
    slices
1 green jalapeño chile, sliced into
    paper-thin rounds
½ cup fresh cilantro leaves, plus
    20 cilantro flowers
8 teaspoons extra-virgin olive oil
Fleur de sel

Blanch the onion in a medium saucepan of lightly salted water for 15 seconds. Drain and submerge in a bowl of ice water just until cold. Drain the onion again and pat dry with paper towels. Put the onion in a small bowl and set aside.

Combine the vinegar, water, sugar, and salt in a heavy small saucepan and bring to a simmer over high heat, whisking to dissolve the sugar and salt. Pour the pickling juice over the onion and set aside until cool. Then cover and refrigerate until very cold. (When the red onion looks very pink, it is thoroughly pickled.)

TO MAKE THE MEYER LEMON GEL

Combine the lemon juice and agar-agar in a heavy small saucepan and bring to a boil over medium-high heat, whisking to dissolve the agar. Continue to boil, whisking constantly, to make sure the agar is fully dissolved, about 1 minute. Pour the mixture into a container and set aside until cool, then cover and refrigerate until cold and set.

TO MAKE THE CEVICHE

Cut the fish on a bias into ⅛-inch-thick slices. Lay the slices in a baking dish and pour enough lime juice over the fish to cover completely. Refrigerate for 25 minutes, or until the fish is opaque.

Transfer the fish to a small baking sheet (discard the lime juice), cover with plastic wrap, and refrigerate until ready to serve.

TO SERVE

Whisk the lemon gel until smooth.

Arrange the fish and tomato slices in four wide soup plates. Sprinkle about 1 tablespoon of the pickled red onion over each serving, then scatter the jalapeño slices and cilantro leaves on top. Drizzle the olive oil over and garnish with the cilantro flowers. Spoon 1 tablespoon of the lemon gel onto one edge of each plate in a stripe, sprinkle fleur de sel over the ceviche, and serve immediately.

TO MAKE THE GRANITÉ

Whisk the beer, simple syrup, and water in a medium bowl to blend. Pour the mixture into an 8-inch square baking pan and freeze until it becomes slushy, stirring every 45 minutes. Continue to freeze the mixture until it is completely frozen.

Using a fork, scrape the granité mixture to create flaky shavings.

TO MAKE THE CORNETS

Stir the corn syrup, butter, sesame oil, and miso in a medium saucepan over medium-high heat until the butter is melted, about 2 minutes. Transfer to a bowl.

Mix the flour, black and white sesame seeds, and ginger in a medium bowl and pour into the warm corn syrup mixture, stirring to mix well. Cover and refrigerate for at least 4 hours, and up to 2 weeks.

When ready to make the cornets, preheat the oven to 350°F. Line large baking sheet with a silicone baking mat. (You only need 6 cornets for this recipe, but there's enough batter so that you can make 12 cornets and then choose the best ones to serve.)

Spoon some of the batter into a pastry bag fitted with a small plain tip and pipe two 3-inch rounds, about 1/8 inch thick, onto the prepared baking sheet, leaving ample space between them to allow for the spread that occurs during baking. Bake for about 10 minutes, or until the disks are golden brown. Remove the baking sheet from the oven and allow the disks to cool for about 30 seconds.

While the disks are still very hot, wrap one around a waffle cone mold and press on the overlap with your hand; hold the cone in place with your hand until it firms up (you may want to wear gloves, either a clean pair of thick rubber gloves or several layers of disposable gloves, to protect your hands from the heat). You can speed up this process by working in front of a fan blowing cool air. Remove the cone from the mold and carefully place it on a parchment-lined tray. Repeat with the second disk, then repeat with the remaining batter. If the disks cool too much, put the baking sheet back in the oven to make them pliable again.

TO PREPARE THE CRABS

Using kitchen shears, cut off the face of each crab behind the eyes. Cut off the tail, tucked under the body, from each crab. Fold back the top halves of each shell and remove the lungs.

Set up three bowls from left to right on the work surface: flour in the first, eggs in the second, and panko in the third. Put the crabs to the left of the bowl with flour and a baking sheet lined with parchment paper to the right of the panko. Bread the crabs by dredging them one at a time in the flour, patting off the excess, dipping them into the eggs, and finally into the panko, and put them on the parchment-lined baking sheet.

Chill six small glasses in the freezer.

TO COOK THE CRABS

Preheat the oven to 200°F. Add enough oil to a large skillet to fill it halfway and heat the oil to 375°F. Cut an X in the bottom of six paper cups, press back the corners of the X, and set the cups upside down on top of the serving plates. Insert a cornet into each cup.

Add 1 crab to the hot oil, gently press on it with a wire skimmer to keep it submerged, and fry until crisp and golden brown, about 1 minute per side. Stand back as the crab fries until you hear a "pop," because the oil has a tendency to splatter as the crab pops. Using tongs, transfer the crab to a baking sheet lined with paper towels, and blot it with more paper towels so it does not absorb too much oil and become soggy as it sits. Transfer to the oven to keep warm, and fry the remaining crabs.

Cut 1 fried crab into 1-inch pieces and gently toss in a large bowl with 1 tablespoon of the spicy mayonnaise. Fill 1 of the cornets with the crab mixture. Repeat with the remaining crabs, mayonnaise, and cornets.

Spoon 1 tablespoon of the mango puree in a pool on top of the crab in each cornet, then drizzle 2 teaspoons of balsamic syrup in a zigzag over the top. Spoon the granité into the frozen glasses, sprinkle with lime zest, and serve immediately.

balsamic syrup

MAKES ½ CUP

One 500 ml bottle balsamic vinegar

Simmer the balsamic vinegar in a deep heavy small saucepan over medium heat until it has reduced to ½ cup, about 35 minutes.

Cool the syrup over an ice bath, then transfer to a squeeze bottle or bowl and store at room temperature for up to 1 week.

mango puree

MAKES 2 CUPS

2 large ripe mangoes (about 2 pounds total),
    peeled, pitted, and cut into chunks

Blend the mango flesh in a blender until smooth. Strain the puree to remove any fibers. Pour the puree into a squeeze bottle or a bowl and refrigerate until chilled, or for up to 1 week.

spicy mayonnaise

MAKES ABOUT 1⅓ CUPS

2 tablespoons Sriracha sauce
1 large egg
1½ teaspoons white wine vinegar

1 teaspoon fresh lemon juice
½ teaspoon fine sea salt
1¼ cups grapeseed oil

Whisk the Sriracha, egg, vinegar, lemon juice, and salt in a medium bowl to blend. Set the bowl on a damp cloth to keep it stable and, whisking vigorously, start to add the oil in a thin, steady stream. As the mayonnaise thickens, add the oil in small increments and whisk until fully incorporated before adding more. The mayonnaise should be very thick. Cover and refrigerate. The mayonnaise can be refrigerated for up to 2 weeks.

One of the first things I always do when I get to Paris is find a little bakery for my favorite sandwich: a perfect baguette filled with ham, butter, and slices of radish and cornichon. There's nothing better. For a second, I was tempted to introduce diners to its glory, but people don't come to LudoBites for a simple sandwich! So I took all the flavors and turned them into a fantastic soup, with chunks of salty ham, crunchy croutons, and a good scoop of the foamy head of a Guinness, because I almost always drink a beer with my Parisian sandwich.

ham-sandwich soup

SERVES 6

SOUP

4 tablespoons unsalted butter
½ yellow onion, diced
1 garlic clove, sliced
8 ounces boiled ham, chopped
3 cups whole milk
1 cup heavy cream
1 cup Chicken Stock (page 39)
Kosher salt and freshly ground
    white pepper

CROUTONS

Six ¼-inch-thick slices rustic
    wheat bread

3 tablespoons unsalted butter, melted
4 ounces Emmental or Swiss cheese,
    cut into thin slices

BROWN BUTTER

4 tablespoons unsalted butter

GARNISHES

Julienned cornichons
Julienned radishes
One 12-ounce bottle Guinness

TO MAKE THE SOUP

Melt the butter in a medium pot over low heat. Add the onion and garlic and cook over low heat, stirring frequently, for 10 to 15 minutes, until the onion is translucent.

Add the ham and cook for another 10 to 15 minutes, stirring occasionally.

Add the milk, cream, and stock, increase the heat to medium-high, and bring to a simmer, stirring occasionally. Reduce the heat to a gentle simmer, cover, and cook for 1 hour, until it releases its flavor and juices.

Strain the soup into a bowl, reserving the onion mixture and broth separately. Working in batches, put the onion mixture into a blender (preferred) or a food processor and puree for 5 minutes, or until finely ground, adding just enough of the reserved broth to allow the mixture to be pureed. Once the mixture is finely ground, gradually add more broth, blending until you have a smooth puree. Pour the puree into a heavy pot or saucepan.

Add any remaining broth and blend thoroughly with an immersion blender. Season to taste with salt and white pepper.

TO MAKE THE CROUTONS

Preheat the oven to 350°F.

Trim the crusts from the bread and cut each slice into 4 rectangles about 1 inch by 1½ inches. Toss the slices in the melted butter and arrange on a baking sheet. Bake until golden brown, 3 to 5 minutes. Set aside. Leave the oven on.

TO MAKE THE BROWN BUTTER

Melt the butter in a heavy small saucepan over medium-high heat, then cook until the butter begins to brown. Remove from the heat; set aside and keep warm.

TO SERVE

Cut the slices of cheese into rectangles similar in size to the croutons. Place the slices of cheese on top of the croutons and bake until the cheese has melted, 2 to 3 minutes.

Pour the soup into six soup bowls. Place the croutons on top of the soup. Drizzle a little brown butter over and around the croutons and sprinkle julienned cornichons and radishes on top of the croutons. Pour the beer into a glass from a distance to create a large head, or blend the beer in a blender to create foam. Spoon the beer foam on top of the soup and serve immediately.

I got the idea for this dish on a vacation with Krissy in Hawaii. The piña colada was her go-to drink. I'd never had one in my life. The memory of the cocktail stuck in my head, and people went crazy first at Bastide and subsequently at LudoBites when I paired it with foie gras—which is not as strange as it might sound. Sweetness and booze are no strangers to foie gras. Plus, how can you resist the fantastic contrast of hot, almost molten, fatty liver, icy coconut sorbet, rum gelée, and crispy pineapple chips?

seared foie gras, pineapple chips, coconut sorbet

SERVES 6

PINEAPPLE ESPUMA
2 cups pineapple juice
5 gelatin sheets
¼ cup water

TOASTED COCONUT
1 coconut

PINEAPPLE CHIPS
½ pineapple
4 cups Simple Syrup (page 300)

SHERRY-MAPLE SYRUP SAUCE
¾ cup cream sherry (preferably Lustau Superior Solera)
½ cup pure maple syrup

RUM GELÉE
1 cup Bacardi silver rum
3 gelatin sheets
¼ cup Simple Syrup (page 300)
¼ cup fresh coconut water

COCONUT SORBET
2 cups unsweetened coconut milk
1 cup Simple Syrup (page 300)

FOIE GRAS
Six 1½-inch-thick slices Grade A foie gras
Sea salt and freshly ground black pepper

Bring the pineapple juice to a boil in a heavy small saucepan. Set aside to cool.

Soak the gelatin sheets in a bowl of cold water until softened, about 5 minutes. Remove the softened gelatin from the water, combine it with the ¼ cup water in a small saucepan, and stir over medium-low heat until it dissolves.

Whisk the gelatin mixture into the pineapple juice. Strain through a fine-mesh sieve. Measure 2 cups of the gelatin mixture. Transfer to a whipped cream canister and refrigerate until set.

TO PREPARE THE TOASTED COCONUT

Preheat the oven to 350°F.

Crack the coconut in half and drain off the coconut water. Remove the white meat, being careful not to break it into small pieces. Peel off the brown skin. Using a mandoline, shave nice slivers of the coconut from a thin side of each piece.

Spread the coconut on a baking sheet and toast in the oven for 10 minutes, or until golden. Set aside to cool.

Reduce the oven temperature to 200°F.

TO MAKE THE PINEAPPLE CHIPS

Remove the rind from the pineapple. Lay the pineapple cut side down on the work surface and cut crosswise in half. Use a 2½-inch ring mold to cut a cylinder from 1 pineapple piece. Using a mandoline or a very sharp knife, cut the pineapple cylinder into 1.5mm paper-thin rounds. Reserve the remaining pineapple for another use—unless you want to make a lot of pineapple chips!

Bring the simple syrup to 165°F in a medium saucepan over medium heat. Add the pineapple slices and cook until translucent, about 5 minutes. Gently remove the pineapple slices from the poaching liquid and drain.

Lay the pineapple slices on a baking sheet lined with a silicone baking mat and bake until dehydrated and thoroughly dry, about 2 hours. Transfer the pineapple slices to

a piece of parchment paper and cool to room temperature; the chips will become crisp as they cool.

MEANWHILE, TO MAKE THE MAPLE SYRUP SAUCE

Simmer the sherry in a heavy deep small saucepan over medium heat until reduced by three-fourths, about 20 minutes. Add the maple syrup and simmer over medium-low heat until reduced and coats the back of a spoon, about 15 minutes. Set aside to cool.

TO MAKE THE GELÉE

Heat the rum in a heavy deep medium saucepan over medium-high heat. Carefully ignite the rum, remove the pan from the heat, and allow to flambé until the alcohol is cooked off, just some small blue flames remain, and the rum is reduced to ½ cup, about 7 minutes. Be careful—the flames will be high!

Meanwhile, put the gelatin in a bowl of ice water to soften, about 5 minutes.

Remove the gelatin from the ice water and stir it into the hot rum until it dissolves. Stir in the simple syrup and coconut water. Blowtorch any bubbles from the top of the mixture.

Transfer the mixture to a 6-by-4-inch pan lined with plastic wrap, or to a pan that holds the mixture in a ¾-inch layer. Refrigerate, uncovered, at least 2 hours until set. The gelée should just be lightly chopped by hand with a knife, and 2 tablespoons of gelée are plated per serving.

TO MAKE THE SORBET

Whisk the coconut milk and simple syrup in a bowl to blend, then strain through a fine-mesh sieve. Transfer to an ice cream machine and freeze according to the manufacturer's instructions.

MEANWHILE, TO PREPARE THE FOIE GRAS

Preheat the oven to 450°F. Using a sharp knife, score both sides of the foie gras in a nice crosshatch pattern. Season both sides of the slices with salt and pepper.

Heat an 8-inch cast-iron skillet over high heat until it begins to smoke (the pan must be very hot to sear the foie gras properly). Sear the scored side of the foie gras slices until browned, about 3 minutes. Turn the slices over and place the pan in the oven until seared on the bottom, about 3 minutes.

TO SERVE

Put the lid on the canister of pineapple espuma and insert 2 nitrous oxide canisters. Run the bottle under hot water until the gelatin mixture melts. Turn the canister upside down and shake the hell out of it for about 1 minute. Hold the canister perpendicular to the plate and squirt some pineapple espuma onto the center of each of six plates. Place a piece of foie gras atop the espuma on each plate. Arrange the rum gelée around the foie gras. Spoon a scoop of coconut sorbet alongside. Drizzle some sherry-maple syrup over, garnish with the pineapple chips and toasted coconut, and serve immediately.

Foie gras is often either served seared, as in the preceding recipe, or as a terrine, but when it's steamed—in this case, inside a leaf of Savoy cabbage—the texture is just incredible, as silky and light as panna cotta. To balance its richness, I add a scattering of pickled turnip (or radishes, if they look nicer at the market) and a simple consommé (clarified in the French style with egg whites) vividly flavored with spicy, funky kimchi.

cabbage-wrapped foie gras, kimchi consommé

SERVES 4

PICKLED TURNIPS

1⅔ cups water
1 cup rice vinegar
½ cup dry white wine
3½ tablespoons granulated sugar
1½ tablespoons kosher salt
5 baby turnips, quartered

KIMCHI CONSOMMÉ

2 cups jarred kimchi
3 cups water
1⅔ cups egg whites (about 11 large whites)

FOIE GRAS

4 large Savoy cabbage leaves
Four 1-inch-thick slices Grade A foie gras
Kosher salt and freshly ground black pepper
4 teaspoons toasted sesame oil

TO MAKE THE PICKLED TURNIPS

Combine the water, vinegar, wine, sugar, and salt in a medium saucepan and bring to a simmer over high heat, stirring to dissolve the sugar and salt. Add the turnips and cook for 1 minute. Remove the saucepan from the heat and set aside to cool.

Transfer the turnips and pickling juice to a container, cover, and refrigerate overnight.

Combine the kimchi and water in a food processor and pulse to coarsely chop the kimchi. Add the egg whites and pulse just to blend. Transfer the mixture to a heavy medium saucepan and bring to a simmer over medium-low heat. Reduce the heat and simmer gently until a coagulated "raft" forms on the top of the egg whites and the broth is clarified (clear), about 45 minutes.

Drape a piece of cheesecloth over the saucepan and submerge a ladle in the broth so that the broth floods into the ladle (the clarified broth will pass through into the ladle without any particles). Transfer the consommé to a small saucepan.

TO PREPARE THE FOIE GRAS

Blanch the cabbage leaves in a large pot of boiling salted water for 1 minute. Drain and submerge the cabbage leaves in a bowl of ice water to cool completely.

Remove the cabbage leaves from the ice water and pat them dry with paper towels. Trim about 1 inch of the thick center rib from each cabbage leaf.

Season the foie gras with salt and pepper. Wrap each piece in a cabbage leaf, as if you were wrapping a gift. Put the stuffed cabbage leaves seam side down in a steamer basket and steam until the internal temperature of the foie gras is 110°F, about 8 minutes.

Meanwhile, just before serving, bring the consommé to a simmer.

TO SERVE

Ladle the hot consommé into four wide shallow bowls. Place the cabbage-wrapped foie gras in the bowls. Drain the pickled turnips and arrange them around the foie gras. Coat the cabbage with the sesame oil, sprinkle with pepper, and serve.

"I ordered the squid, not the pasta," say customers, confused when they receive a plate of tagliatelle in a slightly creamy sauce, topped with a perfect poached egg. Ah, but what looks like noodles is pearly white strips of squid, cooked very, very delicately at a low temperature so it's as tender as fresh pasta.

SERVES 2

squid carbonara

PARMESAN SAUCE

2 cups plus 2 tablespoons Chicken
   Stock (page 39)
1 cup heavy cream
1 cup freshly grated Parmigiano-
   Reggiano cheese

POACHED EGGS

2 large eggs

SQUID CARBONARA

12 cleaned squid bodies
6 tablespoons high-quality lard

About 4 ounces pancetta, cut crosswise
   into 1-inch-long by ½-inch-thick
   lardons
2 teaspoons olive oil
Freshly ground black pepper
2 tablespoons freshly grated
   Parmigiano-Reggiano cheese
12 chive flowers, or thinly sliced fresh
   chives, for garnish

TO PREPARE THE SAUCE

Bring the chicken stock and heavy cream to a simmer in a large saucepan over medium-high heat and simmer until reduced by three-fourths. Whisk in the Parmesan cheese until incorporated. Remove from the heat and set aside. (This makes about 1 cup sauce, more than is needed for the recipe.)

TO POACH THE EGGS USING AN IMMERSION CIRCULATOR

Prepare the circulator for cooking at 150°F. Put the eggs (still in their shells) in the preheated circulator and cook for 45 minutes.

Remove the eggs from the circulator and put in an ice bath to cool—this helps set the white part of the egg without it being watery when served. When ready to serve, put the eggs in the circulator for 15 minutes to rewarm them.

TO POACH THE EGGS USING THE STANDARD METHOD

Bring 6 to 8 quarts lightly salted water to a rolling boil in a deep pot. Crack 1 egg into a ramekin. Remove the pot from the heat and whisk the water briskly to create a vortex, then quickly add the egg to the center of the vortex. Cook just until set, about 2 minutes; as the egg cooks, skim away any foam and loose pieces of egg white that float to the top. Using a slotted spoon, transfer the egg to paper towels to drain. A deep pot helps form a better egg. Repeat with the second egg. Reserve the hot water to rewarm the eggs again just before serving them.

TO PREPARE THE SQUID

Slice each body open lengthwise and open it out so it lies flat. Slice the squid into ¼-inch-wide slices to make "noodles."

Heat the lard in a large sauté pan over medium-low heat. Add the lardons and cook until lightly crisp and golden brown on all sides, 3 to 5 minutes. Remove from the pan and drain on a paper towel.

Heat the oil in a small sauté pan over medium-low heat, swirling it around to coat the bottom of the pan. Add the squid to the pan and cook until just opaque, 10 to 15 seconds. Transfer to a paper towel to drain.

TO SERVE

Place the squid in the center of two plates. Spoon 2 tablespoons of the hot parmesan sauce over each plate of squid. Place the poached eggs on top of the squid and sprinkle pepper over the eggs. Arrange the lardons around the squid plate. Sprinkle a tablespoon of Parmesan onto each plate, so it looks like snow. Garnish with the chive flowers and serve immediately.

Simple, simple, simple: it's my new mantra. Sometimes my simple food verges on the elemental. Here, I poach monkfish slowly in olive oil. The moist, silky flesh sits amid a colorful mélange of still-slightly-crunchy vegetables, which are blanched, simmered in stock, and finished with vadouvan butter, my favorite spice blend. At its essence, the plate is just fish and vegetables, but technique and top-quality ingredients elevate it to a higher plane of deliciousness.

monkfish, légumes de la jardinière, vadouvan

SERVES 6

VEGETABLES
6 yellow baby carrots, stems trimmed
6 orange baby carrots, stems trimmed
6 red baby carrots, stems trimmed
¾ cup fresh English peas
24 sugar snap peas, trimmed
12 baby leeks, trimmed
1 tablespoon all-purpose flour
18 baby turnips, peeled
¾ cup Chicken Stock (page 000)
4 tablespoons unsalted butter
Kosher salt and freshly ground white
  pepper

VADOUVAN BUTTER
8 ounces unsalted butter (preferably
  Plugrá), diced
½ cup Vadouvan (page 48)
Fleur de sel and freshly ground black
  pepper

MONKFISH
8 cups olive oil
Six 5-ounce monkfish fillets
Fleur de sel

TO PREPARE THE VEGETABLES
Blanch the carrots in a large pot of boiling salted water until crisp-tender, about 1 minute. Remove the carrots from the boiling water and submerge them in a large bowl of ice water to cool completely, then transfer to paper towels to drain. Repeat with the peas, snap peas, and leeks, cooking them for about 30 seconds each.

Whisk 4 cups cold water and the flour in a heavy large saucepan to blend and bring to a boil over high heat. Add the baby turnips and cook until crisp-tender, about 2 minutes. Drain and submerge the turnips in the bowl of ice water to cool completely, then transfer to paper towels to dry.

Just before serving, combine the vegetables with the chicken stock in a wide shallow saucepan and bring to a boil over high heat. Boil until the liquid has reduced by three-fourths. Reduce the heat to medium. Add the butter and swirl the pan until the butter is emulsified into the reduced liquid and coats the vegetables. Season to taste with salt and white pepper. Keep warm.

MEANWHILE, TO PREPARE THE VADOUVAN BUTTER

Melt three-fourths of the butter in a heavy medium saucepan over medium heat and cook until the milk solids have separated from the clear butter, about 2 minutes. Add the vadouvan and continue to cook the butter until it turns golden, about 3 minutes. Reduce the heat to low and allow the spices to infuse the butter for 5 minutes, then add the remaining butter and heat it the until the milk solids separate out. Remove from the heat and keep warm.

TO POACH THE MONKFISH

Bring the olive oil to 150°F in a heavy wide pot. Season the monkfish with salt, then submerge it in the oil and poach until it reaches an internal temperature of 140° to 145°F, about 8 minutes. Carefully transfer the fish to paper towels to drain; do not blot the oil from the tops and sides. Season with salt.

TO SERVE

Set the monkfish in the center of six plates. Arrange the vegetables over and around the fish, then spoon the vadouvan butter over. Serve immediately.

Occasionally I look back on a dish and wonder what the hell I was thinking when I came up with it. Lamb, artichokes, and mint is a pretty safe combination—but then there's the smoked eel spiked with curry powder. Wherever it came from, the dish is pretty damn good. Whether you decide to re-create my entire wild dish or not, at least try seasoning the lamb with katsuobushi—my sous chef Syd's inspiration, and a wonderful fusing of land and sea.

Note: To smoke the eel, you'll need a PolyScience smoking gun and a plastic container with a lid.

rack of lamb, fresh goat cheese mousse, smoked eel, artichokes, potato mousseline, mint

SERVES 8

ARTICHOKES

3 large artichokes, cleaned and each
    cut into 8 wedges
Juice of 1 lemon
3 tablespoons olive oil
¼ yellow onion, julienned
½ carrot, thinly sliced
3 garlic cloves, crushed
1 bay leaf
3 fresh thyme sprigs
1 cup dry white wine
About 3 cups Chicken Stock
    (page 39)
Kosher salt

SMOKED EEL

1 tablespoon Madras curry powder
4 cups Dashi (page 29)
½ cup sake
⅓ cup mirin
¼ cup white soy sauce
Two 5-ounce Japanese eel fillets
Fleur de sel

LAMB

Two 8-rib racks of lamb (preferably
    Colorado lamb), frenched
Kosher salt and freshly ground black
    pepper

1 tablespoon olive oil
Pinch of freshly ground katsuobushi
    powder

ACCOMPANIMENTS
Goat Cheese Mousse (recipe follows)
Mint Oil Sauce (recipe follows)
Potato Mousseline (recipe follows)
Fleur de sel

TO PREPARE THE ARTICHOKES

Toss the artichokes with the lemon juice in a medium bowl to coat.

Heat 2 tablespoons of the oil in a heavy large wide skillet over medium heat. Stir in the onion and carrot, then add the garlic, bay leaf, and thyme and sauté until aromatic, about 3 minutes. Add the artichokes and lemon juice, making sure the artichokes are in a single layer, and cook for 1 minute. Add the wine and enough chicken stock so that it is just below the top of the artichokes. Bring to a boil over high heat, then cover the artichokes with a round of parchment paper, reduce the heat to medium, and simmer until the liquid is reduced by three-fourths, about 15 minutes. Remove the paper and simmer until most of the liquid has evaporated; about 15 minutes. Season to taste with salt. Refrigerate the mixture until it's cold.

Preheat the oven to 475°F.

TO PREPARE THE EEL

Put the curry powder in a plastic container with the lid on but with one corner of the lid open. Using a smoking gun, following the manufacturer's instructions, put one end of the smoking tube in the plastic container and fill the container completely with smoke. Immediately seal the container and set the curry powder aside to smoke for about 10 minutes.

Combine the dashi, sake, mirin, soy sauce, and smoked curry powder in a large wide skillet set over medium heat and bring to 122°F. Submerge the eel in the liquid and cook until it is tender when you pinch it, about 10 minutes. Remove from the liquid, set in a plate, and cool in the refrigerator for 20 minutes.

MEANWHILE, TO PREPARE THE LAMB

Season the rack with salt and pepper. Heat the olive oil in a large sauté pan over high heat until smoking. Put the rack of lamb into the pan and caramelize on all sides, about 4 minutes.

Transfer the lamb fat side up to a baking sheet fitted with a rack and roast for 10 minutes, or until the internal temperature is 120°F. Remove from the oven and let rest for 5 minutes.

JUST BEFORE SERVING, TO FINISH THE ARTICHOKES

Heat the remaining 1 tablespoon of oil in a large sauté pan over medium-high heat. Lay the artichokes cut side down in the pan and cook until dark golden brown on the sides, about 2 minutes.

TO SERVE

Cut the eel into eight 2-by-1-inch rectangles. Put the eel skin side down on a baking sheet and, using a blowtorch, brown the meat. Season with fleur de sel. Set 1 eel piece on each of eight plates. Pipe the goat cheese onto the plates alongside the eel. Cut the lamb rack into individual chops. Spoon some mint oil sauce onto each plate and set the chops atop the oil. Put 3 artichoke wedges on top of each chop. Spoon the potato mousseline alongside the chops, season each chop with fleur de sel and a pinch of katsuobushi powder, and serve.

goat cheese mousse

8 ounces soft fresh goat cheese
¼ cup whole milk
1¼ teaspoons xanthan gum

Kosher salt and freshly ground white
pepper

Blend the goat cheese and milk in a food processor until smooth. Add the xanthan gum and puree until smooth, stopping the machine and scraping down the sides of the bowl as necessary. Season to taste with salt and white pepper.

Spoon the mousse into a disposable pastry bag and cut off the tip to make a ¼-inch-wide opening. Refrigerate until ready to use.

mint oil sauce

1 cup lightly packed fresh mint leaves
2 tablespoons fresh flat-leaf parsley
    leaves

¾ cup grapeseed oil
½ teaspoon granulated sugar

Blanch the mint in a large saucepan of boiling salted water for 30 seconds. Drain, transfer to a bowl of ice water to cool, and then drain very well.

Combine the mint, parsley, grapeseed oil, and sugar in a blender and blend until the sides of the blender are hot and it is steaming from the top. Transfer to a jar or other container and refrigerate overnight. Stir before using, so that you serve some of the herb puree along with the green oil.

potato mousseline

2 russet (baking) potatoes (about
1½ pounds total), scrubbed
12 ounces (3 sticks) unsalted butter

½ cup whole milk, or more if needed
Kosher salt and freshly ground white
pepper

Put the potatoes in a large pot of heavily salted water and bring the water to a boil, then lower the heat and simmer gently until a small knife can pierce the potatoes with no resistance, about 45 minutes.

Meanwhile, when the potatoes are almost cooked, heat the butter and milk in a small saucepan over medium heat until the butter is melted and the milk is just warm. Set aside, covered to keep hot.

When the potatoes are cooked, drain them and peel, then quickly put them through a food mill or ricer into a bowl. Using a whisk, quickly mix the butter mixture into the potatoes. If the potatoes do not absorb all the butter and the mixture looks like a separated vinaigrette, add more milk a little at a time, whisking to incorporate it, to restore the emulsion. (Do not add too much milk, or the potatoes will get soupy.)

Using a large silicone spatula, press the mousseline through a strainer into a heat-proof bowl. Cover the mousseline and set the bowl over a saucepan of gently simmering water to keep it hot until ready to serve.

dorade ceviche, heirloom tomato, jalapeño, red onion,
meyer lemon, olive oil (photograph by kevineats.com)

scallop, almond puree, pickled grapes, capers, curry oil,
cauliflower ice cream (photograph by kevineats.com)

spicy soft-shell-crab cone, corona granité (photograph by Eugene Lee)

ham-sandwich soup (photograph by Wesley Wong/eatsmeetwes.com)

seared foie gras, pineapple chips, coconut sorbet (photograph by Lucy Lean/ladlesandjellyspoons.com)

cabbage-wrapped foie gras, kimchi consommé (photograph by Wesley Wong/eatsmeetwes.com)

rack of lamb, fresh goat cheeses mousse, smoked eel, artichokes,
potato mousseline, mint (photograph by kevineats.com)

monkfish, légumes de la jardinière, vadouvan (photograph by Wesley Wong/eatsmeetwes.com)

squid carbonara (photograph by kevineats.com)

goat cheese soup, bacon, tofu, green apple, frisée salad, brioche (photograph by epicuryan.com)

poached egg, potato mousseline, chorizo condiment (photograph by kevineats.com)

raw wagyu beef, somen noodles (photograph by kevineats.com)

mexican-style corn, tomatillo, green onion oil, brown butter powder

(photograph by Tomo Kurokawa of Tomostyle)

confit pork belly, thai choucroute salad, mustard ice cream (photograph by kevineats.com)

hot foie gras dynamite, raw tuna, lychee, cracker puree (photograph by kevineats.com)

seared john dory, saffron risotto, licorice, chanterelles (photograph by kevineats.com)

caramel soufflé, blanco grapefruit, fleur de sel ice cream (photograph by epicuryan.com)

ice cream sundae: pistachio ice cream, bing cherries, hot chocolate sauce, salted pistachios (photograph by kevineats.com)

Beef bourguignon is in my blood. The dish is from Burgundy, like me, and I just love it: the tender meat, the red wine—it tastes like home. All the lovely components are here, just rejiggered. Instead of slowly cooked meat, I use flank steak (*bavette* in French), encased in a salty crust and served pink in the middle. I highlight the texture of the carrots by serving them raw in a slaw, another American preparation that I'd never heard of before I arrived here but that I can't get enough of today. The red-wine-infused butter gets added richness from a dose of bone marrow and texture from the escargots, or snails—though don't they sound much more delicious when referred to in my native tongue?

bavette, escargots, red wine butter, shallot jam, roasted eggplant, carrot slaw

SERVES 6

CARROT SLAW

1 yellow carrot, sliced lengthwise very, very thin

1 orange carrot, sliced lengthwise very, very thin

1 purple carrot, sliced lengthwise very, very thin

¼ cup grapeseed oil

¼ cup mustard oil

¼ cup rice vinegar

2 tablespoons whole-grain mustard

Kosher salt and freshly ground white pepper

SHALLOT JAM

1 tablespoon unsalted butter

6 shallots, thickly sliced

2 tablespoons sherry vinegar

1 tablespoon acacia honey

Kosher salt

1 teaspoon freshly ground black pepper

ROASTED EGGPLANT PUREE

2 eggplants (about 1 pound each)

1 teaspoon kosher salt

⅓ cup extra-virgin olive oil

RED WINE BUTTER

2 cups Burgundy

6 tablespoons unsalted butter, at room temperature

1½ tablespoons coarsely chopped fresh flat-leaf parsley

3 garlic cloves, chopped
¼ teaspoon kosher salt
3 tablespoons finely diced beef bone
    marrow (from about 3 bones)
2 teaspoons olive oil
¾ cup finely chopped canned escargots
    (snails)

STEAKS
Six 7-ounce flank steaks
2 tablespoons olive oil, or more if
    needed
Kosher salt and freshly ground black
    pepper

TO MAKE THE CARROT SLAW

Combine all the carrots with the oils, vinegar, and mustard in a large bowl and toss very well to coat. Season to taste with salt and white pepper. Let stand for 30 minutes before serving. (At the restaurant, I use a Gastrovac to make the carrot slaw: Combine all the ingredients in the Gastrovac and cook for 20 minutes at 40°C, then drain.)

MEANWHILE, TO MAKE THE SHALLOT JAM

Melt the butter in a heavy small saucepan over medium heat. Add the shallots and sauté until translucent, about 2 minutes. Add the vinegar and honey, cover with a round of parchment paper, and cook for 20 minutes. Season with salt to taste and the pepper. (At the restaurant, I use a Gastrovac to make the shallot jam: Combine the butter, shallots, vinegar, and honey in the Gastrovac and add 1 cup grapeseed oil. Cook for 30 minutes at 40°C, then drain and season.)

TO MAKE THE EGGPLANT PUREE

Put eggplants directly on two gas stove burners and char over high heat, turning occasionally, until they are blackened all over and soft in the middle, about 10 minutes.

Cut off the stem and scrape off any dusty white ash from the eggplants, but do not remove the blackened parts. Transfer the eggplant to a food processor, add the salt, and process to a puree. With the machine running, drizzle in the olive oil, processing until well blended.

Transfer the puree to a medium saucepan and cook over medium heat until the excess liquid evaporates and the mixture becomes a thick puree, about 10 minutes. Transfer the puree to a heavy small saucepan and set aside.

Simmer the wine in a heavy small saucepan over medium-high heat until reduced to ¼ cup, about 25 minutes. Cool completely.

Combine the butter, parsley, garlic, and salt in a small food processor and blend well. With the machine running, gradually add the red wine reduction, blending until fully incorporated. Transfer the butter to a small bowl and fold in the bone marrow. Cover and refrigerate until firm.

TO PREPARE THE STEAKS

Using a meat mallet, gently pound the steaks slightly to tenderize. Coat the steaks with the olive oil, then season on all sides with salt (this helps create a great crust on the steaks).

Add enough oil to a large cast-iron skillet to coat the bottom of the pan, then heat the oil over high heat until it begins to smoke. Put the steaks in the pan, reduce the heat to medium-high, and sear the steaks on both sides, turning often so they caramelize gradually. Reduce the heat to low and cook, turning the steaks on all sides until the internal temperature is 128° to 132°F, for rare. Transfer the steaks to a cutting board and let them rest for 3 minutes.

TO FINISH THE BUTTER AND SERVE

Heat the 2 teaspoons olive oil in a heavy large sauté pan over medium-high heat. Add the escargots and sauté until crisp, about 2 minutes. Reduce the heat to medium, add the red wine butter, and swirl the pan until the butter is incorporated and the sauce is emulsified. Remove from the heat.

Meanwhile, reheat the eggplant puree.

Spoon the eggplant puree down the centers of six plates. Slice the steaks across the grain, then shingle them over the eggplant puree. Mound the carrot slaw alongside, and spoon some shallot jam on one edge of each plate. Spoon the butter sauce over the steaks and serve.

My parents divorced when I was a boy. On the Sundays I spent with my father, we'd finish our dinner with *religieuses*, two stacked choux puffs, the top one smaller than the bottom, filled with pastry cream and decorated with fondant icing. It was our special dessert. So the last time I was in Paris with my dad, we went to the famous patisserie Ladurée and bought an incredible purple *religieuse* flavored with violets. My version isn't quite as pretty as Ladurée's but it tastes wonderful.

raspberry religieuse

SERVES 18

PÂTE À CHOUX
½ cup water
½ cup whole milk
Scant 8 tablespoons (scant 1 stick)
    unsalted butter, cut into chunks
1 teaspoon kosher salt
1 teaspoon granulated sugar
1 cup plus 3 tablespoons all-purpose
    flour
5 large eggs
1 large egg white, beaten with 1
    tablespoon water, for egg wash

RASPBERRY PASTRY CREAM
2 cups whole milk
1 vanilla bean, split lengthwise

4 large egg yolks
½ cup granulated sugar
¼ cup cornstarch
10⅔ tablespoons unsalted butter,
    cut into chunks
¼ cup Raspberry Puree
    (recipe follows)

ACCOMPANIMENTS
About 1 cup purchased fondant
Fresh raspberries for garnish

Position a rack in the center of the oven and preheat the oven to 425°F. Line two baking sheets with parchment paper.

Bring the water, milk, butter, salt, and sugar to a boil in a heavy large saucepan. Quickly stir in the flour, breaking up any lumps. Reduce the heat to low and stir until the dough forms a thin film on the bottom of the pan, 2 to 3 minutes.

Transfer the dough to the bowl of a stand mixer fitted with the paddle attachment and beat on medium speed until cool. With the mixer running, add the whole eggs one at a time, beating until fully incorporated.

Transfer the dough to a large pastry bag fitted with a ½-inch plain tip. Pipe 18 larger mounds of dough, 2 inches wide by 1 inch high, onto one of the parchment-lined baking sheets, spacing them about 2 inches apart. Pipe 18 smaller mounds, 1 inch wide by 1 inch high, onto the second sheet, spacing them 1½ inches apart. Very gently brush the egg wash over the puffs.

Bake one sheet at a time until the puffs are lightly golden, about 10 minutes for the smaller puffs and 12 minutes for the larger. Reduce the heat to 350°F and continue to bake until the puffs have dried out and the insides are set, 10 to 15 minutes. Heat the oven to 425°F again before baking the second sheet. Set aside to cool on a rack.

TO MAKE THE PASTRY CREAM

Put the milk in a medium saucepan. Scrape the seeds from the vanilla bean and add the seeds and pod to the milk. Bring to a simmer, then remove from the heat.

Meanwhile, whisk the egg yolks with the sugar and cornstarch in a medium bowl. Whisk in a small amount of the hot milk to temper the eggs, then pour the egg mixture into the saucepan with the remaining milk. Return the pan to medium heat and cook, stirring constantly and scraping the bottom of the pan, until the mixture has thickened to a thick custard. Strain through a fine-mesh sieve into a medium bowl. Immediately stir in the butter and raspberry puree, then set the bowl over a larger bowl of ice water and stir until the pastry cream is chilled. Cover the surface of the custard with plastic wrap and refrigerate for up to 1 day, until needed.

Fill a large pastry bag fitted with a small plain tip with the chilled pastry cream. Pierce a small hole in the bottom of each choux puff and fill with the pastry cream; the puffs should feel heavy.

Heat the fondant in a double boiler.

To coat the tops of the puffs, dip each one in the warm fondant, shake off the excess, hold the puff upside down for a minute to give the fondant a chance to set, and then gently invert and allow the fondant to dry slightly.

While the fondant is still a little tacky, assemble the religieuses by placing the smaller puffs on top of the larger ones. Allow the fondant to dry completely, about 1 hour.

Transfer the puffs to plates or a platter, garnish with fresh raspberries, and serve immediately.

raspberry puree

MAKES ABOUT 1 CUP

1 cup fresh raspberries
2 tablespoons granulated sugar

Combine the raspberries and sugar in a small saucepan and cook over medium heat just until the berries begin to release their juices. Mash the berries; do not strain.

Imagine a big dome of whipped cream covering a bowl of ripe strawberries macerated in a little sugar and topped with chewy macarons. It's a simple, sensational dessert that's 100 percent French. Well, almost—what I don't tell my customers is that I sprinkle Pop Rocks over the strawberries and macarons, so their first bite is a mouth-jolting little thrill. People of all ages love it— when it comes to food, we're all just kids.

macarons, strawberries, chantilly

SERVES 6

MACARONS
¾ cup granulated sugar
3 tablespoons water
½ cup egg whites (about 4 large
   whites), stirred to blend
1¼ cups almond flour
1⅓ cups confectioners' sugar
Pink paste food coloring as desired

EGG WHITE CHANTILLY
¾ cup egg whites (about 6 large
   whites)

¾ cup heavy cream
⅓ cup confectioners' sugar

MACERATED STRAWBERRIES
1 pound fresh strawberries, rinsed
   and hulled
2 tablespoons granulated sugar
3 tablespoons unflavored Pop Rocks
   (optional)

TO MAKE THE MACARONS

Bring the granulated sugar and water to a boil in a small saucepan over high heat, stirring until the sugar is dissolved and brushing down the sides of the pan with a pastry brush dipped in water as necessary to remove any sugar crystals. When the syrup begins to boil, reduce the heat to medium-high, place a candy thermometer in the saucepan, and cook until the thermometer reads 230°F. Letting the syrup continue to cook, pour half of the egg whites into the bowl of a stand mixer fitted with the whip attachment and begin whipping on high speed.

When the syrup reaches 240°F, remove from the heat and slowly drizzle down the side of the bowl into the egg whites, being careful to avoid pouring the syrup onto the whip, which would cause lumps to form. Once all the syrup has been incorporated, continue to whip on high speed until the meringue cools to room temperature.

Line four baking sheets with parchment paper (do not use baking mats). Combine the almond flour, confectioners' sugar, and the remaining egg whites in a large bowl; then add the food coloring until you reach the desired color and mix until very thick. Fold in the meringue.

Spoon the mixture into a pastry bag fitted with a medium plain tip, and pipe 1-inch-by-¼-inch-thick disks onto the prepared baking sheets, spacing them at least 1 inch apart. Allow the macarons to sit uncovered at room temperature for 30 minutes to 1 hour so the surface dries and forms a skin.

Preheat the oven to 350°F.

Slide another baking sheet under each sheet of macarons and bake for about 12 minutes, until puffed but not colored. Transfer the baking sheets to cooling racks and allow the macarons to cool to room temperature, then remove them from the parchment paper. (This recipe makes more macarons than you'll need for this dessert; store the extra macarons in an airtight container at room temperature.)

TO PREPARE THE CHANTILLY

Lightly whisk the egg whites, cream, and confectioners' sugar in a medium bowl just until combined; do not overwhip. Pour the mixture into a whipped cream canister and insert 2 nitrous oxide chargers. Turn the canister upside down and shake vigorously 4 or 5 times.

Test the thickness of the Chantilly by piping some onto a plate; it should be a light whipped foam. If necessary, shake the canister again to thicken the foam. Refrigerate until ready to serve.

TO PREPARE THE STRAWBERRIES

Cut smaller strawberries in half and cut larger berries into quarters, so that you end up with pieces that will fit nicely in a small spoon. Toss the strawberries with the sugar in a medium bowl. Cover the strawberries and refrigerate for at least 1 hour, and up to 8 hours (no longer, or the berries will not have the proper texture).

TO SERVE

Divide the strawberries and their accumulated juice among six shallow bowls. Arrange 6 macarons over the strawberries in each bowl. If using Pop Rocks, sprinkle them over the strawberries and macarons. Cover the macarons in each bowl with a large rosette of Chantilly and serve immediately.

KITCHEN 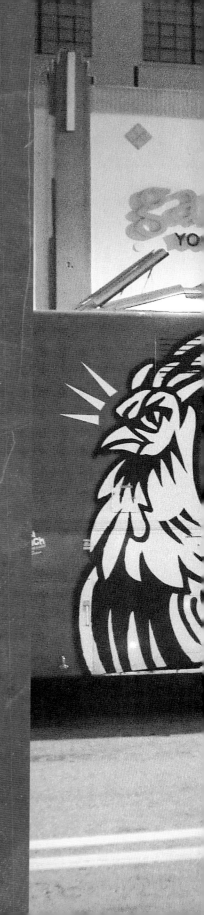 ROSTER

LUDO

SYDNEY (4.0)

JOON (4.0)

DAN (4.0)

GINA (4.0 student hired)

ALEX (intern, later quit)

ED (cooking school intern, later quit)

MICHAEL (cooking school intern)

GRACE (cooking school intern)

FRED (Savage, back for more)

From: XXXX@opentable.com
Date: Thu, Jul 8, 2010, at 5:45 P.M.
Subject: RE: Question for you . . .
To: Kristine Lefebvre <XXXX@gmail.com>

Kristine,

I will check in with engineering, but my sense is that our technology will be able to withstand this. Restaurants like The French Laundry and other popular clients have very high hits rates to those databases.

We really had to come up with a solution to accommodate the next reservations rush, since it had gone so poorly last time around. We decided to stagger the reservation offerings so that they weren't all released at once. At least this way, another system crash wouldn't destroy *all* of our customers' goodwill. Good thing we did, because it was the same story. Insane traffic, system failure. Before we could fire the company responsible for the failures, they quit.

So Krissy had to scramble to find a company that could handle our rabid audience, and she settled on the biggest and best: opentable.com. She tried to explain to them the crazy demand for reservations at our "temporary restaurant housed within another restaurant." I think they thought we were deluded or insane. The e-mail that Krissy received contained a hint of understandably patronizing disbelief. It was a bit like Ticketmaster explaining to a garage band, "Of course, we can handle you. We're used to dealing with the Rolling Stones and Lady freaking Gaga." We weren't small potatoes—LudoBites 4.0 had sold out in just eighteen hours. But, yeah, I get it, we weren't The French Laundry either.

The second round of reservations opened, and guess what? Despite the multiple assurances that their system could handle our needs, it crashed. It had to be rebooted twice. We were fully booked, after a technology-challenged ninety minutes, but Krissy again had to field e-mail after e-mail from some justifiably pissed-off people, including devoted regulars who'd enlisted their entire offices in the race for reservations. Some people accused us of rigging the system and holding back tables for VIPs. If only they knew how many celebrity requests we turned down, and how many entitled Hollywood types Krissy had to reject. As she will say, she can't pull a table out of you know what. As does every restaurant, we reserve one table a night for two seatings for media, family, friends, special requests, and the like, just as concert houses hold seats for reviewers. If it's not booked, we release the reservations to the public. It's a business must.

Fortunately most of our customer service problems were limited to the reservation process, but one disgruntled guy actually decided to launch a personal vendetta against us, and as we heard through the blogger grapevine, he "would make sure we went out of business." I'd kicked him out of an earlier LudoBites, and I guess I'd known he'd eventually resurface. One night, at the height of a busy dinner service, enforcement officers from the Department of Alcoholic Beverage Control stormed in and served us with a notice. Turned out our BYOB policy was illegal. We had absolutely no idea. They told us they typically didn't have time to worry about the BYOB policies of tiny restaurants, what with bigger fish to fry and Skid Row residents boozing on the sidewalks. But someone had complained "multiple times." After about a thousand dollars in legal fees, we decided it just wasn't worth it. We pulled all the wine glasses off the tables and taped a sign on the front door: "We regret to inform you but BYOB is no longer allowed." All of a sudden, we'd gone from BYOB to alcohol-free, losing the $8 corkage charge (that helped bolster our already slim margins). Plus, I'm French. Food deserves wine! Especially food of the caliber we were serving. This development cut to my core as a French chef. We eventually learned the identity of the complainant from another chef, who had a similar BYOB policy and had dealt with the same issues. The blogger told him, "I reported Ludo and I will do the same to you," or something along those lines. Nice guy, huh?

Enough ranting, let me back up for a moment. LudoBites 4.0 was such a success that we decided to stay put at Gram & Papa's and relaunch six weeks after our first run there. As you Americans like to say, if it ain't broke, don't fix it. Well, I guess the menu wasn't broke, but I still decided to change the whole damn thing anyway.

To handle the food, I now had a kitchen staff of seven: my three main guys, Sydney, Joon, aka The Machine, and Dan, a line cook who had worked with us at 4.0. The rest were students from L.A. Trade Tech. At LudoBites, a *stage* is not your typical watch-and-maybe-help-prep kind of gig. These interns are thrown onto the line to learn by doing. The pace of any LudoBites had left even my most experienced crews battered and bloodied; not surprisingly, only two of the four students made it to the end of 5.0.

The experience seems to be especially tough for those second-career students, people who have come from a job in which they were the guys in charge only to be what must feel like slaves in my kitchen. One minute, there they were, extremely successful and on top of their game in the advertising, financial, or entertainment industry. The next moment, they're getting yelled at by some tattooed French asshole. They're working in a place where the correct answer to everything I say is, "*Oui*, chef," where I'm always right—even when I'm wrong. Fred Savage can vouch for this. He joined us again, pitting and pureeing cherries (he missed one pit and had to spend an hour fishing out pit bits from the puree) and piping foie gras icing onto cheese cupcakes (he'd pipe, I'd yell at him to do it again, and better this time). Today I bet you'd find some very pretty cupcakes at the Savage house.

One of my star students was Grace Lee, who not only made it to the end of 5.0 but graduated to paid employee and returned for the next two LudoBites. She had interviewed me for a culinary school project and we'd had a great chat. At the end, she threatened that when we announced the next LudoBites, she'd be after us for an internship. She followed through, and we gave her a shot. I told her flat out that she'd start to have dreams about me, and not nice ones. One night, I remember changing the way I wanted to plate a certain dish five times. When it came time to actually plate one, poor Grace just stood there, staring at an empty dish.

After burning through many gallons of ice cream practicing at home, she'd perfected the art of the one-handed quenelle (not an easy skill). And she learned to taste like a great cook, judging the right amount of, say, salt to add to cauliflower puree by identifying the moment when the puree's flavor reaches the tip of your tongue. I swear it was like watching a kid ride her first two-wheeled bike. I was so proud. It was a great beginning for her.

Thanks to the sustained efforts of my awesome staff, there had been a marked shift in the exposure of our little business, although we hadn't hired a PR person since 3.0. After the big *L.A. Times* story, there was a parade of amazing press, articles from *Time* magazine and feature pieces on NPR and CNN. *France-Amérique* magazine named me the most influential French person in America. As the Twittering masses might say, OMG! WTF!

Still, after the *L.A. Times* critic had disemboweled my entire being at Bastide, I'd decided never to cook for critics again. Not that I wouldn't serve them, but that I wouldn't cook to "please them," that I wouldn't worry about how many stars they did or did not bestow. The opinions I cared about were those of my customers. So we weren't really on the lookout for critics, although it was pretty hard to miss J. Gold when he walked in. We didn't have photos of them on the wall in the kitchen, as many restaurants do. We had even heard from the *L.A. Times* that their critics would never review us because LudoBites wasn't a real restaurant. We certainly weren't on the lookout for critics from New York, let alone Sam Sifton, the then restaurant critic of the *New York Times.*

Unbeknownst to us, he'd managed to wrangle a reservation at the VIP table. Krissy liked to scan the reservation book each night, to see who was coming. She Googled the name he'd given, and traced it to some high-ranking executive from Chase Bank. Good, she told me, in return for giving him the table, she'd ask him to help us refinance our mortgage.

Now, it wouldn't be LudoBites if something fucked-up didn't happen when an important critic showed up. So not only did Krissy end up calling him a wimp when he passed on the cheese course, and not only did we both ask him for help refinancing our mortgage, but on the first night he ate at LudoBites, my kitchen staff and Mike had pissed me off so bad that I'd stormed out of the restaurant half an hour before service. I finally returned an hour later, service in full swing.

A couple of days later, we got a call from someone at the *New York Times*, letting us know they were sending in a photographer to accompany a piece about Mr. Sifton's dinner. Holy shit, we thought, we had actually asked Sam Sifton for mortgage advice! We felt like crawling into a hole and never coming out again.

We waited anxiously for the review. When the day came, Krissy ran up to me with a printout in her hand and a tear in her eye. The review, she said, was bad. Really bad. I wasn't exactly surprised. We'd been open for less than a week. More than half of our kitchen staff had no previous professional culinary experience. Wait, why was Mike giggling? Why was Krissy cracking a smile? We gathered the entire staff up front before service and read them the article. I could hear the crack in Krissy's voice as she read:

"[The dishes are] a series of vaguely Asian, deeply French and fairly Californian experiments that manage at once to be both simple in flavor and amazingly complex in execution.

"The entrees at LudoBites are, in contrast to current East Coast restaurant trends, reliably as good as the appetizers that precede them.

"The first night eating all this was an amazement. The second was about ten times better—each dish perfectly executed, with every flavor in place, every temperature correct, every plate a fully realized piece of art. It was only the fifth night the restaurant had been open."

We were so proud, so honored, and completely humbled. This was the *New York* "freaking" *Times,* and their food critic not only took the time to understand who we were, what my food was about, but he embraced it for all that is was and wasn't. We told everyone on the staff to get and keep a copy of the review because these things don't happen often and may never happen again to any of us. We never intended to have to deal with restaurant critic reviews, that was the point, but this article single-handedly defined what LudoBites had to be from this day forward. Every guest from that night on would expect the same experience had by Mr. Sifton, regardless of their understanding of food and restaurants. Almost an impossible challenge. It makes me think about the chefs in France, how they fight for that third Michelin star and once they receive it they spend the rest of their careers trying to keep it. It is a dangerous game. Bernard Loiseau is a perfect example.

On our final night, we supplemented our regular dinner service with the LudoTruck. We'd been working on it for months, using it for private parties and events. This was its coming-out party. We parked it out front selling fried chicken balls to the line of three hundred–plus people. It was a way to welcome fans who couldn't score reservations and to thank customers who wanted one last taste. It turned into a sort of impromptu block party. Even Hollywood Jesus showed up. Maybe that's how we'd made it through another LudoBites intact—someone from above was looking out for us.

My chef friend Art Smith hosted a barbecue at his house in Chicago and made a naan bread that I just loved. Krissy loved it even more. She insisted I add naan to my menu, and guys, trust me, when your wife is that passionate about something, you do what she says. Being French, I can't have bread without butter, so I whipped up this subtly sweet, salty spread to serve alongside.

vadouvan naan, salted coconut butter

SERVES 8

NAAN

3½ cups all-purpose flour

3 tablespoons Vadouvan (page 48)

1 tablespoon instant yeast

2 teaspoons kosher salt

1 teaspoon baking powder

2 teaspoons black sesame seeds

½ cup whole milk

½ cup whole-milk yogurt

1 jumbo egg

2 tablespoons grapeseed oil, plus more for brushing the griddle

2 tablespoons honey

COCONUT BUTTER

½ pound (2 sticks) unsalted butter, at room temperature

½ cup unsweetened coconut milk (stirred before measuring)

2 tablespoons honey

2 teaspoons fleur de sel

TO MAKE THE NAAN

Mix the flour, vadouvan, yeast, salt, baking powder, and sesame seeds in a bowl.

Combine the milk, yogurt, egg, grapeseed oil, and honey in the bowl of a stand mixer fitted with the dough hook and mix well. Add the dry ingredients and mix on low speed for 5 minutes, or until a smooth, elastic dough forms.

Transfer the dough to an oiled bowl large enough to allow the dough to double in size, cover with plastic wrap, and set aside in a warm, draft-free place to rise for about 2 hours, or until doubled in size.

Gently press the dough down, then cover it again and allow it to rise until doubled in size, about 1 hour.

MEANWHILE, TO MAKE THE COCONUT BUTTER

Combine all the ingredients in the bowl of the stand mixer, fitted with the whisk attachment, and mix on low speed until the coconut milk is incorporated into the butter. Increase the speed to high and whip until the butter is light and fluffy, about 3 minutes. Spoon the butter into small ramekins and set aside at room temperature.

TO COOK THE NAAN

Heat a cast-iron griddle over medium-low heat.

Meanwhile, gently press the dough down, divide into eight 4-ounce portions, and form into balls. Roll out each ball of dough into about a 7-inch disk using as little flour as possible to keep the dough from sticking to your work surface.

When the griddle is very hot, brush it with oil, place 1 of the dough disks on it, and cook until golden brown on the first side, about 2 minutes. Flip the naan and cook until golden brown spots form on the bottom, about 2 minutes. Keep warm while you cook the rest of the naan.

TO SERVE

Arrange the warm naan in a basket or on a platter and serve the coconut butter alongside.

Nothing to see here—just your normal cheese-and-chicken-liver cupcake. Inspiration struck when I wanted to serve chicken liver mousse but found myself searching for a replacement for plain old toast. A dip of my finger into the rich, fatty, creamy liver brought to mind some kind of wonderful savory icing. Aha, why not use it to top cupcakes? The key is to make the cupcakes *à la minute*, so they're warm and wonderful, but then to let them cool just slightly, so the liver doesn't melt too much. The timing is easy to get right at home, but it was incredibly difficult at frenetic LudoBites. And then, even when we did get it right, we'd have a table of, say, eight bloggers sharing one cupcake and passing it around so everyone could take a photo. Guys, I'd think, the icing is melting. Eat the fucking thing already!

cheese cupcake, chicken liver chantilly, kumquat, cornichons

SERVES 8

CHICKEN LIVER CHANTILLY
3 tablespoons Brown Butter (page 223)
1 large yellow onion, thinly sliced
1 pound chicken livers, fat and sinew removed
⅓ cup sherry vinegar
Kosher salt and freshly ground white pepper
¾ cup heavy cream

CUPCAKES
3 jumbo eggs
2 tablespoons whole milk
6 tablespoons unsalted butter, melted
¾ teaspoon kosher salt
4 ounces Cantal cheese, finely shredded
2 ounces Emmental cheese, finely shredded
⅔ cup all-purpose flour
2 teaspoons instant yeast
Nonstick cooking spray

ACCOMPANIMENTS
¾ cup Kumquat Puree (recipe follows)
24 cornichons, julienned

Heat 2 tablespoons of the brown butter in a large sauté pan over medium heat. Add the onion and sauté until golden brown, about 8 minutes. Using a slotted spoon, transfer the caramelized onion to a bowl and set aside.

Add the remaining 1 tablespoon brown butter to the pan and increase the heat to medium-high. Add the chicken livers and cook until they are deep brown on the outside but still rare in the center, about 3 minutes. Stir in the caramelized onion and deglaze the pan with the sherry vinegar, scraping up any browned bits on the bottom of the pan. Simmer until most of the vinegar has evaporated, about 2 minutes.

Using a slotted spoon, transfer the liver and onion mixture to a food processor. Blend until smooth. Season to taste with salt and pepper.

Transfer the mixture to a metal bowl and set it over another bowl filled with ice water. Cover with plastic wrap and refrigerate until the liver mixture has completely cooled but is not chilled and firm.

Whisk the heavy cream to stiff peaks. Stir one-fourth of the whipped cream into the liver mixture to lighten it a bit. Then gently fold in the remaining whipped cream. Cover and refrigerate for at least 2 hours, and up to 2 days (no longer).

TO MAKE THE CUPCAKES

In the bowl of a stand mixer fitted with the whip attachment, whisk the eggs until frothy, about 4 minutes. Add the milk, melted butter, and salt and whip for 10 to 15 seconds. Toss both cheeses with the flour in a small bowl, so the cheeses do not clump together, then add the cheese mixture and yeast to the milk mixture and mix until all the flour is moistened and a dough forms.

Remove the bowl from the mixer stand, cover with plastic wrap, and let the mixture rise in a warm, draft-free place for 45 minutes, or until the dough is doubled in size.

Meanwhile, preheat the oven to 350°F. Line 8 muffin cups with paper liners and spray the paper liners generously with nonstick spray.

Using a 2-ounce portioning scoop (or a level ¼-cup measure), scoop the batter into the paper liners. Bake for about 12 minutes, or until a toothpick inserted into the center of a cupcake comes out clean. Invert the cupcakes onto a rack and turn right side up.

TO SERVE

Fit a large pastry bag with a star tip and fill with the chicken liver Chantilly. Starting at the edges and working toward the center, pipe a large rosette of Chantilly on top of each warm cupcake.

Spoon about 1 tablespoon of the kumquat puree next to the rim of a small plate, then place the tip of a spoon in the center of the puree and quickly drag the spoon across the puree toward the opposite side of the plate. Repeat with seven more plates, then place a frosted cupcake in the center of each plate. Top with the julienned cornichons and serve.

kumquat puree

MAKES 1⅓ CUPS

8 ounces kumquats
1 cup sugar
½ cup water

Combine the whole kumquats, sugar, and water in a heavy medium saucepan and bring the water to a boil, stirring to dissolve the sugar. Reduce the heat to low to maintain a gentle simmer and cook, uncovered, stirring occasionally and pressing down on the kumquats once they start to soften, until the kumquats are very tender, about 2 hours.

Drain the kumquats; reserve the cooking liquid. Blend the kumquats in a blender until smooth, adding enough of the cooking liquid to form a puree with the consistency of a sauce. Cover and refrigerate for up to 2 weeks. Serve chilled.

What I love about my job is that just when you think you've eaten it all, someone proves you wrong. One afternoon I joined my friend Craig for lunch at the private sushi bar at Matsuhisa and ate a dish that was just *wow*! Perfectly cooked somen noodles. Beautiful bigeye tuna. Sesame oil. Three components transformed into something unbelievably good. It really opened my mind about simple food. I decided I wanted to serve something like it, but with my own twist, of course. Here that means cold noodles cradling beef tartare tossed with peanut vinaigrette, adorned with little cubes of candied watermelon, and sprinkled with miso powder.

raw wagyu beef, somen noodles

SERVES 6

PEANUT VINAIGRETTE
¼ cup grapeseed oil
¼ cup reduced-sodium soy sauce
2 tablespoons toasted sesame oil
1½ tablespoons granulated sugar
¼ cup roasted peanuts, finely chopped
2 tablespoons finely chopped
   peeled fresh ginger
1½ tablespoons finely chopped garlic
1 fresh Thai chile, finely chopped
¼ teaspoon freshly ground black pepper

DRIED MISO
⅓ cup yellow miso

CANDIED WATERMELON
1½ cups water
1 cup granulated sugar
¾ cup fresh mint leaves
Thirty ½-inch cubes seeded
   watermelon

BEEF AND NOODLES
One 3½-ounce bundle somen noodles
1 pound Wagyu beef top-round,
   julienned
Fresh micro mint leaves for garnish

TO PREPARE THE VINAIGRETTE
Whisk the grapeseed oil, soy sauce, sesame oil, and sugar in a medium bowl until the sugar is dissolved. Whisk in the peanuts, ginger, garlic, chile, and pepper. Cover and refrigerate.

TO MAKE THE DRIED MISO

Preheat the oven to 200°F. Line a baking sheet with a silicone baking mat.

Spread the miso in a very thin, even layer over the baking mat. Bake until the miso is dry and golden brown, about 1½ hours. Turn the oven off and leave the miso in the oven until it is crisp and brittle, about 3 hours.

Grind the miso in a spice grinder or clean coffee grinder until it forms a powder. (You won't need all of the dried miso for this recipe; store the remaining miso in a sealed glass jar at room temperature for other uses.)

TO PREPARE THE WATERMELON

Combine the water and sugar in a small saucepan and bring to a boil over high heat, stirring to dissolve the sugar. Add the mint and set aside, covered, to cool slightly, then refrigerate the syrup until cold.

Add the watermelon cubes to the mint syrup and marinate in the refrigerator for 30 minutes.

Remove the watermelon cubes from the mint syrup and keep refrigerated.

TO SERVE

Cook the noodles in a large saucepan of boiling salted water over high heat, stirring, for 1½ minutes. Drain the noodles in a sieve and rinse them under cold water, stirring them with chopsticks to remove all of the outer starch (this helps the noodles to be served cold without sticking together). Drain the noodles and arrange them in the center of six ceramic bowls.

Gently toss the beef in a medium bowl with some of the peanut vinaigrette to coat. Put the beef mixture on top of the noodles. Spoon some more peanut vinaigrette over the beef and noodles to glaze. Scatter the watermelon cubes around the beef and noodles. Garnish with the micro mint leaves and some of the dried miso and serve.

At LudoBites, I often operate by different arithmetic than most restaurants do. In this case, for instance, salad + salad = soup. I took two French salads—goat cheese melted on toast with simply dressed greens and the famous *salade Lyonnaise*, frisée with lardons—and fused their flavors into an elegant soup.

goat cheese soup, bacon, tofu, green apple, frisée salad, brioche

SERVES 8

GREEN APPLE-CELERY CONDIMENT
1 green apple, coarsely chopped
6 celery stalks, coarsely chopped
1½ teaspoons vitamin C powder
2 teaspoons agar-agar

GOAT CHEESE MOUSSE
8 ounces soft fresh goat cheese
1 cup heavy cream
Kosher salt and freshly ground black pepper
⅛ teaspoon xanthan gum

CRISPY BACON
8 ounces applewood-smoked bacon, cut crosswise into ¼-inch strips
3 tablespoons grapeseed oil

SOUP
3 cups Chicken Stock (page 39)
1 pound soft fresh goat cheese
Kosher salt and freshly ground white pepper

BRIOCHE TOAST
Eight ½-inch-thick slices brioche
2 tablespoons olive oil
1 teaspoon chopped fresh thyme
¾ teaspoon chopped fresh rosemary
½ teaspoon finely grated lemon zest

SALAD
4 cups tender yellow frisée lettuce leaves
¼ cup 1-inch-long pieces fresh chives
1½ tablespoons olive oil
1½ tablespoons fresh lemon juice
Kosher salt and freshly ground black pepper

GARNISHES
¼ cup ½-inch cubes firm tofu
¼ cup diced green apple (with skin)
Chive flowers

TO MAKE THE GREEN APPLE CONDIMENT

Juice the apple (with the skin) and celery with the vitamin C.

Measure 1 cup of the juice and pour it into a heavy small saucepan. Add the agar-agar and bring the juice to a boil over high heat. Reduce the heat to low and simmer very gently, stirring, until the agar is dissolved, about 10 minutes. Transfer to a container and refrigerate until cold and set.

Once the apple mixture is cold, mix it in a blender until smooth, then return to the refrigerator.

TO MAKE THE MOUSSE

Pulse the goat cheese, heavy cream, and salt and pepper to taste in a food processor just until blended. Sprinkle the xanthan gum powder over the mixture and pulse again to blend. Spoon the mousse into a pastry bag and refrigerate until cold.

TO PREPARE THE BACON

Sauté the bacon in a heavy small saucepan over medium heat until it begins to brown, about 4 minutes. Add the grapeseed oil and cook over medium-low heat until the bacon is brown and crisp, about 16 minutes.

Drain the bacon and discard the oil, then drain the bacon on paper towels.

Preheat the oven to 375°F.

TO MAKE THE SOUP

Bring the chicken stock to a boil in a heavy medium saucepan over high heat. Using an immersion blender, slowly add the goat cheese, blending until smooth. Season to taste with salt and white pepper. Keep warm.

TO PREPARE THE BRIOCHE TOAST

Using a 2¾-inch round cutter, cut out a round from each slice of bread. Arrange on a heavy baking sheet, then brush the olive oil over both sides of the brioche. Bake until the toasts are golden brown and crisp, about 5 minutes per side.

Remove from the oven and immediately sprinkle each toast generously with the thyme, rosemary, and lemon zest.

TO MAKE THE SALAD

Toss the frisée and chives in a medium bowl with the olive oil and lemon juice to coat. Season to taste with salt and pepper.

TO SERVE

Place a brioche toast in the center of each of eight soup plates. Pipe a generous amount of the goat cheese mousse on top of each toast. Scatter the tofu, green apple, and crispy bacon around the toasts. Place a spoonful of the apple condiment on the rim of each plate. Mound the frisée salad on top of the mousse. Pour the hot soup around the toasts, garnish with chive flowers, and serve.

In America, people eat eggs almost exclusively as a morning meal. Yet when I was growing up, every Sunday night, my grandma would make omelets with whatever leftover vegetables were in her fridge. In France, it was more like roast chicken for lunch, eggs for dinner. So nearly every LudoBites menu has had eggs on it. This dish had perhaps the most enthusiastic following, probably because of the potato mousseline—basically butter and cream. Oh, and a little potato too. Just ask Sam Sifton, the *New York Times* restaurant critic, who shared the dish with his companion on his first visit and, on his second, ordered one for everyone at his table. His exacts words: "Its effect is narcotic."

poached egg, potato mousseline, chorizo condiment

SERVES 6

CHORIZO CONDIMENT
3 ounces hot Spanish chorizo (preferably Palacios brand), casing removed and meat finely diced
½ cup olive oil

POTATO MOUSSELINE
2 russet (baking) potatoes (about 1½ pounds total), scrubbed

12 ounces (3 sticks) unsalted butter
½ cup whole milk, or more if needed
Kosher salt and freshly ground white pepper

POACHED EGGS
6 large eggs

TO MAKE THE CHORIZO CONDIMENT
Combine the chorizo and oil in a food processor and process for 10 minutes, or until it has almost formed a smooth paste; stop the machine occasionally to scrape

down the sides of the bowl. Transfer the mixture to a bowl and set aside at room temperature.

Put the potatoes in a large pot of heavily salted water and bring the water to a boil, then lower the heat and simmer gently until a small knife can pierce the potatoes with no resistance, about 45 minutes.

Meanwhile, when the potatoes are almost cooked, heat the butter and milk in a small saucepan over medium heat until the butter is melted and the milk is just warm. Set aside, covered to keep hot.

When the potatoes are cooked, drain them, peel, and quickly put them through a food mill or ricer into a bowl. Using a whisk, quickly mix the butter and milk into the potatoes. If the potatoes do not absorb all the butter and the mixture looks like a separated vinaigrette, add more milk a little at a time, whisking to incorporate it, to restore the emulsion. (Do not add too much milk, or the potatoes will get soupy.)

Using a large silicone spatula, press the mousseline through a strainer into a bowl. Cover the mousseline and set the bowl over a saucepan of gently simmering water to keep it hot until ready to serve.

TO POACH THE EGGS USING AN IMMERSION CIRCULATOR

Prepare the circulator for cooking at 150°F. Put the eggs in the preheated circulator and cook for 45 minutes.

Remove the eggs from the circulator and put into an ice bath to cool—this helps set the white part of the egg without it being watery when served. When ready to serve, put the eggs in the circulator for 15 minutes to rewarm them.

TO POACH THE EGGS USING THE STANDARD METHOD

Bring 6 to 8 quarts lightly salted water to a rolling boil in a deep pot. Crack 1 egg into a ramekin. Remove the pot from the heat, and using a whisk, stir the water briskly to create a vortex, then quickly add the egg into the center of the vortex. Cook just until set about 2 minutes; as the egg cooks, skim away any foam and loose pieces of egg white that float to the top. Using a slotted spoon, transfer the egg to paper towels to drain. Repeat with the remaining eggs. Reserve the water to rewarm the eggs just before serving them.

TO SERVE

Stir the chorizo condiment, then spoon about 1 tablespoon of it into the bottom of six small serving bowls.

If using the circulator method for the eggs, one at a time, crack the eggs open onto a dish, use a large spoon to scoop up the egg, leaving behind any straggling whites, and place in the bowls. If using the standard poaching method, dip the eggs into the reserved water just until rewarmed, then drain quickly on paper towels and place in the bowls. Cover each egg with about ⅓ cup of the potato mousseline and serve immediately.

Sometimes I don't know how my cooks put up with me. When a dish strikes me, I want to make it immediately, and I'll march into the kitchen to demand that prep stops and menus change, all to satisfy my urge to cook whatever has popped into my head. This happened after I ate great Chinese barbecue with my friend Will. I felt like I just had to transfer those flavors to foie gras—I could barely sleep that night! I even begged Will, who's Chinese, to find the ingredients for me, because after spending some sleepless hours online looking for recipes, I decided that he, an Asian guy, would have much more success scouting out red preserved bean curd and zhu hou sauce than a Frenchman.

hot foie gras, chinese barbecue sauce, miso-eggplant terrine

SERVES 6

BARBECUE SAUCE
1¼ cups granulated sugar
5 tablespoons red yeast rice paste
¼ cup water
2 tablespoons red preserved bean curd
2 tablespoons salt
2 tablespoons hoisin sauce
2 tablespoons Asian sesame paste
2 tablespoons rose essence liquor, (preferably Mei Kuei Lu Chiew brand)
2 tablespoons zhu hou sauce
2 teaspoons soy sauce
½ teaspoon Chinese five-spice powder

CUCUMBER COUSCOUS
1 hothouse cucumber, peeled

FOIE GRAS
Six 1½-inch-thick slices Grade A foie gras
Sea salt and freshly ground black pepper
6 slices Miso Eggplant Terrine (recipe follows)

TO MAKE THE BARBECUE SAUCE

Combine all the ingredients in a heavy small saucepan and bring to a boil over medium-high heat. Strain the sauce through a fine-mesh sieve into a small bowl and let cool.

Cover the sauce and refrigerate overnight so all of the flavors meld together. Return the sauce to room temperature before using.

TO MAKE THE CUCUMBER COUSCOUS

Cut the cucumber lengthwise in half and scrape out the seeds with a spoon. Slice the cucumber thickly and put the slices in a food processor. Pulse until the cucumber is chopped into pieces the size of couscous. Drain the cucumber in a fine-mesh sieve set over a bowl and refrigerate for 30 minutes.

TO COOK THE FOIE GRAS

Preheat the oven to 450°F.

Using a sharp knife, score one side of the slices of foie gras into a nice crosshatch pattern. Season both sides of the slices with salt and pepper.

Heat two large cast-iron skillets over high heat until they begin to smoke (the pan must be very hot to sear the foie gras properly). Sear the scored side of the foie gras slices in the skillets until browned, about 2 minutes. Turn the slices over and place the skillets in the oven until they are seared on the bottom, about 3 minutes. Transfer the foie gras to a plate lined with paper towels to absorb excess oil.

Lay a slice of eggplant terrine on one side of each plate. Set the foie gras alongside the eggplant. Spoon the barbecue sauce over the foie gras. Spoon a scoop of the cucumber couscous onto each plate and serve.

eggplant terrine

10 SLICES

4 eggplants (each about 1 pound)
2 tablespoons kosher salt
1 cup mirin rice wine
1 cup sake
1 cup yellow light miso paste
1 cup heavy cream

2 whole eggs
2 large egg yolks
2 tablespoons mirin
2 tablespoons sake
Nonstick cooking spray
1 tablespoon olive oil

Peel the eggplants and cut each in half lengthwise. Cut each half of eggplant again lengthwise into ½-inch-thick slices. Salt the eggplant on both sides and place them on 3 baking sheets for 1 hour. Rinse the eggplant under water to remove the salt.

Blend the mirin rice wine, 1 cup of sake, and miso in a blender for 30 seconds to blend well. Place the eggplant slices in a large roasting pan and pour the marinade over the eggplant. Toss the eggplant to coat them completely in the marinade. Cover and refrigerate overnight, occasionally turning and rotating the eggplant to marinate evenly.

Preheat the convection oven to 325°F.

Spray the inside of an 11¾-by-4¼-by-3-inch-deep terrine mold with pan spray. Line the pan bottom and sides with plastic wrap so there are no air bubbles. Drain eggplant in a colander then gently squeeze each piece of eggplant to remove the excess liquid. Lay the eggplant pieces in a single layer on a clean towel to continue to remove any excess marinade.

Whisk the cream, eggs, egg yolks, mirin, and sake in a medium bowl to blend. Add just enough of the custard to cover the bottom of the terrine mold. Place the eggplant slices lengthwise into the terrine mold and lay them down just as you would see a brick house. With every layer pour some custard to coat the eggplant. Layer the eggplant until you are ⅛-inch from the top of the mold. Place 1 layer of plastic wrap on top of the terrine and cover with foil.

Place the terrine in a water bath and bake until the center of the terrine reaches 155°F on an instant read thermometer, about 1 hour and 50 minutes. Place the terrine on a baking sheet and remove the foil. Set an empty terrine mold on top of the filled eggplant terrine to weigh it down and help form tight layers when the terrine is unmolded. Refrigerate overnight until set.

Invert the terrine onto a cutting board and remove the mold and plastic lining. Using an electric meat carving knife, cut the ends of the terrine so that the ends are straight since the ends of the terrine are on a bias. Then, cut the terrine into ½-inch-thick slices.

When ready to serve, heat the oil in a large nonstick sauté pan over medium heat. Lay the eggplant slices in the pan and cook until caramelized on both sides, about 4 minutes per side.

On the streets of L.A. and Mexico City, vendors sell grilled corn slathered with mayo, rolled in cheese, and spritzed with lime. I can't get enough of it. Of course, I gave it my own spin for LudoBites, adding a lively, spicy tomatillo salsa and a drizzle of green onion oil. Instead of mayo, I make a warm cream infused with wasabi to add another dimension of spice.

mexican-style corn, tomatillo, green onion oil, brown butter powder

SERVES 4

BROWN BUTTER POWDER
1 cup tapioca maltodextrin
½ teaspoon kosher salt
1 tablespoon Brown Butter
  (recipe follows)

WASABI CREAM
½ fresh wasabi root
1 cup heavy cream
¼ teaspoon kosher salt

CORN
4 ears yellow corn, husked
Kosher salt
2 tablespoons Brown Butter (recipe
  follows)

ACCOMPANIMENTS
About 1⅓ cups Tomatillo Salsa,
  warm (recipe follows)
About 6 tablespoons Green Onion Oil
  (recipe follows)
½ cup fresh cilantro leaves

TO MAKE THE BROWN BUTTER POWDER

Put ¾ cup of the tapioca maltodextrin and the salt in the bowl of a stand mixer fitted with the whisk attachment and mix well.

Warm the brown butter in a saucepan just until it is melted but not hot. Pour the butter onto the powder and mix on low speed until all of the butter is incorporated. Scrape the bowl to make sure no butter has settled on the bottom. Sprinkle the

remaining ¼ cup maltodextrin over the butter mixture and mix until all the butter is absorbed and the mixture is powdery and light. Set aside.

TO MAKE THE WASABI CREAM

Peel the wasabi root and grate enough on a Japanese grater (oroshigane) to equal about 2 tablespoons. Combine the grated wasabi, cream, and salt in a heavy medium saucepan and simmer over medium-low heat until the cream is reduced by half and thickened, about 15 minutes. Cover and keep hot.

TO PREPARE THE CORN

Blanch the corn in a pot of lightly salted boiling water for 1 minute, then put the corn in a large bowl of ice water to cool completely.

Drain the corn, cut the ends off the cobs, and cut each cob crosswise into 4 pieces. Pat the corn thoroughly dry.

Heat a large cast-iron skillet over medium heat until it begins to smoke. Season the corn with salt. Add 1 tablespoon of the brown butter and add half of the corn to the hot pan and cook, turning occasionally, until the corn is golden brown on all sides, about 7 minutes. As the corn cooks, it will pop, so take care, and use a splatter guard if necessary.

Remove the pan from the heat and wave a blowtorch over the corncobs until the kernels are charred. Transfer the corn to a plate and keep warm. Wipe out the skillet and repeat with the remaining tablespoon of brown butter and corn.

TO SERVE

Spoon the salsa into the center of four plates. Put 4 pieces of corn, cut sides up, atop the sauce on each plate. Spoon the green onion oil around the corn, then sprinkle the top of the cobs generously with the brown butter powder. Smear a spoonful of the wasabi cream onto each plate, garnish with the cilantro leaves, and serve.

green onion oil

½ cup grapeseed oil
7 green onions, sliced
2 tablespoons coarsely chopped fresh
   flat-leaf parley

½ teaspoon kosher salt

Combine the oil, green onions, parsley, and salt in a Vitamix blender and blend on high speed until the side of the blender is very hot, about 2 minutes. You should be able to see the steam come out of the hole from the blender top. That indicates that it is ready to be turned off.

Pour the oil mixture into a glass jar, then refrigerate uncovered overnight so that the oil turns green and it infuses the oil with scallion flavor. When ready to use do not strain and use the oil and its solids for serving.

tomatillo salsa

MAKES 3 CUPS

1 pound tomatillos, husks removed,
   rinsed
¼ Spanish yellow onion, thinly sliced
½ cup (packed) cilantro leaves
1 jalapeño chile, thinly sliced (with
   seeds)

3 garlic cloves, thinly sliced
2 tablespoons fresh lime juice
Kosher salt

Blanch the tomatillos in a saucepan of simmering salted water until they begin to soften and lose some of their bright green color, about 3 minutes. Transfer the tomatillos to a plate and set aside to cool completely.

Place the tomatillos in a blender, then add the remaining ingredients and pulse until the tomatillo is smooth and the rest of the ingredients are roughly chopped.

brown butter

2 sticks unsalted butter, cut into
   1-inch pieces

Melt the butter in a heavy small saucepan over low heat, then increase the heat to medium-high and cook the butter, stirring constantly, until it turns a dark golden brown, about 4 minutes. Set the pan in a bowl of ice water to stop the cooking (if you don't do this, the butter will turn too dark), then allow the brown butter to sit at room temperature until it is completely cool but still fluid.

Only the truly jaded can deny the siren song of dynamite sauce—you know, the creamy, spicy sauce that you get at some less-than-traditional sushi bars. Of course it goes well with raw tuna, typical partner, but I promise you it also goes well with foie gras, which is rich and flavorful enough to stand up to the heat. Add the aromatic sweetness of lychee and a little crunch from crumbled crackers, and you truly have a dynamite dish.

hot foie gras dynamite, raw tuna, lychee, cracker puree

SERVES 6

DYNAMITE SAUCE
1 cup Kewpie mayonnaise
2 tablespoons orange tobiko caviar
4 teaspoons garlic-chile sambal sauce (preferably Hoy Fung), or more to taste

FOIE GRAS
Six 1½-inch-thick slices Grade A foie gras
Fine sea salt and freshly ground black pepper

TUNA
1 pound sushi-grade center-cut bigeye tuna, cut into ½-inch dice
9 fresh lychees, peeled, pitted, and quartered
2 tablespoons toasted sesame oil
Fleur de sel

ACCOMPANIMENTS
½ cup Cracker Puree (recipe follows)
6 edible purple violets
6 edible yellow violets

TO MAKE THE SAUCE
Using a rubber spatula, fold the mayonnaise, caviar, and sambal sauce together in a small bowl. Add more sambal sauce, if you like, and refrigerate until ready to serve.

TO PREPARE THE FOIE GRAS
Preheat the oven to 450°F. Using a sharp knife, score one side of each slice of foie gras in a nice crosshatch pattern. Season both sides of the slices with salt and pepper.

Heat two large cast-iron skillets over high heat until the pans begin to smoke (the pans must be very hot to sear the foie gras properly). Sear the scored side of the foie gras slices in the skillets until they are browned, about 2 minutes. Turn the slices over and place the skillets in the oven until seared on the bottom, about 3 minutes. Transfer the foie gras to a plate lined with paper towels to absorb any excess oil.

TO PREPARE THE TUNA

Using chopsticks, gently fold the tuna and lychees together in a medium bowl until well mixed. Drizzle the sesame oil over the mixture, sprinkle with salt, and fold gently until incorporated.

TO SERVE

Set a slice of foie gras on one side of each plate. Spoon the dynamite sauce generously over the foie gras to cover it. Use a blowtorch to sear the top of the dynamite sauce and brown it lightly. Mound the tuna mixture on the other side of the plates. Smear some cracker puree on one edge of each plate. Garnish with the flowers and serve.

cracker puree

MAKES ⅔ CUP

12 saltine crackers
8 tablespoons (1 stick) unsalted
    butter, cut into 1-inch pieces, at
    room temperature

Kosher salt

Pulse the crackers in a food processor until broken into coarse crumbs. Add half of the butter and pulse to blend. Add the remaining butter, pulsing to blend to a nearly smooth puree. Season to taste with salt. Keep at room temperature until ready to serve.

This is choucroute garnie gone crazy. Instead of serving a warm sauerkraut and meat dish with mustard, I turn the mustard into ice cream and the fermented cabbage into a raw slaw. As if that weren't enough, I sneak shredded green papaya and jicama into the cabbage and hit it all with a Thai-inspired vinaigrette. And the pork belly confit sports an Asian glaze.

confit pork belly, thai choucroute salad, mustard ice cream

SERVES 8

THAI VINAIGRETTE

¼ cup water

¼ cup fish sauce (preferably Three Crab brand)

¼ cup fresh lime juice

5 garlic cloves, finely chopped

4 teaspoons packed palm sugar, crushed

3 Thai chiles, seeded and finely chopped

FRIED SHALLOTS AND LOTUS ROOT

8 ounces shallots

One 6-inch piece lotus root, peeled

Soybean or canola oil

PICKLED RED ONION

½ cup sherry vinegar

⅓ cup water

¼ cup dry white wine

2 tablespoons granulated sugar

A sachet made with 1½ teaspoons coriander seeds and 1½ teaspoons black peppercorns, tied in a square of cheesecloth

1 small red onion, julienned

SALAD

8 fingerling potatoes

½ Savoy cabbage, finely julienned (about 3 cups)

½ jicama, peeled and finely julienned (about 3 cups)

¼ green papaya, peeled, seeded, and finely julienned (about 2 cups)

12 Thai basil leaves, halved or quartered if large

Juice of 1 lime, or to taste

8 pieces Confit Pork Belly (recipe follows), hot and glazed

Mustard Ice Cream (recipe follows)

TO MAKE THE VINAIGRETTE

Combine all the ingredients in a saucepan and bring to a boil. Transfer to a bowl and let cool.

Cover the vinaigrette and refrigerate overnight to meld the flavors.

TO PREPARE THE SHALLOTS AND LOTUS ROOT

Using a mandoline, slice the shallots into ⅛-inch-thick rings. Cut the lotus root into ⅛-inch-thick slices. (You'll have about 1½ cups sliced shallots and 2 cups lotus root.)

Add enough oil to a heavy large saucepan to fill it halfway and heat the oil over medium heat to 300°F. (Use a deep-fry thermometer to regulate the temperature of the oil; if it's higher than 300°F, it will be too hot.) Working in batches, fry the lotus root slices until golden brown, about 3 minutes (they will shrink to about half their original size). Using a spider or a wide-meshed spoon, lift the lotus root chips from the oil, draining well, then transfer to a baking sheet lined with paper towels. Repeat with the shallots, frying them just until they are pale golden (they will continue to darken as they cool), and gently lay them on the paper towels so they maintain their shape. The shallots will become crisp as they cool; so don't pile them on the paper towels.

TO PREPARE THE PICKLED ONION

Combine the vinegar, water, wine, sugar, and sachet in a heavy small saucepan and bring to a boil over high heat, stirring to dissolve the sugar.

Put the onion in a bowl and pour the hot vinegar mixture over it. Set aside until the onion is completely cooled and pickled. When the onion looks very pink, it is thoroughly pickled. Drain before serving.

TO PREPARE THE SALAD

Steam the potatoes for about 20 minutes, until just tender. Set the potatoes aside until they are just cool enough to handle.

While the potatoes are still hot, peel off the skin with a small paring knife, then cut the potatoes lengthwise in half. Place on a tray, cover, and refrigerate the potatoes until cold.

Toss the cabbage, jicama, papaya, basil leaves, 2 tablespoons of the pickled onion, and ½ cup each of the fried shallots and lotus root in a large bowl with enough of the vinaigrette to coat. Season to taste with the lime juice.

Place a piece of hot pork belly on each of eight plates. Mound the salad on top of the pork belly, spoon a scoop of the ice cream alongside, and serve immediately.

confit pork belly

SERVES 8

BRINE
8 cups water
½ cup honey
⅔ cup kosher salt
3 tablespoons coarsely crushed
   garlic
6 large fresh thyme sprigs
4 fresh flat-leaf parsley sprigs
2 fresh rosemary sprigs
2 bay leaves
1 tablespoon coarsely cracked
   black peppercorns

One 2½-pound piece fresh pork
   belly
5 pounds high-quality lard

GLAZE
⅓ cup honey
⅓ cup red wine vinegar
⅓ cup reduced-sodium soy sauce
¼ teaspoon Chinese five-spice
   powder
1½ teaspoons cornstarch, mixed with
   2 teaspoons water

TO BRINE THE PORK BELLY

Combine the water, honey, salt, garlic, thyme, parsley, rosemary, bay leaves, and peppercorns in a large saucepan and bring to a boil. Remove from the heat and let the brine cool until lukewarm.

Put the pork belly in a large container and pour the brine over it. Cover and refrigerate for 24 hours.

Remove the pork belly from the brine (discard the brine) and return to the refrigerator until you're ready to prepare the confit.

TO PREPARE THE CONFIT
Preheat the oven (preferably a convection oven, with the fan on low) to 225°F.

Melt the lard in a heavy large rondeau over medium-low heat and bring it to 150°F. Put the pork belly skin side down in the lard, making sure it is completely covered. Put a heavy pan on top of the belly to keep it submerged. Transfer the pot, uncovered, to the oven and cook for 4 hours, or until the pork is tender.

Carefully transfer the pork, skin side down, to a baking sheet or baking pan large enough to allow the belly to lie flat. Lay a sheet of parchment paper on top of the pork, put another pan on top, and put a weight in the pan to compress the pork belly. Refrigerate overnight.

TO PREPARE THE GLAZE
Combine the honey, vinegar, soy sauce, and five-spice powder in a heavy small saucepan and bring to a boil over high heat. Whisk the cornstarch mixture, then whisk into the glaze to blend and return the glaze to a boil. Reduce the heat to medium-low and simmer for 1 minute. Remove from the heat and set aside. Cover to keep warm.

TO HEAT AND GLAZE THE PORK
Preheat the oven to 450°F.

Remove the weight from the pork belly. Trim the edges neatly and cut the pork into 8 pieces.

Heat a heavy large skillet over medium heat. Add the pork belly pieces and cook until golden brown and heated through, about 3 minutes per side. (If the pork pieces are brown but not hot throughout, transfer them to a baking sheet and bake until they are hot, about 5 minutes.) Brush the glaze over the pork pieces.

mustard ice cream

MAKES ABOUT 1½ CUPS

1 cup whole milk
¼ cup heavy cream
3 tablespoons Dijon mustard

⅛ teaspoon turmeric
6 large egg yolks
1 tablespoon granulated sugar

Combine the milk and cream in a heavy medium saucepan and bring just to a simmer over medium heat, then whisk in the mustard and turmeric.

Meanwhile, whisk the yolks and sugar in a medium bowl to blend. Gradually whisk the cream mixture into the yolks. Return the mixture to the saucepan and stir constantly over medium heat until the custard thickens and an instant-read thermometer registers 165° to 170°F, about 4 minutes; do not boil.

Strain the custard through a fine-mesh sieve into a medium bowl. Set the bowl over a bowl of ice water and stir the custard until it is cold.

Transfer the custard to an ice cream maker and freeze according to the manufacturer's instructions. Serve, or pack the ice cream into a freezer container, cover with plastic wrap, and freeze until firm.

I love to take a nice, ordinary plate of food—in this case, fish with rice—and make it more interesting. To figure out how, I often look to my past. I remember eating a particularly lovely saffron risotto at the restaurant La Calendre, in Padua, Italy, where they'd sneaked in a little licorice. When I worked at Pierre Gagnaire, the chef brilliantly slipped licorice into a dish of chanterelle mushrooms. So I took one of my favorite fish, firm-fleshed John Dory, perched it on top of an homage to La Calendre's risotto, and spooned over a frothy emulsion of chanterelles.

seared john dory, saffron risotto, licorice, chanterelles

SERVES 4

CHANTERELLE EMULSION
1 tablespoon olive oil
2½ ounces chanterelle mushrooms, rinsed and coarsely chopped
½ teaspoon kosher salt
2 tablespoons finely minced shallots
1¼ cups whole milk
1½ teaspoons soy lecithin

SAFFRON RISOTTO
About 4 cups Chicken Stock (page 39)
2 tablespoons olive oil
3 tablespoons finely chopped shallots
⅓ cup Chardonnay

Small pinch of saffron threads
¾ cup Carnaroli rice
½ cup freshly grated Parmigiano-Reggiano cheese
¼ teaspoon licorice powder
Kosher salt

JOHN DORY
3 tablespoons olive oil
Four 4-ounce skinless John Dory fillets
Kosher salt and freshly ground white pepper

Heat the oil in a heavy small saucepan over high heat. Add the chanterelles and ¼ teaspoon of the salt and sauté until the chanterelles are tender and beginning to brown, about 4 minutes. Reduce the heat to low, add the shallots, and sauté until the shallots are translucent, about 1 minute. Add the milk, soy lecithin, and the remaining ¼ teaspoon salt and bring to a simmer.

Using an immersion blender, blend the mixture for 2 minutes, or until the mushrooms are pureed. Remove from the heat and let steep for 20 minutes.

Strain the mushroom mixture through a fine-mesh sieve into another small saucepan. Set aside.

TO MAKE THE RISOTTO

Bring the chicken stock to a boil in a small saucepan over high heat, then reduce the heat to low and cover the saucepan to keep the stock hot.

Heat the oil in a heavy small saucepan over medium-low heat. Add the shallots and sauté until translucent, about 3 minutes. Add the wine and saffron and simmer until the wine is reduced by half, about 2 minutes. Set the saucepan aside.

Stir the rice in a dry medium saucepan over medium heat until it is hot, about 1 minute. Pour in the wine and shallot mixture and set a timer for 20 minutes. Add 1 cup of the hot stock and simmer, stirring often until the broth is almost absorbed, about 4 minutes. Continue adding stock 1 cup at a time, allowing each addition to be absorbed before adding the next and stirring often, until the rice is tender and the mixture is creamy, about 20 minutes total; at the 16-minute mark, be sure to add only enough stock so that the rice is slightly loose. Stir in the cheese and licorice powder, then season to taste with salt. Remove from the heat.

MEANWHILE, TO PREPARE THE JOHN DORY
Preheat the oven to 425°F.

Heat 1½ tablespoons of the oil in each of two heavy large sauté pans over high heat until it begins to smoke. Season the fillets with salt and white pepper. Lay 2 fillets in each sauté pan, immediately transfer the sauté pans to the oven, and cook until the fish is opaque on the top, about 5 minutes. Turn the fish over and set the pans aside for 1 minute.

TO SERVE
Spoon the risotto onto four plates. Set the fillets atop the risotto.

Return the mushroom milk to a simmer and, using the immersion blender, blend the milk until frothy. Skim the froth from the top with a spoon and spoon the froth over the fish. Serve immediately.

TO PREPARE THE MORELS

Heat the oil in a heavy medium saucepan over medium-high heat. Add the morels and a pinch of salt and sauté until the morels begin to soften, about 3 minutes. Reduce the heat to medium-low, add the shallot, and sauté until tender, about 2 minutes. Add the cream and ¼ cup of the wine, bring to a simmer, and simmer until the cream is reduced and thickened, about 15 minutes.

Add the remaining 2 tablespoons wine and simmer for 1 minute to cook off the alcohol. Season to taste with salt and pepper. Cover and keep hot.

TO PREPARE THE GARLIC-CHEESE BUBBLES

Bring the cream to a simmer in a heavy small saucepan over medium heat and simmer until it is reduced by half, about 10 minutes.

Whisk in the cheese, garlic, and salt. Using an immersion blender, blend the mixture until smooth, then blend in the milk. Cover and keep hot.

TO PREPARE THE VEAL

Heat a heavy cast-iron skillet over low heat until it is very hot. Season the veal with salt and pepper. Add the oil to the skillet, then lay the veal in the skillet. Turn the meat quarter turns at a time every 2 minutes; the oil should sizzle lightly, so adjust the heat accordingly. Keep cooking and turning the veal until the internal temperature reaches 132°F, about 8 minutes per side. Transfer the veal chops to four plates and let rest while you finish the dish. Set the pan aside.

MEANWHILE, TO PREPARE THE ASPARAGUS

Blanch the asparagus in a large pot of boiling salted water just until bright green but still very crisp, about 1 minute. Drain and transfer to a bowl of ice water to cool completely. Remove the asparagus from the ice water and pat dry.

Heat the oil in a large sauté pan over medium-high heat. Add the asparagus and sauté until heated through, about 2 minutes. Season to taste with salt and white pepper.

TO PREPARE THE OYSTERS AND SERVE

Heat the cast-iron skillet until it is very hot. Add the oysters and sear on both sides to lightly char them, about 1 minute per side. Arrange the oysters on top of the veal.

Arrange the asparagus alongside the veal. Stir the chives into the warm wine sauce and spoon the sauce around the veal. Using the immersion blender, blend the hot Parmesan sauce until it's frothy. Skim the froth from the top with a spoon, spoon it over the veal, and serve immediately.

Caramel goes so well with salt, so when I decided to serve this warm, featherlight soufflé—which I learned to make while working for Marc Meneau. I wanted to give it some salinity. But instead of just sprinkling on the flakes of fleur de sel, I put them into an ice cream, which melts onto the warm soufflé. To work the angle between the sweet of the soufflé and the salt of the ice cream, I finish it off with a little acid in the form of Oro Blanco grapefruit, which is a cross between an acidless pomelo and a white grapefruit.

caramel soufflé, blanco grapefruit, fleur de sel ice cream

SOUFFLÉS
2½ cups whole milk

5 large eggs, separated

2¼ cups granulated sugar, plus 2 tablespoons for coating the soufflé dishes

⅓ cup all-purpose flour

¼ cup water

Butter for the soufflé dishes

ACCOMPANIMENTS
Blanco Grapefruit (recipe follows)

Fleur de Sel Ice Cream (recipe follows)

TO MAKE THE SOUFFLÉS

Bring the milk to a boil in a heavy medium saucepan.

Meanwhile, using an electric mixer, beat the egg yolks and 6 tablespoons of the sugar in a large bowl until light, thick, and fluffy, about 5 minutes. Mix in the flour. Gradually mix in the hot milk, then return the mixture to the saucepan and whisk over medium-low heat until the pastry cream thickens and bubbles begin to break on the surface, about 2 minutes. Transfer the pastry cream to a large bowl. Press plastic wrap directly onto the surface of the pastry cream and set aside.

Combine 1½ cups of the sugar and the water in a heavy small saucepan and stir over medium heat until the sugar dissolves, about 3 minutes. Boil without stirring, swirling the pan occasionally for even cooking until the caramel turns a deep amber brown and just begins to smoke, about 8 minutes; brush down the sides of the pan with a wet pastry brush as necessary to remove any sugar crystals.

Immediately whisk the hot caramel into the pastry cream. Press plastic wrap directly onto the surface of the caramel cream and refrigerate until cold, at least 3 hours.

Preheat the oven to 400°F. Butter six 9-ounce soufflé dishes and coat with 2 tablespoons sugar. Put the dishes on a heavy baking sheet.

Whisk the caramel cream to loosen it. Using an electric mixer on medium-low speed, beat the egg whites in a large bowl until soft peaks form. Gradually beat in the remaining 6 tablespoons sugar, then continue beating just until firm peaks form. Fold the egg whites into the caramel cream just until blended; do not overmix.

Divide the soufflé batter equally among the prepared soufflé dishes. Bake the soufflés until they puff but are still moist in the center, about 20 minutes.

TO SERVE

Place a scoop of blanco grapefruit and a scoop of ice cream and serve immediately.

blanco grapefruit

MAKES 2 CUPS

1 Oro Blanco grapefruit (about 1¼ pounds)
½ cup granulated sugar

2 tablespoons cold water
2 gelatin sheets

Cut the top and bottom off the grapefruit; reserve them. Stand the grapefruit on one of the cut ends and slice from top to bottom in order to remove the rind and some of the white pith. Cut all the rind into ¼-inch squares.

Working over a bowl, remove the grapefruit segments from the membranes, letting them drop into the bowl. Squeeze the juices from the membranes over the segments. Set aside.

Put the rind in a small saucepan, cover with cold water, and bring the water to a boil. Drain the rind in a sieve, rinse thoroughly under cold water, and return the rind to the saucepan. Cover with cold water again, and repeat the boiling and rinsing process 4 more times.

Return the rind to the saucepan, add the sugar and water, and bring to a boil. Add the grapefruit segments and juice and boil for 5 minutes. Remove from the heat.

Soak the gelatin in a bowl of cold water until it softens, about 5 minutes.

Remove the softened gelatin from the water, add it to the hot grapefruit mixture, and stir until the gelatin is dissolved. Pour the mixture into a container, cover, and refrigerate until set, about 1 hour. Stir to loosen before serving.

fleur de sel ice cream

MAKES ABOUT 3 CUPS

10 jumbo egg yolks
½ cup sugar

¾ teaspoon fleur de sel
2 cups whole milk

Bring the milk to just below a simmer in a heavy medium saucepan over medium-high heat.

Meanwhile, whisk the egg yolks, sugar, and fleur de sel in a large bowl until creamy and lemon-colored. Slowly add one-third of the hot milk to the egg mixture, whisking constantly. Pour the tempered egg mixture back into the remaining milk and cook over low heat, stirring constantly with a silicone spatula, until the custard thickens enough to coat the back of a wooden spoon, about 10 minutes; do not allow the custard to simmer.

Pass the custard through a fine-mesh strainer into a large bowl. Set the bowl over another bowl of ice water and cool the custard completely, stirring often. Cover the custard and refrigerate until very cold, at least 6 hours.

Freeze the custard mixture in an ice cream maker following the manufacturer's instructions. Pack the ice cream into a freezer container and cover with plastic wrap pressed directly on top of the ice cream and then with the lid. Freeze until scoopable.

When I was nineteen, I was living in Paris and working for one of the most famous chefs in all of France. I was tasting and helping to cook the food, including some truly amazing ice creams and pastries. And almost every Sunday, on my day off, I'd go to Boulevard St.-Germain and eat at McDonald's. I always started with a Big Mac and finished with a caramel sundae with peanuts—I loved it. Ever since then, I've been infatuated with sundaes, from more sophisticated versions like this one to the lowbrow ones you find at McDonald's.

ice cream sundae: pistachio ice cream, bing cherries, hot chocolate sauce, salted pistachios SERVES 6

PISTACHIO ICE CREAM
10 jumbo egg yolks
½ cup granulated sugar
2 cups half-and-half
⅓ cup pistachio paste

CHERRIES IN SYRUP
8 ounces Bing cherries, pitted
1 cup granulated sugar

HOT CHOCOLATE SAUCE
1 cup light corn syrup
8 ounces bittersweet chocolate
   (72% cacao), chopped
4 tablespoons unsalted butter

SALTED PISTACHIOS
4 ounces pistachios
1 tablespoon unsalted butter
1½ teaspoons kosher salt

VANILLA CHANTILLY
1 cup heavy cream
1 tablespoon confectioners'
   sugar
½ vanilla bean, split lengthwise

Whisk the egg yolks and sugar in a large bowl until creamy and lemon colored.

Meanwhile, bring the half-and-half to just below a simmer in a heavy medium sauce-pan over medium-high heat. Slowly add half of the hot half-and-half to the egg mix-ture, whisking constantly. Pour the tempered egg mixture back into the remaining half-and-half, add the pistachio paste, and cook over low heat, stirring constantly with a silicone spatula, until the custard thickens enough to coat the back of a wooden spoon, about 10 minutes; do not allow the custard to simmer.

Strain the custard through a fine-mesh strainer into a medium bowl. Set the bowl over another bowl of ice water and stir until cold. Cover and refrigerate overnight.

Freeze the custard mixture in an ice cream maker following the manufacturer's in-structions. Pack the ice cream into a freezer container and cover with plastic wrap pressed directly on top of the ice cream and then with the lid. Freeze until scoopable.

TO PREPARE THE CHERRIES

Combine the cherries and sugar in a heavy small saucepan and bring to a simmer over medium heat, stirring to dissolve the sugar. Increase the heat to high and boil until the mixture reaches 230°F on a candy thermometer, about 8 minutes. Set aside to cool.

Pour half of the cooled cherry mixture into a container. Blend the mixture remain-ing in the saucepan with an immersion blender until coarsely pureed. Pour into the unblended cherries, cover, and set aside.

TO MAKE THE CHOCOLATE SAUCE

Combine the corn syrup, chocolate, and butter in a large microwave-safe bowl and heat in the microwave on high for 30-second (or shorter) intervals, stirring be-tween each interval, until the chocolate and butter are melted and the sauce is well blended. Set aside. (The sauce can be made ahead, and covered and refrigerated until ready to serve.)

Preheat the oven to 350°F.

Spread the pistachios in a single layer on a heavy baking sheet and bake for about 8 minutes, until toasted and fragrant. Set aside to cool completely.

Melt the butter in a heavy medium sauté pan over low heat and continue cooking until brown, about 5 minutes. Immediately add the pistachios and salt and toss to coat the pistachios evenly.

Pour the pistachios onto a paper-towel-lined baking sheet and set aside to cool.

TO MAKE THE CHANTILLY

Combine the cream and sugar in a small bowl. Scrape the seeds from the vanilla bean and add the seeds to the cream. Whisk lightly just to blend the vanilla and sugar with the cream.

Pour the cream into a whipped cream canister and insert 1 nitrous oxide charger into the canister. Turn the canister upside down and shake vigorously about 5 times. Test the thickness of the cream—it should be lightly whipped. Shake canister again, if necessary.

TO SERVE

Warm the chocolate sauce if necessary: If using a microwave, do so in 30-second, or shorter, intervals; or stir the sauce in a heavy small saucepan over low heat until warm.

Put a scoop of pistachio ice cream in each of six glass dessert cups and cover with 1 tablespoon of the cherries and syrup. Place another scoop of ice cream on top, and cover with 3 tablespoons hot fudge sauce. Pipe a rosette of whipped cream on top, sprinkle 1 tablespoon of the salted pistachios on top of the whipped cream, and serve immediately.

When I was little, my grandmother would pick me up at school and walk me home. We'd always pass a bakery along the way, but we'd walk right by—except for those occasional happy days when she'd let me go in and get my favorite treat, the little almond-flavored cakes called *financiers*. They were baked twice a day, so they were always fresh and often still warm. I channeled those happy moments for this dessert, adding vivid green matcha tea powder for its color and sweetness-tempering bitterness. Please note the batter needs to be refrigerated overnight to produce restaurant-quality results.

matcha green tea cake, red berries, mascarpone mousse

SERVES 12

MATCHA GREEN TEA CAKE
Brown Butter (page 223)
¾ cup all-purpose flour, plus more
    for the pan
½ cup matcha tea powder
½ cup very hot water
2½ cups confectioners' sugar
1½ cups almond flour
1⅔ cups egg whites (about 10 large
    whites)

MACERATED BERRIES
8 ounces fresh blackberries
8 ounces fresh raspberries
About 3 tablespoons granulated sugar

MASCARPONE MOUSSE
3 gelatin sheets
1⅓ cups heavy cream
4 large egg yolks
½ cup granulated sugar
1¼ cups mascarpone cheese,
    at room temperature

TO MAKE THE TEA CAKE
Using some of the brown butter, coat an 11¾-by-4-by-3-inch-deep baking pan, then dust the pan with flour; tap out any excess flour.

Whisk the matcha powder and hot water in a small heatproof bowl to blend to a paste.

In the bowl of a stand mixer fitted with the paddle attachment, mix the confectioners' sugar, almond flour, and ¾ cup all-purpose flour on low speed for 30 seconds to combine. Add the matcha mixture and mix on low speed for 30 seconds to combine. With the mixer running, gradually add the egg whites, adding more only as fast as they are absorbed by the flour mixture and scraping the bowl as needed. Mix in the reserved ¾ cup brown butter.

Pour the batter into the prepared baking pan. Cover with plastic wrap and refrigerate overnight.

The next day, preheat the oven to 350°F. Bake the cake for about 1 hour, or until a toothpick inserted into the center comes out with just a few small crumbs attached. Set the pan on a cooling rack and cool the cake for about 10 minutes. Invert the cake onto the rack and remove the pan. Allow to cool to room temperature.

TO MACERATE THE BERRIES

Toss the berries with 3 tablespoons sugar in a small bowl. Using the back of a fork, coarsely crush the berries to release some of their juices, leaving some berries intact. Sweeten the berries with more sugar if necessary. Cover the berries and refrigerate for at least 1 hour, and up to 8 hours (no more, for the optimal texture).

TO MAKE THE MOUSSE

Soak the gelatin in a bowl of cold water to soften, about 5 minutes. Remove the gelatin from the water and place it in a very small saucepan; set aside.

Whisk the cream to soft peaks in a large bowl.

Whisk the egg yolks and sugar vigorously in another bowl until pale yellow and thick. Whisk in the mascarpone to blend completely.

Add 2 tablespoons of the whipped cream to the gelatin and stir over low heat just until the gelatin is fully dissolved. Pour the hot gelatin mixture into the remaining

whipped cream and whisk to combine, then immediately fold the cream mixture into the mascarpone mixture. Refrigerate until set, about 2 hours, or up to 1 day.

TO SERVE

Cut the cake into twelve ¾-inch-thick slices and place a slice off center on each of twelve plates. Spoon a small pile of berries alongside the cake—using about ⅓ cup of berries for each serving. Place a scoop of mascarpone mousse on top of each pile of berries. Spoon any remaining berries around the cake and serve.

KITCHEN  ROSTER

LUDO

SYDNEY (4.0 and 5.0)

JOON (4.0 and 5.0)

DAN (4.0 and 5.0)

FRANK

GRACE (student intern, 4.0 hired)

MICHELLE (cooking school intern)

YUKI (cooking school intern)

After the onslaught of amazing press throughout LudoBites 4.0 and 5.0, we got so tired of reading about ourselves, I can only imagine how sick L.A. was of reading anything concerning us or hearing the name LudoBites. But we needed to work, LudoBites was now our full-time business model, and if we didn't work, we didn't make any money. We had also just learned that after a very trying seven-year journey our surrogate was pregnant. With twins. Now we really needed to work.

The more press, the more attention, the more pressure. I will always cook my best, but I never intended for LudoBites to grow into this monster it had become. It all started out as a simple little restaurant for friends and had grown into a temporary restaurant that crashes the world's largest reservation system.

We'd spent the past two years living out of suitcases. When I left for Vegas, we rented out our home in Sherman Oaks. After I returned from Vegas, we shacked up in a leaky-roofed, mold-ridden rental in Manhattan Beach, then decamped to a friend's guest room in Los Feliz. This worked for a while.

But you can't start a family out of a suitcase. At the end of LudoBites 5.0, we moved back to our little house in the Valley. It was time to think about getting ready for our family. We started to wonder if we could possibly do LudoBites 6.0 in the Valley. Why not? We managed to produce our two most successful LudoBites to date in a part of downtown Los Angeles that Sam Sifton from the *New York Times* equated with the opening scene of the Michael Jackson *Thriller* video. Skid Row had become our part of town. But the Valley was a whole other animal. We love our house and our neighborhood, but it does not scream progressive dining experiences. But hell, this is LudoBites and we are going to make a selfish decision. For once, we'd have a five-minute commute to work.

By coincidence, the restaurant space that way back in 2007 we'd tried to rent from a completely unreasonable landlord—the very failed deal that pushed us over the cliff and sent us hurtling toward LudoBites—was available again. And we found out that the unfortunate leaseholder, chef Andre Guerro, was still held hostage by that same damn landlord. He had officially closed his restaurant Max, briefly operated the space as Maché and now was left stuck with a nonoperational restaurant he was using as a catering kitchen and to house his full liquor license. It was five minutes from our house. We gave Andre a call.

We had never done LudoBites at a chef-driven restaurant before. A clash of egos was inevitable. Andre is a really nice guy who likes to talk and talk. At one of our early meetings, as Krissy and I listened to him tell us about what his customers liked to eat and drink, I had flashbacks to L'Orangerie and Bastide—the very reasons I'd decided to work for myself. These would be *my* customers: LudoBites, for all its ups and downs, was successful because I did what I wanted. When we got home from the meeting, Krissy immediately modified our agreement to state, in bold, "Ludo will create and have complete control over the menu for the Event."

The space was, more or less, the same as it had been when it'd almost become our permanent home a few years back: About sixty seats inside, a bar in back that sat six, and a patio that sat another twelve. The kitchen was long and narrow, with a decent line. To get from the expo station to the dishwasher station, you had to duck under a metal shelf that held plates for service. The place had been closed for a couple of months, so it needed some freshening up—but by this point, that would be a cinch. We brought in our tableware, some paintings for walls, and two communal tables we had built for the patio to accommodate walk-ins. An unexpected boost added to our excitement—Sam Sifton contacted Krissy and asked if he could announce the opening. How cool, we thought! The launch of our temporary restaurant, now in the Valley, of all places, broadcast by the *New York Times*. One more reason we love Twitter.

It was somewhat thrilling to think that our little experiment had crashed the world's largest online reservation system, but for Krissy, the consummate host, it had been devastating. She felt that she had failed her customers, who, because of the intimate nature of LudoBites, also seemed like friends. So she spent hours on the phone with the folks at OpenTable to make sure the disaster wouldn't be repeated.

OpenTable pulled out all the stops. They even agreed to disable an element of the system that could possibly cause crashes. Their rep told the *Times*: "In preparation for

LudoBites 6.0, we disabled the feature and tested the service in our lab by simulating the levels of search volume we expect to see with this highly popular restaurant. . . . The system performed flawlessly."

The day the reservations were to go up for grabs, Krissy, our Webmaster, and an OpenTable rep gathered in our home office, along with two friends manning video cameras meant to capture the resounding success. Instead, they captured an hour and twenty minutes of pure agony. The site went down. Krissy freaked out. The rep was on the phone nonstop, at one point saying dolefully, "We need to shut down the whole system." Krissy hit Twitter, trying to offer reservation info in real time. Her Twitterfeed, @Frenchchefwife, became a trending topic a title typically bestowed on things like earthquakes and Justin Bieber. Poor customers, and poor Krissy. She spent every free moment for the next few days sending e-mails of contrition to the disappointed, the frustrated, and the furious, all people who had done everything right but didn't get a fair chance to book a table. OpenTable ultimately published a lengthy "Open Apology to Ludo and Krissy Lefebvre + LudoBites Lovers."

We had no time for regrets, because despite the insanity, we were fully booked and had a restaurant to open. But we'd gotten pretty good at this by now. We had hired a bunch of waiters from Max; Jan, the other partner at Max, was going to bartend; and we even had two sommeliers. It was the largest and most experienced staff we'd ever had. We even had time to do a staff tasting of the menu, a requisite part of the process for just about every other restaurant in the world but a rarity on Planet LudoBites. An hour before we opened, a line had formed for the walk-in tables.

Still, 6.0 began on a sour note. Andre volunteered to expedite opening night, and I was thrilled to have him helping—at first. Soon it became clear that we wanted to do expediting our way and he wanted to do it his way. In what would be a recurring theme in this LudoBites, Andre and his staff still wanted to do things their way. The tickets were fucked, everyone was pissed, and for the second half of night one, Andre just sullenly stood around and watched. It felt like shit to push him out, but the coup d'état was essential.

The stress of the push and pull between my staff and Andre's even got to Joon, my rock. He really was like a machine. Usually he only said two things: "Yes, chef," and "Right away, chef." He shut up and got things done. But one particularly crazy night, he cracked. All of a sudden I heard, "Don't touch it! Don't touch it!" Could that bloodcurdling shriek be coming from . . . Joon? He was sweating and screaming. Suddenly, nobody was allowed to touch the plates he turned out except Krissy. I had to laugh. Later on, though, we looked at our computer system's nightly report. Of the 378 plates we put out that night, Joon had made 246. He had a right to freak out.

Another issue to contend with was the Valley itself. The area has a bit of a reputation. Diners here, people say, have more provincial palates than sophisticated city eaters. I still think that's bullshit. But I must admit, we did confront a few incidents of infuriating culinary ignorance. The one that continues to traumatize Krissy and me until this day was the Sous-Vide Chicken Debacle.

I'm not a big fan of sous-vide cooking, but there was a Cryovac at Max, so I figured I'd use it to make one dish on the menu, a deboned half chicken marinated in olive oil and smoked paprika to rev up the flavor and color, then poached slowly in a vacuum-sealed bag, which kept the lean meat incredibly succulent and, yes, slightly pink but decidedly cooked through. Then I seared it to add a bit of mouthwatering crunch.

Well, a table of six women insisted that the chicken was raw and they sent it back to the kitchen. Our lovely server walked into the kitchen and explained. Mistakes happen, so I dutifully checked and I confirmed that the chicken was perfectly cooked. All was well. Until a few minutes later, when I saw the server crying. The women, it turned out, had kept arguing with her and telling her she was a terrible waitress. That was it. I was out

there in a flash. I told them their chicken was cooked and if they didn't like it, well, that was too bad. And how dare they speak so disrespectfully to their server? They kept at it, and suddenly I thought to myself, What the fuck am I doing? I'm standing out here, when I should be cooking, fighting with six women about chicken! I pronounced them ignorant and informed them that they were paying for the chicken, whether they ate it or not. If they refused, I'd call the police.

I must say, Jan, the other co-owner of Max, was a godsend. Although she was working long days churning out pastry for The Oinkster, their other restaurant, she would show up every night with a smile on her face, quickly attending to any issues we had, and then spend the rest of the evening muddling and mashing the ingredients for the Ludo "Coq" tails. Her dedication was impressive.

For the most part, 6.0 ran smoothly, but something odd happened. By any significant measure, it was a smash hit. We were making good money, and Andre was too. We had plenty of servers, a full bar, and even sommeliers working the tables. Yet with all that came a formality, a stuffiness, that didn't quite fit. Turns out that working in borrowed spaces with borrowed staff is a little like speed dating. Some people surprise and enrapture you. But others, while they might look great on paper, leave you feeling unmoved. We missed Mike Ilic's hospitality. We even missed Skid Row. We learned that the success of LudoBites transcended typical measures, that magic was more important than money.

As a kid, I'd look forward to my four o'clock snack (in France they call this a *goûter*), rummaging through the refrigerator for something tasty to top my baguette. Rarely did I seek out anything sweet. I'd push aside the jar of Nutella and reach for the Laughing Cow cheese. Sometimes I'd take my dad's tin of sardines and mash them with the cheese, an unlikely combination that I love to this day. In keeping with the casualness of my childhood snack, this recipe is incredibly simple, the smoked butter (no, I didn't make smoked butter as a kid) nothing more than a mixture of good butter and store-bought smoked salt.

smoked butter, sardine–laughing cow cheese

smoked butter

MAKES 4 OUNCES

8 tablespoons unsalted French butter, at room temperature

½ teaspoon fine smoked salt

In the bowl of a stand mixer fitted with the paddle attachment, beat the butter and smoked salt on medium speed until the butter is creamy and lighter in color. Transfer the butter to a sheet of plastic wrap, shape the butter into a log, and roll up in the plastic, twisting the ends to seal. Refrigerate the butter until cold.

Slice the butter crosswise into disks when serving.

sardine–laughing cow cheese   MAKES ABOUT 8 OUNCES

One 6-ounce package Laughing Cow
Original Creamy Swiss cheese

1½ ounces olive-oil-packed sardines,
drained, backbones removed

In the bowl of a stand mixer fitted with the paddle attachment, beat the cheese and sardines on medium speed until well blended. Spoon the cheese mixture into small ramekins and serve or refrigerate for up to 2 days until ready to serve.

I still can't believe that this simple dish, a Vietnamese-inspired jumble of shredded fruits and vegetables paired with slices of raw fish, became one of the signature dishes of 6.0. The salad is so bright and exciting: crispy raw jicama and green papaya and crunchy fried shallots and basil, all dressed with lime juice and fish sauce. I favor hamachi (yellowtail) here for its delicate flavor, luxurious fat content, and silky texture, but I recommend using whatever looks best at the market—perhaps another white-fleshed fish like striped bass, or even scallops or tuna.

hamachi, vietnamese salad

SERVES 6

FRIED SHALLOTS AND LOTUS ROOT

8 ounces shallots

One 6-inch piece lotus root, peeled

Soybean or canola oil

PICKLED RED ONION

½ cup sherry vinegar

⅓ cup water

¼ cup dry white wine

2 tablespoons granulated sugar

1½ teaspoons coriander seeds and 1½ teaspoons black peppercorns tied in a square of cheesecloth

1 small red onion, julienned

SALAD

3 cups finely julienned peeled green papaya

3 cups finely julienned peeled jicama

½ green banana, peeled and julienned

½ cup loosely packed fresh cilantro leaves

⅓ cup loosely packed small fresh Thai basil leaves (halved or quartered if large)

About ½ cup Vietnamese Vinaigrette (recipe follows)

Juice of 2 limes (about ¼ cup)

Twenty-four ¼-inch-thick slices hamachi fillet (about 12 ounces total)

TO PREPARE THE SHALLOTS AND LOTUS ROOT

Using a mandoline, slice the shallots into ⅛-inch-thick rings. Cut the lotus root into ⅛-inch-thick slices. (You'll have about 1½ cups sliced shallots and 2 cups lotus root.)

Add enough oil to a heavy large saucepan to fill it halfway and heat the oil over medium heat to 300°F. (Use a deep-fry thermometer to regulate the temperature of the oil; if it's higher than 300°F, it will be too hot.) Working in batches, fry the lotus root slices until golden brown, about 3 minutes (they will shrink to about half their original size). Using a spider or a wide-meshed spoon, lift the lotus root chips from the oil, draining well, then transfer to a baking sheet lined with paper towels. Repeat with the shallots, frying them just until they are pale golden (they will continue to darken as they cool), and gently lay them on the paper towels so they maintain their ring shape. The shallots will become crisp as they cool; don't pile them on the paper towels.

TO PREPARE THE PICKLED ONION

Combine the vinegar, water, wine, sugar, and sachet in a heavy small saucepan and bring to a boil over high heat, stirring to dissolve the sugar.

Put the onion in a bowl and pour the hot vinegar mixture over it. Set aside until the onion is completely cooled and pickled (when the onion looks very pink, it is thoroughly pickled). Drain before serving.

TO ASSEMBLE THE SALAD

Combine the papaya, jicama, banana, ⅓ cup of the cilantro, ¼ cup of the basil, half of the shallots, half of the lotus root chips, and ⅔ cup of the pickled red onion in a large bowl. Toss with enough vinaigrette to coat, then toss with lime juice to taste.

TO SERVE

Lay 4 hamachi slices on each of six plates. Mound the salad on top of the hamachi. Garnish with the remaining basil, cilantro, lotus root chips, and shallots and serve immediately.

vietnamese vinaigrette

MAKES ABOUT 1 CUP

⅓ cup water
¼ cup fish sauce (preferably Three
    Crab brand)
¼ cup fresh lime juice

5 garlic cloves, finely chopped
2 tablespoons crushed palm sugar
3 Thai chiles, seeded and finely
    chopped

Combine all the ingredients in a small saucepan and bring to a boil over medium-high heat. Transfer to a bowl and set aside to cool. Cover and refrigerate overnight to meld the flavors.

I'm a big fan of mackerel, especially when it's marinated in the Japanese style. The texture of that fish, not cooked but transformed by acid and salt, reminds me of ceviche. So I decided to sauce it with Peruvian-style *leche de tigre,* the milky white liquid left after fish has been marinated for ceviche, which you slurp up after you've devoured the cured seafood. The merging of the two cultures is not so odd when you consider that Peru has long been home to a significant Japanese population. Right before serving, I sprinkle a little sugar over the fish and hit it with a blowtorch to create a crackling, slightly bitter caramelized shell.

At LudoBites we had some *leche de tigre* on hand from scallops we'd marinated for another dish, but this recipe shows you how to make your own, using meaty fish bones.

marinated mackerel, leche de tigre, purslane, brûléed leeks

SERVES 4

LECHE DE TIGRE

8 ounces meaty white fish bones

1 cup fresh lime juice

12 sprigs fresh cilantro

3 garlic cloves, thinly sliced

1 jalapeño chile, thinly sliced into rounds

MACKEREL

½ cup reduced-sodium soy sauce

⅓ cup rice vinegar

¼ cup mirin

1 tablespoon granulated sugar

Four 6-ounce Spanish or Japanese mackerel fillets with skin

About 3 tablespoons granulated sugar

BABY LEEKS

12 baby leeks, root ends trimmed

2 tablespoons olive oil

Kosher salt

GARNISHES

32 purslane leaves

20 borage flowers

TO MAKE THE LECHE DE TIGRE

Combine all the ingredients in a bowl or other nonreactive container, cover, and refrigerate for 5 hours.

Strain the leche de tigre into a bowl, pressing on the solids. Discard the solids and refrigerate the liquid.

TO PREPARE THE MACKEREL

Whisk the soy sauce, vinegar, mirin, and sugar in a bowl until the sugar is dissolved. Put the mackerel skin side down in a baking dish and pour the marinade over it, turning to coat. Cover and refrigerate for 40 minutes.

Remove the mackerel from the marinade and cut each fillet crosswise into 4 equal pieces. Put on a plate, cover, and refrigerate until ready to serve.

TO PREPARE THE LEEKS

Blanch the leeks in a large saucepan of lightly salted boiling water for 1 minute. Drain the leeks and submerge them in a bowl of ice water just until they're cold, then remove from the ice water and drain on paper towels. Pat dry with more paper towels.

Heat the oil in a large sauté pan over high heat until it begins to smoke. Reduce the heat to medium, add the leeks, with a pinch of salt, and cook, turning occasionally, until the leeks are dark brown on all sides, about 12 minutes. Using tongs, transfer the leeks to paper towels to drain.

TO SERVE

Put the mackerel pieces skin side up on the back of a baking sheet. Sprinkle the sugar evenly over the skin to coat lightly. Using a blowtorch, melt the sugar until it is caramelized and browned.

Arrange 4 pieces of mackerel on each of four plates. Arrange 3 baby leeks on each plate. Drizzle 3 tablespoons of the leche de tigre over and around the fish on each plate. Garnish each with 8 purslane leaves and 5 borage flowers and serve immediately.

Back at LudoBites 4.0, I fell in love with the idea of gently cooking squid and using it instead of the pasta in carbonara, in part to delight in people's initial confusion ("Wait, where's the squid?") and in part to witness their conversion to excitement ("Wait, this *is* squid!"). Yet this is LudoBites, so I didn't want to do carbonara again. Why not put to use my love of pad Thai? My version— deconstructed, reimagined, and refined—hits all the notes that make the original such a pleasure to eat.

squid pad thai

SERVES 4

PEANUT COMPOUND BUTTER

2 garlic cloves

3 tablespoons white wine vinegar

⅓ cup toasted peanuts

1 stalk lemongrass, trimmed and tender inner part thinly sliced

1 fresh kaffir lime leaf, very finely chopped

3 tablespoons finely chopped peeled fresh galangal

3 tablespoons finely chopped peeled fresh ginger

2 teaspoons peanut oil

¼ teaspoon ground coriander

¼ teaspoon ground cumin

A couple drops of pure coconut extract

8 tablespoons (1 stick) unsalted butter, cut into pieces

SPICY TOFU PUREE

4 ounces firm tofu, cubed

¼ cup whole milk

2 dried Thai bird chiles, finely chopped

½ teaspoon xanthan gum

Kosher salt

PAD THAI SALAD

12 seedless red grapes, thinly sliced

1 cup bean sprouts, washed

½ cup thinly julienned peeled black radish

2 green onions, thinly sliced on a sharp bias

4 large shrimp, peeled, deveined, and sliced into ¼-inch-wide pieces

2 teaspoons peanut oil

Kosher salt and freshly ground white pepper to taste

SQUID

2 tablespoons clarified butter or peanut oil

12 cleaned squid bodies, cut lengthwise into ¼-inch-wide strips

Kosher salt and freshly ground white pepper, to taste

Ground dried Thai bird chiles for garnish (optional)

TO MAKE THE COMPOUND BUTTER

Put the garlic in a small saucepan, add enough water to cover, and bring the water to a boil; drain. Repeat 2 more times.

Put the garlic in a small bowl and add the white wine vinegar and 3 tablespoons water. Cover and refrigerate for at least 3 hours, and up to 3 weeks.

Drain the garlic and add it to a food processor, along with the peanuts, lemongrass, kaffir lime leaf, galangal, ginger, peanut oil, coriander, cumin, and coconut extract. Process to a paste, stopping the machine occasionally and scraping the bowl. Gradually blend in the butter.

TO MAKE THE TOFU PUREE

Blend the tofu, milk, and chiles in a blender until smooth. With the blender running on medium-high speed, slowly stream the xanthan gum into the vortex. Increase the speed as needed to maintain the vortex and continue to blend until no vortex appears on high speed. Season to taste with salt. Transfer the tofu puree to a container, cover, and refrigerate until cold, or for up to 1 week.

JUST BEFORE SERVING, MAKE THE SALAD

Combine all the ingredients in a medium bowl and toss well.

TO PREPARE THE SQUID

Melt the clarified butter in a heavy large sauté pan over medium heat. Add the squid, season with salt and pepper, and sauté until the squid begins to turn opaque, about 45 seconds. Add 6 tablespoons of the peanut compound butter and toss until the butter melts and coats the squid, about 2 minutes.

TO SERVE

Divide the squid and peanut sauce among four rimmed soup bowls. Top each with a mound of the salad. Using a small metal spoon, scrape about 1 tablespoon of the tofu puree onto the rim of each bowl. If desired, garnish the rims of the bowls with a light sprinkling of ground Thai chile.

In France, we have a well-known dish of oil-cured herring served with potato salad. That was my jumping-off point here. And I must have jumped way off, because I swapped herring with salmon and chilled strands of somen (my noodle fetish again) stand in for the starch. Adorning it all are ribbons of raw carrot, red wine vinaigrette, and glassy orbs of salmon roe singed with a blowtorch so they take on a fantastic smokiness but still retain their pop-in-your-mouth texture.

salmon, somen noodles, raw rainbow carrots

SERVES 4

CARROTS
1 orange rainbow carrot
1 purple rainbow carrot
1 red rainbow carrot

NOODLES
One 3½-ounce bundle somen noodles
Twenty ⅛-inch-thick slices Marinated
    Salmon (recipe follows)

VINAIGRETTE
¼ cup oil reserved from marinated
    salmon
2 tablespoons red wine vinegar
Kosher salt

¼ cup salmon roe for garnish

TO PREPARE THE CARROTS

Scrub the carrots, but do not peel them. Using a mandoline, shave the carrots lengthwise into paper-thin slices. Put the shaved carrots in a bowl of ice water and set aside for 10 minutes.

Drain the carrots, put in a small bowl, and refrigerate until you're ready to serve.

TO PREPARE THE NOODLES

Cook the noodles in a large saucepan of boiling salted water, stirring, for 1½ minutes. Drain the noodles in a sieve and rinse them under cold water, stirring the noodles with chopsticks to remove the surface starch (this helps keep noodles that will be served cold from sticking together). Drain the noodles and put them in a small bowl.

TO SERVE

Mound the noodles in the center of four plates. Arrange 5 salmon slices in a straight line on top of the noodles on each plate. Toss the carrots and gently scatter them on top of the salmon.

TO MAKE THE VINAIGRETTE

Whisk the oil and vinegar in a small bowl to blend. Season to taste with salt. Drizzle 1½ tablespoons of the vinaigrette over the salmon, noodles, and carrots on each plate.

Put the salmon roe on a small baking sheet. Using a blowtorch, slightly char the salmon roe, without popping it. Spoon the salmon roe evenly around the noodles and serve immediately.

marinated salmon

MAKES ABOUT 4 POUNDS

One 4-pound side Scottish salmon
(preferably Loch Duart)
3 cups Diamond kosher salt

2 tablespoons juniper berries, ground
About 4 cups grapeseed oil

Line a large baking sheet with parchment paper and put the salmon skin side down on the parchment paper. Pour the kosher salt evenly over the salmon until it is completely covered. Cover with plastic wrap and refrigerate for 2 hours.

Brush the salt off the salmon and rinse the salmon under cold water to wash off any remaining salt. Dry the salmon with paper towels.

Put the salmon skin side down in a roasting pan. Sprinkle the juniper berries over the salmon, then pour enough oil over the salmon so that it is completely submerged. Cover with plastic wrap and refrigerate for 24 hours.

Remove the salmon from the oil, draining it well; reserve ¼ cup of the oil for the vinaigrette in the main recipe. Remove the skin from the salmon. Using a large slicing knife, cut the salmon against the grain into ⅛-inch-thick slices.

When my grandfather Gilbert was still alive, he had a little condo on the beach in Antibes, in the South of France. A few steps away, there was this little place that was barely a restaurant, closer to a bar, with just three or four dishes on the menu, and that's where he and I would have lunch. I almost always ordered *moules frites*, the classic brothy, steamy bowl of mussels with crispy fries. I loved the broth most of all, the oceanic flavor of the shellfish juices mingling with shallots and the zing of white wine, all of it just begging to be sopped up with nice bread. Even though the dish, like most essentially simple food, can be difficult to do well, I know my customers would be disappointed if I served them something so straightforward. So I decided to distill that lovely broth into a creamy velouté, spiked with the Moroccan spice blend ras el hanout. Thin, crispy fries complete the memory for me—my grandpa, me, and fantastic *moules frites*.

moroccan mussel velouté, small fries

SERVES 4

BROTH
2 cups Chardonnay
1 shallot, thinly sliced
1 tablespoon unsalted butter
2 pounds black mussels, scrubbed and
   debearded

MOROCCAN VELOUTÉ
½ teaspoon saffron threads
1 cup heavy cream
1 tablespoon ras el hanout
1 tablespoon unsalted butter
Kosher salt and freshly ground white
   pepper

FOR SERVING
1 large heirloom tomato (about 10
   ounces), cut into ½-inch cubes
1 tablespoon extra-virgin olive oil, plus
   more for drizzling over the soup
1 tablespoon sherry vinegar
12 fresh purple small basil leaves
1 orange
Kosher salt and freshly ground white
   pepper
Small Fries (recipe follows)

TO MAKE THE BROTH

Combine the wine, shallot, and butter in a heavy large pot and bring the wine to a boil over high heat. Stir in the mussels, cover, and cook, stirring occasionally, just until the shells open, about 5 minutes. Remove the pot from the heat and let stand for 5 minutes.

TO MAKE THE VELOUTÉ

Remove the mussels from the pot and remove the meat from the shells; set the meat aside and discard the shells.

Strain the cooking liquid through a fine-mesh sieve into a bowl, then return the liquid to the pot and bring it to a boil. Crumble in the saffron, add the cream, and bring to a simmer. Simmer until the cream is slightly reduced, about 5 minutes.

Stir in the ras el hanout and half of the mussels. Using an immersion blender, blend the mixture until smooth. Blend in the butter. Season the velouté to taste with salt and white pepper.

TO SERVE

Combine the tomato, oil, vinegar, basil, and remaining mussels in a large bowl. Using a Microplane, grate the zest from half of the orange over the tomato mixture. Stir in the hot velouté. Season to taste with salt and white pepper.

Divide the soup among four small soup bowl, and drizzle with olive oil. Mound the small fries on a plate.

small fries

2 big russet (baking) potatoes (about 1 pound each)
About 8 cups grapeseed oil

Kosher salt and freshly ground white pepper

Peel the potatoes. With a mandoline, cut them lengthwise into shoestring-sized strips (known as *pommes pailles*, or straw potatoes). Put the potatoes in a large bowl of ice water and stir to release some of the starch (the water will turn cloudy), then transfer the potatoes to a colander and rinse them under cold running water. Drain well.

Line a large baking sheet with paper towels and scatter the potatoes over them. Pat the potatoes dry with more paper towels.

Add enough oil to a large deep pot to fill it one-third full, and heat the oil to 375°F over medium-high heat. Working in small batches, fry the potatoes until crisp and golden, about 3 minutes; be careful not to add too many potatoes at one time, or the oil may bubble up and overflow. Using a spider, remove the potatoes from the oil and transfer them to another baking sheet lined with paper towels. (Return the oil to 375°F before adding each new batch of potatoes.) Immediately sprinkle the hot fries with salt and white pepper.

Nothing against seared foie gras or a classic terrine, but when you serve as much of the luxurious stuff as I do, you like to come up with different ways to cook it. As it turns out, poaching foie gras turns the lobe of liver into a wobbly, almost Jell-O-like, masterpiece. I go a step further and use rice-wine-vinegar poaching liquid, so the foie is sort of pickled. Then I sear the liver in a hot pan to add color and lacquer it with honey to balance the acidity. The result is so unlike what diners are used to that some people swear they've never liked foie gras until they tasted this version, while others swear that I don't know how to cook the liver or that I buy lobes of shitty quality. Sometimes my favorite dishes are also the most polarizing ones.

pickled foie gras, autumn fruits chutney, rose

SERVES 4

ROSE SYRUP
¼ cup rose water
2 tablespoons Simple Syrup (page 300)
Pink food coloring paste
½ teaspoon xanthan gum

PICKLED FOIE GRAS
3 cups rice vinegar
1 cup acacia honey plus ½ cup for
   roasting
½ cup water
3 tablespoons grated peeled fresh ginger
   (with Microplane)

2 tablespoons ground cumin
1 (1½-pound) whole foie gras lobe
Fleur de sel de Guérande

ACCOMPANIMENTS:
1⅓ cups Autumn Fruit Chutney
   (page 274)
2 tablespoons diced Granny Smith apple
   (with peel)
2 tablespoons diced peeled Anjou pear
2 tablespoons pineapple, peeled, cored,
   and diced
16 edible fresh rose petals (preferably
   multi-colored)

Combine the rose water and simple syrup in a very small saucepan and bring the mixture to a boil over high heat. Then set the saucepan in a bowl of ice water to cool.

Add just enough of the pink coloring paste to create a nice light pink color. Using an immersion blender, blend in the xantham gum to thicken the sauce. Set aside at room temperature.

TO PREPARE THE FOIE GRAS

Combine the rice vinegar, 1 cup of the honey, water, ginger, and cumin in a heavy large saucepan and bring it to a simmer over high heat, stirring to dissolve the honey. Remove the pan from the heat and let rest until the poaching syrup at 149°F, about 15 minutes. Use a low flame to maintain this temperature, then add the whole foie gras and poach it until the center of the lobe reaches 132°F, about 30 minutes. At this point the foie gras will be very delicate, so using a large wide spatula carefully lift the foie gras out of the poaching liquid and set it on a baking sheet.

Heat a large nonstick sauté pan over medium heat until it is hot. Carefully lay the whole poached lobe of foie gras in the pan and cook until golden brown on all the sides, about 3 minutes. Add the remaining ½ cup of honey to the pan and baste the honey over the foie gras for about 1 to 2 minutes. Transfer the foie gras to a cutting board and slice it crosswise into ½-inch-thick slices, then season each slice with fleur de sel.

TO SERVE

Spoon about ⅓ cup of the fruit chutney into the center of each of 4 large plates. Top with the foie gras slices, dividing equally. Garnish with the diced fruits and rose petals. Spoon a dollop of the rose syrup alongside the foie gras on each plate and serve.

One winter when I was little, I watched in amazement (and, to be honest, a bit of terror) as the men in my family bled a just-slaughtered pig, catching the red liquid in a basin and then whisking it away to turn it into boudin noir, or blood sausage, flavored with warm spices like nutmeg and ginger. (The pig was then butchered and some of it was roasted for that night's dinner, the rest preserved as charcuterie.) As the weather got cold during this run of LudoBites, my mind turned to that rustic sausage. I took the flavors of the sausage and channeled them into a warm terrine, smooth and light like custard, with crunchy fried onions, apple "caviar," and apple vinaigrette.

boudin noir pudding, apples, fried onions

SERVES 8

BLOOD SAUSAGE TERRINE
1 tablespoon olive oil
2 onions (about 1 pound), finely diced
8 ounces pork back fat, finely diced
4 ounces smoked bacon, finely diced
3 garlic cloves, finely chopped
1 small Fuji apple, peeled, cored, and cut into ¼-inch dice
½ cup dry red wine
2 cups pig's blood
⅓ cup heavy cream

VINAIGRETTE
¼ cup granulated sugar
1 cup apple cider vinegar
1¼ cups fresh apple juice
1 vanilla bean, split lengthwise

GREEN APPLE CAVIAR
2 green apples, cored and coarsely chopped
Three 500 mg vitamin C tablets
¼ teaspoon (0.5 g) sodium alginate
1 tablespoon (10 g) calcium chloride

FRIED ONIONS
Canola oil for deep-frying
1 large onion, sliced into very thin rings (⅛ inch thick)
1 cup all-purpose flour
Kosher salt and freshly ground white pepper

1 Pink Lady apple or other in-season apple, cored (not peeled) and cut into julienne

Preheat the oven to 320°F.

Heat the oil in a heavy large skillet over medium heat. Add the onions and sauté until translucent, about 8 minutes. Add the back fat, bacon, and garlic and sauté until some of the fat renders and coats the onions, about 3 minutes. Stir in the apple and cook, stirring often, until the mixture becomes a beautiful golden brown color, about 20 minutes.

Add the red wine, reduce the heat to medium-low, and simmer gently for about 5 minutes until slightly reduced. Add the blood and cream and stir until the mixture reaches 130°F, about 5 minutes. Transfer to a blender and puree until smooth.

Strain the terrine mixture through a fine-mesh sieve and pour into a 4-cup terrine mold (6 inches long by 3¾ inches wide by 3½ inches deep). Set the mold in a roasting pan and fill the roasting pan with enough warm water to come halfway up the sides of the terrine. Bake until the mixture has set, about 10 minutes. Remove the terrine from the water bath, let cool, then refrigerate overnight.

TO MAKE THE VINAIGRETTE

Melt the sugar in a heavy small saucepan over medium heat, without stirring but tilting and rotating the pan so that the sugar melts evenly, and cook until it becomes a golden brown caramel, about 5 minutes. Add the vinegar, stirring to deglaze the pan, and bring to a boil. Add the apple juice and simmer until the mixture reduces to a syrupy consistency, about 30 minutes. Remove from the heat.

Scrape the seeds from the vanilla been and stir the seeds into the apple vinaigrette (reserve the pod for another use, if desired). Set the vinaigrette aside to cool completely.

TO MAKE THE GREEN APPLE CAVIAR

Combine the apples and vitamin C tablets in a Vitamix and puree. Strain the apple mixture through a fine-mesh sieve into a bowl, pressing on the solids to release as much juice as possible; discard the solids. Mix ¾ cup of the apple juice and the alginate in a small bowl to blend. Let stand for 15 minutes.

Stir the apple juice mixture once and let stand for 15 minutes again; the mixture will thicken.

Mix the calcium chloride with 4 cups cold water in a medium bowl. Fill a third bowl halfway with cold water.

Using a spoon or a dropper, drop the apple juice mixture into the calcium water to form balls. The balls should be about three times the size of regular caviar. Let the balls soak for 2 minutes, then gently remove them from the calcium water and rinse in the third bowl of cold water.

Preheat the oven to 350°F.

TO PREPARE THE FRIED ONIONS

Pour 3 inches of oil into a heavy large pot or deep fryer. Heat the oil to 350°F (over medium heat if using a pot). Separate the onion slices. Working in small batches, toss the slices in the flour to coat completely, shake the excess flour off the slices and deep-fry until golden brown and crisp, 2 to 3 minutes (be sure to allow the oil to return to 350°F before adding each batch). Using a slotted spoon, transfer the onions to paper towels to drain. The onion rings will be crisp and delicate, so handle them carefully to ensure they stay intact. Immediately season the hot onion rings to taste with salt and white pepper.

TO SERVE

Run a small knife under hot water, then run it around the edges of the terrine. Set the mold in a bowl of hot water just long enough to loosen the terrine from the bottom of the mold, about 3 minutes. Invert the terrine mold onto a carving board and gently tap the mold to release the terrine. Trim the edges of the terrine if necessary. Using a large hot moistened knife, cut the terrine into ¾-inch-thick slices. Place the slices on a baking sheet and bake until heated through, 8 to 10 minutes.

Meanwhile, toss the julienned apple in a medium bowl with enough of the vinaigrette to coat.

Using a spatula, transfer the slices of terrine to plates. Spoon the green apple caviar on top of the slices, then top with the fried onions. Spoon the julienned apple and vinaigrette around the slices of terrine and serve.

hamachi, vietnamese salad (photograph by kevineats.com)

smoked butter, sardine-laughing cow cheese (photograph by kevineats.com)

marinated mackerel, leche de tigre, purslane, brûléed leeks

(photograph by Wesley Wong/eatsmeetwes.com)

salmon, somen noodles, raw rainbow carrots (photograph by Anne Fishbein)

squid pad thai (photograph by Wesley Wong/eatsmeetswes.com)

moroccan mussel velouté, small fries (photograph by Wesley Wong/eatsmeetswes.com)

cod, smoked potato, pickled bell pepper, pil-pil sauce, amaranth
(photograph by Wesley Wong/eatsmeetswes.com)

galbi steak, steamed cabbage, kimchi sauce (photograph by gastronomyblog.com)

jidori™ half chicken, 65°C egg, chanterelles, chorizo froth (photograph by kevineats.com)

pickled foie gras, autumn fruit chutney, rose (photograph by Donovan Unks)

john dory, jalapeño nage, broccolini, potato chips (photograph by kevineats.com)

suntory-yamazaki-whiskey rib eye, smoked shishito peppers (photograph by kevineats.com)

crème fraîche panna cotta, caramel caviar (photograph by kevineats.com)

warm carrot cake, coconut, thai curry, mango sorbet, kaffir lime oil
(photograph by gastronomyblog.com)

cantal cheese pick-up sticks, white chocolate, candied black olives
(photograph by Wesley Wong/eatsmeetwes.com)

U8 TES VERSION 007

gram & papa's
227 E. 9th Street · DownTown L.A. 90015

ug 3 - Sept 10
servations July 14 at 4:00
Opentable

c dates and further info to be posted at
udobites.com & www.facebook.com/ludobites

RESERVATION CALENDAR

Sun	Mon	Tue	Wed	Thu	Fri	Sat
	August 1	2	3	4	5	6
7	8	9	10	11	12	13
14	15	16	17	18	19	20
21	22	23	24	25	26	27
28	29	30	31	September 1	2	3
4	5	6	7	8	9	10

LU8 BITES VERSION 007

gram & papa's
227 E. 9th Street · DownTown L.A.

onion tart, caramelized onions, bottarga (photograph by Colin Young-Wolff)

jamaican fried chicken wings (photograph by Wesley Wong/eatsmeetwes.com)

bouillabaisse milk shake (photograph by Wesley Wong/eatsmeetwes.com)

salt-cod panna cotta, smoked tapioca, potato-mousseline ice cream (photograph by Shayla Del)

dorade ceviche, cucumber water, purslane (photograph by kevineats.com)

squid, black ash, chorizo cream (photograph by Wesley Wong/eatsmeetwes.com)

egg, sea urchin, caviar, champagne beurre blanc (photograph by kevineats.com)

duck, cherry sauce, spicy saucisse, beets, radish (photograph by Colin Young-Wolff)

époisses cheese risotto, hazelnuts, egg yolk, herb salad (photograph by Wesley Wong/eatsmeetwes.com)

tandoori octopus, yogurt, cauliflower, grapefruit (photograph by Colin Young-Wolff)

lavender tropézienne (photograph by Shayla Deluy)

peach melba vacherin, lavender chantilly cream (photograph by kevineats.com)

You see the plate and the dish just looks like fish and potatoes, a great team, sure, but nothing exciting. But the fish is slowly poached to supreme silkiness, the soft potatoes are infused with liquid smoke and capped with crispy shards of potato, and it's all sauced with a puree of pickled bell peppers to provide bright flavor and a painterly splash of color, along with an incredible mayo-like emulsion of fish, olive oil, and garlic called pil-pil. Pil-pil is typically used to poach fish, but here I decided to use just a little as a condiment that still brings the flavors of Basque country alive. This recipe combines all of my favorite parts of Basque cuisine in one dish.

cod, smoked potato, pickled bell pepper, pil-pil sauce, amaranth

SERVES 4

SMOKED POTATOES
8 fingerling potatoes (about 1 pound total)
10 cups water
¼ cup liquid smoke
Kosher salt
1 tablespoon extra-virgin olive oil
Pinch of fleur de sel

COD
6½ cups extra-virgin olive oil
Four 5-ounce skinless cod fillets

Fleur de sel
¼ cup fresh micro amaranth leaves

ACCOMPANIMENTS
16 Potato Chips (recipe follows)
Pickled Red Pepper Puree (recipe follows; about ¾ cup)
Pil-Pil Sauce (recipe follows; about ½ cup)

TO PREPARE THE POTATOES
Put the potatoes in a medium saucepan and add enough water to cover them by 2 inches. Add the liquid smoke and enough salt so the water tastes slightly salty and bring to a simmer over high heat. Simmer for 10 minutes, or until a knife glides

in and out of a potato smoothly. Drain the potatoes and place them on a baking sheet to cool; then refrigerate them until cold.

TO PREPARE THE COD

Heat the olive oil to 150°F in a saucepan large enough to hold the cod in a single layer. Add the cod to the hot oil and poach until the internal temperature reaches 140° to 145°F, about 20 minutes.

MEANWHILE, TO FINISH THE POTATOES

Cut them lengthwise in half, and steam them until they are hot, about 5 minutes. Toss the potatoes in a small bowl with the olive oil and fleur de sel.

When the cod is cooked, carefully transfer the fillets to paper towels to drain the oil. Season the cod with fleur de sel.

TO SERVE

Place a cod fillet on each of four plates. Arrange 4 fingerling potato halves on each plate. Set a potato chip on each fingerling potato. Spoon a dollop each of the red pepper puree and the pil-pil sauce alongside the cod on each plate and serve. Garnish with amaranth leaves.

pil-pil sauce

MAKES ABOUT 2½ CUPS

2 cups olive oil
4 ounces meaty cod bones
2 large hard-boiled eggs
¾ cup water

1 garlic clove
1 teaspoon kosher salt
½ teaspoon freshly ground white
  pepper

Combine the olive oil and cod bones in a medium saucepan, pressing on the bones to submerge them completely. Slowly bring the oil to 140°F and cook the bones for 2 hours, or until the water from the fish and bones is released. Remove from the heat and remove the bones.

Using an immersion blender, blend the oil with the released liquid for 30 seconds. Strain the oil through a fine-mesh sieve into a container and refrigerate overnight.

The next day, the oil will have separated from the liquid. Carefully pour the oil into another container, leaving the liquid that has settled at the bottom behind; discard the liquid.

Peel the hard-boiled eggs and separate the whites and yolks; discard the yolks. Put the egg whites, water, garlic, salt, and white pepper in a blender and puree until smooth. With the blender running, gradually blend in enough of the cod-infused oil to form a smooth, creamy sauce. If the sauce is too thick, add a little more water to loosen it. Transfer the sauce to a container and keep cool. Refrigerate if not using immediately; bring to room temperature to serve.

pickled red pepper puree   MAKES A SCANT 1¼ CUPS

3 red bell peppers (about 1¼ pounds total), cored, seeded, and thinly sliced
½ cup sherry vinegar
½ cup water
3 tablespoons dry white wine

3 tablespoons granulated sugar
1½ tablespoons smoked paprika
½ teaspoon kosher salt
2 garlic cloves, crushed
1 bay leaf

Combine all the ingredients in a large saucepan and bring to a boil, then reduce the heat and simmer gently until the peppers are very tender, about 30 minutes. Transfer the pepper mixture to a container and set aside to cool; then refrigerate overnight.

Drain the peppers and discard the pickling liquid. Puree the peppers in a blender on high speed until very smooth. Press the puree through a fine-mesh sieve into a container. Cover and refrigerate for up to 2 days. Bring to room temperature before using.

potato chips

1 large russet (baking) potato (about
   1 pound)
About ⅓ cup Clarified Butter
   (page 31)

Kosher salt and freshly ground white
   pepper

Preheat a convection oven to 350°F with the fan on low speed.

Peel the potato. Using a mandoline, cut it into 1/16-inch-thick slices.

Line two heavy large baking sheets with parchment paper. Brush clarified butter over the parchment paper to coat. Sprinkle salt and white pepper all over the buttered paper. Lay the potato slices in a single layer on the baking sheets, spacing them so they do not touch. Brush clarified butter lightly over the potatoes and sprinkle with salt and white pepper. Place another sheet of parchment paper over the potatoes on each pan and set a baking sheet on top of the paper. Bake for about 45 minutes, until dark golden brown. After the chips have baked for 20 minutes, begin to check for doneness every 10 minutes.

Using a metal spatula, transfer the potato chips to a baking sheet lined with paper towels to drain. Serve warm.

This is French food of the Michel Guérard era—pristine and light, without rivers of cream and lakes of butter. To be sure, there's a little butter in the *nage*, a classic French poaching liquid for fish, but it's mostly white wine. Oh, and jalapeño, which I adore for its lip-tingling heat and its grassy flavor, plus a last-minute dose of yuzu kosho, a bright, salty paste of Japanese citrus and chile. And because I like the idea of American fish and chips I have used potato chips again as a garnish. Like so much of my food, the dish is France-meets-L.A.

john dory, jalapeño nage, broccolini, potato chips

SERVES 4

BROCCOLINI
12 ounces baby broccolini, stalks
    removed

JALAPEÑO NAGE
8 tablespoons (1 stick) unsalted butter
½ onion, julienned
5 jalapeño chiles, seeded and thinly
    sliced into rounds
3 cups dry white wine
1 cup water
¾ teaspoon yuzu kosho
Kosher salt

JOHN DORY
Four 6-ounce skinless John Dory
    fillets

GARNISHES
¼ cup assorted fresh herbs, such
    as tarragon, parsley, and chervil
    leaves and chopped chives
20 Potato Chips (page 283)

TO PREPARE THE BROCCOLINI
Blanch the broccolini in a large saucepan of boiling salted water for 1 minute. Drain and then add the broccolini to a large bowl of ice water to cool completely. Drain again and pat the broccolini dry with paper towels.

TO PREPARE THE JALAPEÑO NAGE

Melt 4 tablespoons of the butter in a large saucepan over medium heat. Add the onion and jalapeños and cook until tender, about 10 minutes. Add the wine and water and bring to a boil; then reduce the heat to medium-low and simmer gently for 20 minutes to infuse the liquid. Remove the pan from the heat and let steep for 20 minutes.

Strain the nage through a fine-mesh sieve into a skillet; discard the solids. Using an immersion blender, mix in the yuzu kosho and the remaining 4 tablespoons butter to blend. Season the nage to taste with salt.

TO PREPARE THE JOHN DORY

Bring the nage to 175°F over high heat, then reduce the heat to maintain the temperature. Lay the fish in the *nage* and cook until just opaque throughout, about 5 minutes.

TO SERVE

Lay the fish in four shallow soup plates and pour ½ cup of the nage over the fish in each plate. Add the broccolini florets to the nage and cook just until they are heated through; sprinkle with the herbs. Garnish each serving with 5 potato chips, propping them on top of broccolini and fish so they don't soften in the nage, and serve.

It almost killed me, this dish. People kept sending it back, because I'd decided to prepare the chicken sous-vide, the gentle heat doing such lovely things to the lean meat, but when you cook sous-vide, the chicken still looks slightly pink even though it's completely cooked. "No, it's not raw, and yes, I'm sure," I told table after table to no avail. What a shame! I mean, I was so proud of this dish. The flavors are rustic: they make you feel like you are eating at a farm. And all the components are prepared just right: incredibly moist chicken encased in crispy skin, a precisely poached egg, and salty, fatty chorizo as a light froth.

jidori™ half chicken, 65°c egg, chanterelles, chorizo froth

SERVES 2

CHICKEN

1 half Jidori™ chicken (3 to 4 pounds), thighbone removed
5 tablespoons olive oil
2 tablespoons plus 2 teaspoons smoked paprika
Kosher salt

EGG

1 very fresh large egg

CHANTERELLES

8 ounces chanterelle mushrooms, halved if large
1½ tablespoons olive oil
Kosher salt

2 tablespoons minced shallots
2 teaspoons finely diced garlic
2 teaspoons very finely chopped fresh flat-leaf parsley
Freshly ground white pepper

CHORIZO FROTH

2 ounces hot Spanish chorizo (preferably Palacios brand), casing removed and thinly sliced
1 cup whole milk
½ cup heavy cream
¼ teaspoon kosher salt
⅛ teaspoon granulated sugar
1 teaspoon soy lecithin

TO PREPARE THE CHICKEN

Prepare an immersion circulator for cooking at 140°F. Meanwhile, put the chicken, 3 tablespoons of the oil, and 2 tablespoons of the paprika in a sous-vide bag and vacuum-seal it at 99.9%.

Put the bag of chicken into the preheated circulator and cook for 1½ hours. Remove the chicken from the circulator and put it into an ice bath to cool.

TO PREPARE THE EGG

Prepare the circulator for cooking at 149°F (or 65°C). Put the egg in the preheated circulator and cook for 45 minutes. Remove the egg from the circulator and put it into an ice bath to cool—this helps set the white part of the egg without it being watery when served.

TO PREPARE THE CHANTERELLES

Fill a large bowl halfway with cold water. Put the chanterelles in the water, press them to the bottom of the bowl, gently stir them to loosen the dirt. Lift out the mushrooms and put them in a fine-mesh sieve to drain. Dump out the water, rinse out the bowl, and repeat the process 2 times, or until the water looks clean. Drain the mushrooms in the sieve for 5 minutes, then put them on paper towels to drain further.

TO PREPARE THE CHORIZO FROTH

Combine the chorizo, milk, cream, salt, and sugar in a small saucepan and bring to a slow simmer over medium-low heat; do not allow the mixture to boil. Reduce the heat and simmer very gently for 20 minutes.

With an immersion blender, break up the chorizo into smaller chunks, to add more flavor and color to the mixture. Strain the chorizo cream through a fine-mesh sieve and return to the saucepan. Using the immersion blender, mix the lecithin into the cream. Cover and keep hot.

Put the chicken and egg in the circulator, set at 149°F, for 15 minutes to rewarm them. Set the egg aside. Open the bag and transfer the chicken to a cooling rack to drain the excess liquid, then pat the chicken dry with paper towels.

Season the chicken on both sides with salt and sift the remaining 2 teaspoons paprika over it. Heat the remaining 2 tablespoons oil in a large sauté pan over medium-high heat until it begins to smoke. Using a large fish spatula, lift up the chicken and put it skin side down in the pan, then reduce the heat to medium and cook slowly to render the fat from the skin and make it crisp, rotating the chicken as needed, about 8 minutes. Turn the chicken over and cook until golden brown on the bottom, about 2 minutes. Set the chicken on paper towels to drain.

MEANWHILE, TO FINISH THE MUSHROOMS

Heat the olive oil in a medium sauté pan over medium-high heat until it begins to smoke. Add the mushrooms and cook, without stirring, until they are golden brown on the bottom, about 5 minutes. Season with a pinch of salt, then toss the mushrooms and reduce the heat to medium. Sprinkle the shallots over the mushrooms and toss. Reduce the heat to low and cook until the shallots and mushrooms are tender, about 2 minutes. Add the garlic and parsley, season with salt and pepper, and sauté until the garlic is tender and fragrant, about 2 minutes. Season the mushrooms to taste with salt and pepper.

TO SERVE

Put the chicken on a large plate and spoon the mushrooms alongside it. Gently crack the egg and place it alongside the chicken and mushrooms.

Using the immersion blender, blend the hot chorizo cream until frothy, then skim off the bubbles and spoon them over the egg to cover. Serve immediately.

This is it, the perfect steak. First, you take a perfect cut of beef, the fat-stippled rib eye, and marinate it in whiskey. Booze and beef is a common pairing in France, where cooks flambé steak au poivre with Cognac. But you don't often taste the spirit. Here the crust that forms on the outside of the steak has this incredible smokiness. It's so flavorful that you don't need a drop of sauce. Just a handful of smoky blistered shishito peppers, which I treat with a blowtorch and a smoking gun in my kitchen, but which you could instead toss for a minute or two in a very hot pan until charred.

Note: If you want to smoke the peppers, you'll need a PolyScience smoking gun, some whiskey-barrel wood chips, and a plastic container with a lid.

suntory-yamazaki-whiskey rib eye, smoked shishito peppers

SERVES 2

STEAKS
Two 12-ounce rib-eye steaks, well trimmed
⅔ cup Suntory Yamazaki single-malt whiskey
2 tablespoons olive oil

Kosher salt and freshly ground black pepper

SHISHITO PEPPERS
12 shishito peppers
Fleur de sel

TO MARINATE THE STEAKS
Combine the steaks and whiskey in a resealable plastic bag. Force out the extra air, then seal the bag and refrigerate overnight.

Lay the peppers on the back of a baking sheet and wave the flame of a blowtorch over the peppers, stopping to turn them occasionally until they are blackened on all sides and slightly wilted.

Put the peppers in a plastic container, cover but leave one corner of the lid open. Using the smoking gun, following the manufacturer's instructions, put one end of the smoking tube into the plastic container and to fill the container with smoke. Immediately seal the container and set the peppers aside to smoke for about 10 minutes.

TO COOK THE STEAKS

Heat the oil in a heavy large sauté pan over medium-high heat until it begins to smoke. Drain the steaks (do not pat them dry) and season on both sides with salt and pepper. Add the steaks to the sauté pan and cook until they are dark brown on both sides but still medium-rare in the center, about 2½ minutes per side. Transfer the steaks to a cutting board and let rest for 5 minutes.

TO SERVE

Slice the steaks and lay the slices on two plates. Arrange the peppers around the steaks, season them with fleur de sel, and serve.

The worst part about being a chef is that people never invite you to dinner. Friends worry that I won't like what they cook or that I'll judge them for turning out food that doesn't take ten hours, a blowtorch, and two hundred dollars' worth of foie gras. It's crazy! Because what they don't realize is how often I'm inspired by home-cooked meals. Like the time Will, my friend and the Ferdinand Magellan of many of my best Asian meals, invited me to have dinner with his family. His mother-in-law cooked *galbi* (Korean-style marinated short ribs) that was so good I gave up on polite conversation and started peppering her with questions about all her secrets. By the end of the night, she'd given me a recipe and Will's wife gave me a Korean cookbook. At LudoBites, I tweaked the marinade and applied it to flavorful, wonderfully chewy hanger steak, then embellished it with a fun deconstruction of kimchi: steamed cabbage doused with a butter infused with typical kimchi seasonings.

galbi steak, steamed cabbage, kimchi sauce

SERVES 6

STEAK

½ cup granulated sugar

⅓ cup water

¼ cup corn syrup

⅓ cup rice vinegar

¼ cup soy sauce

2 tablespoons toasted sesame oil

1 ounce fresh ginger, peeled and grated on a Microplane

2 garlic cloves, grated on a Microplane

¾ teaspoon freshly ground black pepper

6 (7-ounce) hanger steaks

1½ tablespoons olive oil

KIMCHI SAUCE

1 gelatin sheet

½ cup water

3 ounces unsalted butter, diced

1½ tablespoons rice vinegar

2 teaspoons Three Crab fish sauce

2 teaspoons fresh daikon, peeled and finely grated

2 teaspoons fresh ginger, peeled and finely grated

2 teaspoons sambal sauce

½ teaspoon garlic, finely grated

½ teaspoon honey

CABBAGE

4 green cabbage leaves
4 red cabbages leaves
2 teaspoons olive oil
Kosher salt

ACCOMPANIMENTS

Bone Marrow (page 294)
Pickled Vegetables (page 295)
6 shiso leaves, halved

TO PREPARE THE STEAKS

Combine the sugar, water, and corn syrup in a small saucepan and bring to a boil over medium-high heat, stirring until the sugar is dissolved, about 3 minutes. Remove the pan from the heat and add the vinegar, soy sauce, sesame oil, ginger, garlic, and black pepper. Using an immersion blender, blend the ingredients well. Cool the marinade completely.

Combine the steaks and the marinade in a container. Cover and refrigerate for 4 hours. Drain the marinade from the steaks then keep the steaks covered and refrigerated until you're ready to cook them.

TO MAKE KIMCHI SAUCE

Place the gelatin in a bowl of ice cold water and set aside until the gelatin softens, about 5 minutes. Meanwhile, bring the ½ cup of water to a boil in a small saucepan over high heat. Add the butter and blend with an immersion blender. Add the vinegar, fish sauce, daikon, ginger, sambal sauce, garlic, and honey, then blend well again with the immersion blender. Remove the gelatin from the ice water and stir it into the butter mixture until it is dissolved. Keep the sauce hot.

TO PREPARE CABBAGE

Boil water in a large saucepan. Add a little salt to the boiling water.

Using a 2-inch-round cutter, cut out 18 disks each of green cabbage leaves and red cabbage leaves.

Cook the green cabbage disks in the boiling water for 30 seconds, then remove the cabbage disks from the boiling water and transfer them to a bowl of ice water to cool. Remove the cabbage disks from the ice water and pat them dry with paper towels. Repeat with the red cabbage disks.

Heat the 1½ tablespoons of olive oil in a heavy large sauté pan over medium-high heat. When the pan begins to smoke, add the steaks. Reduce the heat to medium-low and cook the steaks until they are very dark on all sides (due to the marinade caramelizing) and the internal temperature of the steak registers 130°F to 135°F on an instant-read meat thermometer, about 3 minutes per side. Transfer the steaks to a cutting board and let rest for 3 minutes before slicing.

Meanwhile, steam the cabbage disks in a Japanese bamboo steamer until they are hot. Remove the cabbage disks from the steamer and toss them in a small bowl with the 2 teaspoons of olive oil and season them with salt.

Lay the green and red cabbage disks on 6 large plates. Spoon the kimchi sauce over the cabbage. Lay the steak slices on top of the cabbage. Place 2 slices of marrow alongside the steaks on each plate and top each plate with 3 slices of each pickled vegetable. Garnish with the shiso leaves and serve.

bone marrow

SERVES 6

BRINE

4 cups water

2 tablespoons hickory smoke powder

1 tablespoon kosher salt

6 beef marrow bones (about 1¾ pounds)

COOKING

2 tablespoons kosher salt

1 tablespoon hickory smoke powder

Sel de Guérande

TO BRINE THE MARROW BONES

Combine 4 cups of water, smoke powder, and salt in a small saucepan over high heat and stir just until the water is warm and the salt dissolves. Set the brine aside to cool to room temperature. Place the marrow bones in a container and cover with the brine (the bones should be completely submerged in the brine). Cover and refrigerate overnight.

Drain the bones; discard the marinade. Place the bones in a large saucepan, then add enough cold water to cover the bones completely (about 6 cups of water). Add the kosher salt and smoke powder and set the pan over medium-low heat. Bring the water to 175°F, then allow the bones to cook at this temperature for 2 minutes, or until bone marrow is very hot on the outside. Cooking the bones at this temperature and for just a couple of minutes ensures the marrow doesn't melt too much. Remove the bones from the water and set them aside until they are cool enough to handle. Using a paring knife, cut between the bone and the marrow to loosen the marrow and remove the marrow intact as a cylinder. Place the marrow in a bowl of ice water until it is firm again (like the same texture of cold butter). Cut the marrow into ¾-inch-thick rounds.

TO SERVE

Place the marrow slices on a sizzle platter or on the back of a heavy baking sheet. Using a blow torch, wave the flame over the top of the marrow slices until they are charred on top. Sprinkle the marrow with sel de Guérande and serve.

pickled vegetables

SERVES 6

2 cups water
1 cup rice vinegar
½ cup distilled white vinegar
2 tablespoons granulated sugar

1 cauliflower, florets only
1 small kohlrabi, peeled
1 watermelon radish

Combine the 2 cups of water, rice vinegar, white vinegar, and sugar in a small saucepan and bring to a simmer over high heat.

Cut the cauliflower florets, kohlrabi, and radish on a mandolin into 1-mm-thin slices. Place the cauliflower, kohlrabi, and radish slices in 3 separate vacuum bags and divide the pickling liquid among the bags, adding enough to each bag to submerge the vegetables completely. Set the bags aside until completely cooled. Vacuum seal the bags at 99% and refrigerate overnight.

Strange and wonderful, this unassuming stack of batons, arranged like the sticks that make up the children's game pick-up sticks, makes a surprising cheese course. Some of the sticks are firm Cantal cheese, others are white chocolate, and one is nearly impossible to distinguish from the other until you pop it in your mouth. The sweet and salty counterpunch is mirrored in the bits of candied Moroccan olives scattered on top, providing color and little explosions of flavor.

cantal cheese pick-up sticks, white chocolate, candied black olives

SERVES 4

CANDIED BLACK OLIVES
½ cup granulated sugar
½ cup water
30 oil-cured Moroccan black olives, pitted

PICK-UP STICKS
4 ounces high-quality white chocolate, chopped

One 4-ounce block (at least 5-inches long) Cantal cheese

YELLOW ASH
1 cup cubed baguette
3 tablespoons Clarified Butter (page 31)
2 teaspoons Madras curry powder

Extra-virgin olive oil

TO PREPARE THE CANDIED OLIVES

Preheat the oven to 100°F.

Combine the sugar and water in a heavy small saucepan and bring to a boil over medium-high heat, stirring until the sugar dissolves. Continue to boil, without stirring, until the mixture is syrupy, about 5 minutes.

Add the olives and cook over medium-low heat, without stirring, until the syrup reduces and coats the olives, about 10 minutes.

Spread the olives on a nonstick baking sheet so that they do not touch (discard the syrup) and bake for 3 hours, or until dry and crisp. Let the olives cool completely, then finely chop them. Set aside.

MEANWHILE, TO PREPARE THE PICK-UP STICKS

Cover a small baking sheet with plastic wrap. Stir the white chocolate in a small heatproof bowl set over a saucepan of simmering water until melted and smooth. Pour the melted chocolate onto the prepared baking sheet and spread it into a 9-by-6-inch rectangle. Refrigerate until the chocolate is set.

Cut the chocolate into 5-inch-long by ½-centimeter-wide sticks. Keep the sticks refrigerated.

Cut the cheese into 5-inch-long by ½-centimeter-thick sticks.

TO PREPARE THE ASH

Preheat the oven to 350°F.

Toss the bread cubes in a small bowl with the clarified butter to coat. Arrange the bread cubes on a baking sheet and bake until golden brown and crisp, about 15 minutes. Cool.

Combine the toasted bread cubes with the curry powder in a food processor and pulse until they become fine crumbs. Transfer the ash to a container and set aside at room temperature.

TO SERVE

Arrange the cheese and chocolate sticks on four plates so that they look like pick-up sticks. Sprinkle the candied olives and yellow ash over the pick-up sticks and the plates. Drizzle extra-virgin olive oil over and serve.

People always ask me where my inspiration comes from and I always give the same answer: everywhere. This dish is proof of that. I was having dinner at a Thai restaurant in L.A. called Talesai as a guest of the owner when I had an incredible curry dish with carrots. For some reason I immediately thought, I want these exact flavors in a dessert. Well, here you go. You like carrot cake, right? Then you have to try this. At LudoBites, we baked each cake to order, so it comes to the table warm, with the icing melting on top and a quenelle of icy mango sorbet on the side.

warm carrot cake, coconut, thai curry, mango sorbet, kaffir lime oil

SERVES 12

CREAM CHEESE FROSTING
8 tablespoons (1 stick) unsalted butter, at room temperature
8 ounces cream cheese, at room temperature
½ cup confectioners' sugar
1 tablespoon Thai yellow curry paste
⅛ teaspoon pure coconut extract

CAKES
1½ pounds carrots, peeled and cut crosswise into 1-inch chunks

2 cups all-purpose flour
1 tablespoon ground cinnamon
1 tablespoon baking powder
1 teaspoon kosher salt
4 jumbo eggs
1½ cups granulated sugar
1¼ cups grapeseed oil
1¼ cups chopped walnuts

ACCOMPANIMENTS
Mango Sorbet (recipe follows)
Kaffir Lime Oil (recipe follows)

TO MAKE THE FROSTING
In the bowl of a stand mixer fitted with the paddle attachment, beat the butter, cream cheese, confectioners' sugar, and curry paste until smooth and fluffy. Mix in the coconut extract. Use when cakes are baked, or transfer the frosting to a covered container and refrigerate for up to 2 days; allow the frosting to come to room temperature before using it.

Cook the carrots in a large saucepan of boiling water for about 25 minutes, until very tender.

Drain the carrots and puree in a blender until smooth. Measure out 2 cups of carrot puree to use in the cakes (reserve any remaining puree for another use).

Preheat the oven to 375°F. Butter and flour twelve 3-inch ring molds with 2-inch-high sides.

Stir together the flour, cinnamon, baking powder, and salt in a medium bowl.

Fit the stand mixer with the whip attachment and beat the eggs and sugar in the (clean) mixer bowl on high speed for 3 minutes. With the mixer running, slowly stream in the oil. Turn off the mixer and add the carrot puree, then mix on medium speed until fully incorporated. Turn off the mixer, add the dry ingredients, and mix on low speed until fully incorporated, about 30 seconds; do not overmix. Stir in the walnuts.

Spoon the batter into the prepared molds, dividing it equally. Bake for 25 minutes, or until a toothpick inserted into the center of a cake comes out with just a few crumbs attached. Cool slightly.

TO SERVE

Unmold the warm cakes and place 1 cake on each plate. Spoon the frosting onto the cakes. Spoon a scoop of mango sorbet onto each plate. Divide the kaffir lime oil among twelve small ramekins and serve them alongside the cakes for drizzling.

mango sorbet   MAKES ABOUT 3 CUPS

1 cup mango puree
1 cup Simple Syrup (recipe follows)
½ cup water

Stir together all the ingredients in a medium bowl. Freeze in an ice cream maker following the manufacturer's instructions.

Pack the sorbet into a freezer container and cover with plastic wrap pressed directly on the surface of the sorbet and then with the lid. Freeze until scoopable. (If you freeze the sorbet overnight, allow it to soften slightly before scooping it.)

simple syrup

MAKES 3 CUPS

2 cups water
²⁄₃ cup plus 1 tablespoon glucose or
   corn syrup
½ cup granulated sugar

Combine all the ingredients in a small saucepan and bring to a boil over high heat. Remove from the heat and allow the syrup to cool, then cover and refrigerate. The syrup will keep for a few months.

kaffir lime oil

MAKES ABOUT 1 CUP

½ cup fresh kaffir lime leaves
½ cup grapeseed oil

Combine the leaves and oil in a small saucepan and heat to 250°F. Remove the pan from the heat and let steep for 1 hour. Strain the oil into a container; discard the leaves. Store for up to 2 weeks.

This dish first appeared on my menu at Bastide. I love sweet salted caramel from Brittany and I wanted to create a dessert that played off this sweet-salty balance, but I did not want to just use salt. So I thought, why not replace the salt with caviar? Sounds logical, no? The oceanic salinity of the caviar would balance out the sweetness of the caramel, and the silky smooth creamy panna cotta finishes the triangular balance. I am only quoting Krissy here—she says, "It's the world's most perfect dessert."

crème fraîche panna cotta, caramel caviar

SERVES 16

Nonstick cooking spray or
    grapeseed oil
8 ounces crème fraîche (preferably
    Bellwether Farms brand)
1 cup heavy cream
1 cup whole milk
⅓ cup sugar

1 vanilla bean, split lengthwise
5 gelatin sheets
⅔ cup Caramel Sauce (recipe
    follows)
3 ounces American sturgeon caviar
Fleur de sel

TO PREPARE THE PANNA COTTA

Lightly coat an 8-inch square baking pan with cooking spray (or grapeseed oil). Press a sheet of plastic wrap into the pan, being careful not to wrinkle the plastic and making sure it is pressed into the corners. (Be careful not to tear the plastic: lift it away from the sides, then gently work it into the corners.) Use a flat plastic object (such as a credit card wiped clean with alcohol) to remove any large wrinkles, running a flat edge from the center of the pan out to the edges.

Stir the crème fraîche, cream, milk, and sugar in a large saucepan to blend. Scrape the seeds from the vanilla bean and stir the seeds and pod into the cream mixture. Bring to a simmer, stirring occasionally, over medium heat.

Meanwhile, soak the gelatin sheets in a bowl of cold water until softened, about 5 minutes.

Remove the softened gelatin from the water and add it to the hot cream mixture. Stir over medium-low heat until the gelatin dissolves. Transfer the cream mixture to a bowl and set it over another bowl of ice water; discard the vanilla pod. Using a silicone spatula, stir the cream mixture until it is cold and just beginning to thicken. (This will ensure that the vanilla seeds are suspended throughout the panna cotta.) Do not allow the mixture to thicken too much, and do not mix with a whisk, as that would incorporate air.

Pour the cream mixture into the prepared baking pan. Set the pan on a level surface in the refrigerator and refrigerate until the panna cotta is set, at least 6 hours, and up to 2 days.

TO SERVE

Invert the panna cotta onto a cutting board and gently pull off the plastic wrap. Using a very sharp knife dipped in warm water, cut the panna cotta into 1-inch-wide strips, then cut once across the strips to cut them in half.

Pour about 2 teaspoons of caramel sauce into the center of each plate. Using an offset icing spatula, spread the sauce in each plate into a rectangular shape about 6 inches by 2 inches. Using the spatula, carefully set the strips of panna cotta on top of the caramel sauce. Gather up some of the caviar in a line along the edge of a knife, then drop it onto the panna cotta strips in a line down the center, using about

2 teaspoons for each rectangle; repeat with the remaining caviar. Sprinkle a few grains of fleur de sel over each panna cotta and serve.

caramel sauce
MAKES ABOUT 1½ CUPS

1 cup granulated sugar
¼ cup water

1 cup heavy cream

Combine the sugar and water in a heavy small saucepan and bring to a boil over medium-high heat, stirring until the sugar dissolves. Boil without stirring until the caramel turns a very dark amber, occasionally brushing down the sides of the pan with a wet pastry brush to remove any sugar crystals and swirling the pan for even cooking, about 9 minutes. Test the darkness of your caramel by dipping a spoon into the caramel and dotting some of it onto a white plate (it will appear darker in the saucepan than it actually is, and checking with a white plate will ensure it is the proper color).

Remove the pan from the heat and slowly add the cream (the mixture will bubble vigorously). Using a long whisk, stir over low heat until the sauce is smooth. Let cool completely, then refrigerate until cold before serving.

KITCHEN  ROSTER

LUDO

GREG

JOON (4.0, 5.0, and 6.0)

GRACE (5.0 and 6.0)

SAM (lived in Utah)

ELODIE (2.0 and 3.0)

ROSANNA (hired for the last week)

RYAN (intern)

NIKKI (student)

SHARON (intern)

SABEL (student)

ERIKA (student)

ILA (blogger/student/intern)

FRED (Savage, just couldn't get enough)

In the seven months since the last LudoBites in Los Angeles, not only had Krissy and I gone on a cross-country tour to shoot a show for the Sundance Channel, setting up LudoBites for one night in each of six cities and discovering incredible food and people along the way, but we'd also celebrated the birth of our twins, Rêve and Luca. Their birth ushered in a rare glimpse of permanence in what had been for the last four years a provisional existence.

It was time to come back home, by which I mean L.A., and also, we'd realized, Gram & Papa's. Krissy and I had never felt so comfortable as we did there with the owner, Mike Ilic. He was like family, and our relationship was full of love and respect and dysfunction. With the twins and our crazy travels, we yearned to reinhabit a familiar place, like slipping on an old pair of jeans. Mike welcomed us back with open arms. LudoBites 7.0—or, as we came to call it, "007"—was born.

There was one problem. And it was a biggie. Sydney, my sous chef, my rock, had been swooped up by Joe Pytka to take over the stoves at Bastide. Joon "the Machine" and Frankie from 6.0 both joined him. My team was gone. Keeping employees at a pop-up restaurant is tough. It's one thing for Krissy and me to accept the impermanence and unpredictability. LudoBites is our show, our gamble, our glory. For our employees, it's just a job. To make matters worse, Krissy wouldn't be around as much, her time now dominated by our two little miracles.

OpenTable was on board again, and after the disastrous showings in 5.0 and 6.0, they seemed eager to prove they could handle the LudoBites reservations mob. This time the company's servers in San Francisco, which had the bandwidth to handle the traffic, would handle the reservations. Usually Krissy got to watch as the reservations were booked in real time, even as the system crashed. Not this time. She would have to sit at home, her only window into the process an OpenTable guy on speakerphone.

Reservation day came: July 14, Bastille Day, commemorating French independence. We had decided on the date hoping, superstitiously, that its symbolism (as LudoBites was the product of my own newfound independence) would bring us some luck. Krissy was sitting at our dining room table with a representative from OpenTable, counting down until our reservations went live at 4:00 P.M. She was so nervous: we had no Plan B—this had to work. Her trembling finger was hovering over her keyboard, ready to tell our Twitter and Facebook followers with a single click that the reservation system was live. 3, 2, 1 . . . Krissy clicked and we waited.

But not for long. Requests for reservations spiked to 120 per second. After a little more than 30 seconds, the voice on speakerphone reported that every available reservation, for twenty-two nights of service and two seatings per night, was gone. Bullshit, Krissy thought, sure the system had crashed again—how else could you explain it? OpenTable double-checked. There had been no crash: we were fully booked in under a minute.

It worked, maybe a little too well. While the folks at OpenTable celebrated, Krissy became more and more upset. Because once she told our Web guy to send out the e-blast announcing that we were fully booked (sent at 4:01 P.M. and processed by 4:06 P.M.), the e-mails came in fast and furious.

One of the coolest things about LudoBites is that there aren't the typical walls separating Krissy and me from the customers. Until this LudoBites, Krissy had responded to every single e-mail that came in. But this openness can be difficult too. In most restaurant operations, a marketing person or other employee deals with the wave of e-mails, weeding out those that are irrelevant or cruel. Not in our case. The wave engulfed Krissy, who had spent so much time and energy making customers happy from the moment they made a reservation to the time they left the restaurant. Now she was drowning in a bog of lamentation and outright vitriol. Some simply expressed frustration: "I logged on at 4:01 and it says you're out of tables. This sucks." Others decided to be assholes: "Fuck you, take me off the mailing list."

So, on this day of triumph, I came home to see Krissy crying. For her, the unhappy customers outweighed the success. She spent hours answering nasty e-mails, trying to explain the situation. The next morning, we were leaving with the twins for New York for a ten-day press tour for LudoBites America, which was about to air its first episode. Finally, Krissy did something she'd never done before. She stopped

answering the e-mails that were still flooding her inbox. The twins needed to be put to bed. Our travel plans had to be figured out. You can't make everyone happy. And family comes first.

Fortunately, by now I had found my kitchen team. In typical Joe Pytka fashion, he had closed Bastide again, and while Sydney was quickly snatched up by the Patina Group, Joon was ready to join us. The Machine was back! A great cook named Greg Bernhardt, who had worked at some of L.A.'s finest restaurants, would be my sous chef. They'd join Grace, my star student turned paid employee. Plus, I felt really good about the new menu, for which I both drew from my past (perfect scrambled eggs, an archetypal *Tropézienne*) and incorporated some of the cool ingredients and techniques I'd learned about on our road trip (including a gelée made from the spicy, vinegary liquid that sauces North Carolina barbecue).

Of course there were problems. For a couple of nights, we accidentally hosted a theme night: LudoBites, Sauna Edition. Hundred-degree weather and a busted AC made for a hot, steamy dining room one night for a private event for a group of bankers, all dressed in suits, and another night for our regular customers. It was miserable, the bouillabaisse milk shakes melting before they reached the tables and Krissy going from table to table holding a dusty old fan turned to high to offer everyone a few minutes of relief.

But most of my stress came from my students, my wonderful, hardworking employees—whom I occasionally wanted to put in the Robot Coupe. I had more students working at 007 than at any other LudoBites. Many of them had never worked in a restaurant kitchen. I wasn't sure how many of these green cooks would survive until the end. Sharon, a self-starter, was an ambitious home cook who brought in photos of stuff she'd made at home when she interviewed with me. I thought, Why not, let's

give her a go. If she falls on her face, she falls on her face. She was a perfectionist, for sure. One night, she was on the verge of tears when her tarts didn't look identical. I was almost OK with that, but I wasn't OK when she broke Kitchen Rule #1: she got into an argument with me in the middle of service. Maybe being a father had softened my heart, because instead of firing her on the spot, I gave her homework. She wrote "I will not argue with chef" one hundred times. Another student, Sabel, forgot to cross off the names of dishes from the tickets that told the kitchen staff what orders had already been delivered to diners, leading the kitchen to make twice as many duck breasts and chicken wings as we needed, I made her write my commandment to never fucking do that again a hundred times as well.

I even came close to firing Grace about three times. One night, she made only a third of the red wine mayo that she was supposed to. Instead of telling her to hit the road, I threw the bowl of mayo against the wall. I'm such an asshole sometimes, and that night, I ended up looking the part, my white chef's jacket spattered with red, looking as if I'd chosen to wear polka dots or had lost a knife fight.

Elodie, one of the first of the employees we hired while they were dining at LudoBites 1.0, had returned to help out. She was a hard worker and very talented, but she could really drive Mike and me nuts, always complaining that the fridge was broken or the oven wasn't good enough. Mike and I looked at each other, and thought, *No shit!* We were trying to put out life-changing food in a kitchen built for cooking turkey burgers. There's no complaining at LudoBites. You just have to make things happen with what you have.

As each LudoBites winds down, the craziness typically subsides. Krissy and I have time to circulate, chatting with new customers and posing for photos with friends and regulars. But on the second-to-last night, investigating the reason for our computer's shoddy behavior, we found it sitting in a pool of water on the floor upstairs. The computer was dead. This meant no printers for orders coming into the kitchen, no credit card processing, no nothing. Krissy was handwriting tickets, totaling checks on scrap paper, scribbling down credit card info, and praying that the payments could be processed later. That was a long night. Thank God there was light at the end of the tunnel.

The last night came, and to my surprise, every single one of the students had made it to the end. Sharon, Sable, Ryan, Nikki, Ila, and Erika, I'm proud of you guys. And of Fred Savage too, who graduated from peeling grapes to plating dishes on the line. After the final plate had gone out, Krissy and I shared a celebratory drink with the staff and began to feel that strange and familiar combination of relief and sadness. The stress would be over for a while, but this particular moment in time—the good, the bad, and the ugly—was gone forever. We went home that last night, kissed the twins good night, had a few shots of tequila, and passed out ourselves, wondering what was next.

KEVIN EATS A LOT

The blogger Kevin Eats is a maniac. He prides himself on being the first blogger to post about a restaurant, so he *always* has to eat on opening night. He had good luck during the first six iterations of LudoBites, but for 007, he too was screwed like so many by the "gone in sixty seconds" reservation process. What was he to do? Well, he just showed up. At 5:30 P.M. on opening night. Krissy saw him at the door, looking sheepish, and wondered what he was doing here. His name wasn't on the reservation list. We had no walk-in tables at Gram & Papa's. He said he was there hoping for a no-show. As service began, he stood close to Krissy, peering over her shoulder as she crossed off the names of arriving customers. It wasn't looking good. Finally, there was just one name left, a reservation for four. Only two people showed up. They were so apologetic, they offered to share their table with Kevin, who was still standing next to Krissy looking like a puppy who'd just spotted a big bone. So, yes, Kevin got to write about opening night at LudoBites 007. Because of the obsessiveness of people like him, we have an incredible permanent record of our temporary restaurant, a sort of online scrapbook put together by a thousand friends. In fact, a quarter of the photos in this book were taken by Kevin. Like I said, Kevin is a maniac. And we're so thankful for it.

There are many reasons I stopped serving bread at LudoBites, but most important among them: people eat bread, bread, and more bread, and then they're no longer hungry for my food. I wanted to start the meals off with something substantial but also interesting. So I crossbred two distinguished French tarts, the tarte flambée of Alsace and the pissaladière of Nice. Both share thin, crispy crusts covered with slow-cooked onions, but from there I pick and choose, adding the refreshing crème fraîche of the tarte flambée and the briny element of the pissaladière, replacing the latter's olives and anchovies with intense grated bottarga.

onion tart, caramelized onions, bottarga

SERVES 4

CARAMELIZED ONIONS

8 tablespoons (1 stick) unsalted butter
5 yellow onions (about 3 pounds), halved lengthwise and thinly sliced lengthwise
Pinch of kosher salt
2 teaspoons granulated sugar

DOUGH

½ cup lukewarm water (105° to 110°F)
1½ teaspoons active dry yeast
1½ cups all-purpose flour

1¼ teaspoons kosher salt
1 teaspoon olive oil

TOPPINGS

⅔ cup crème fraîche
¼ cup fromage blanc or plain Greek yogurt
About 2 ounces bottarga (preferably from Sicily or Sardinia)
Fleur de sel and freshly ground white pepper
About 1½ tablespoons fresh thyme leaves

TO CARAMELIZE THE ONIONS

Melt the butter in a large deep skillet over high heat until it bubbles. Add the onions and salt and cook until the onions are translucent, about 12 minutes. Add the sugar and cook over medium-low heat, stirring often, until the onions are browned and look caramelized, about 2 hours. Transfer the onions to a fine-mesh sieve set over a bowl to drain and cool.

MEANWHILE, TO MAKE THE DOUGH

Gently stir the water and yeast in a small bowl, then set aside until bubbles form on top of the mixture, about 5 minutes.

Sift the flour into the bowl of a stand mixer. Set the bowl in the mixer stand, fit it with the dough hook, and mix in the salt. Add the yeast mixture and mix in on low speed. With the machine running, add the oil and keep mixing until the dough has formed a shiny ball.

Transfer the dough to a work surface and divide it into 4 equal pieces. Shape each piece into a ball and set the balls on a lightly floured baking sheet. Cover the dough with a slightly dampened towel and let rise in a warm, draft-free place for 50 minutes, or until doubled in size.

TO PREPARE THE TARTS

Put a baking stone on the bottom rack of the oven and preheat the oven to 425°F.

Mix the crème fraîche and fromage blanc in a small bowl to blend.

On a lightly floured surface, roll out 1 dough ball into an oval about ⅛ inch thick and about 10½ inches long by 6½ inches wide. Transfer the dough to a floured pizza paddle. Spread about 3 tablespoons of the cream mixture over the dough, then scatter about ¼ cup of the caramelized onions on the top of the cream, spreading them with an offset spatula to cover the cream but without mixing it into the cream too much. Transfer the tart to the preheated baking stone and bake until you see some golden brown marbling on the top of the tart and the crust is golden brown on the bottom, about 12 minutes. Repeat with the remaining dough and toppings.

TO SERVE

Grate enough of the bottarga over the tarts as they come out of the oven to make a nice, uniform yellow layer. Sprinkle a small pinch of fleur de sel and some white pepper over each tart. Sprinkle about 1 teaspoon of thyme leaves over each tart, and serve immediately.

I can't bear to write a LudoBites menu that neglects chicken. I love to cook it, because the meat is a showcase for technique: without good technique, you won't have good chicken. Here the Jamaican flavor comes from the spice blend, a flavor-packed mixture of coriander seeds, allspice, cardamom, and other seasonings. But my technique is very French. After I brine the chicken wings, I plunge them into gently bubbling fat, which keeps the wings incredibly moist as they cook, then roast them to crisp the skin. The result is everything you've ever dreamed chicken wings could be.

At the restaurant, we thought it'd be nice to provide plastic gloves to the diners who ordered these, to spare them sticky, yellowish fingers. It resulted in some odd scenes. A few customers who spoke little English didn't understand their waiter's instructions and kept the gloves on throughout the meal. And chef Jon Shook, of Animal and Son of a Gun, who left his table for a cell phone call during dinner, was spotted chatting outside, gloves still on.

jamaican fried chicken wings

SERVES 8

BRINE
6 cups water
½ cup sugar
½ cup kosher salt

CHICKEN
24 chicken wings (about 5½ pounds)
5 ounces chicken skin
7 pounds high-quality lard
Cornstarch for dredging

JAMAICAN SAUCE
2 tablespoons black peppercorns

1 tablespoon coriander seeds
1 tablespoon annatto seeds
1½ teaspoons cumin seeds
¾ teaspoon whole allspice
2 tablespoons turmeric
1 tablespoon ground cardamom
1 teaspoon Madras curry powder
⅔ cup honey
1½ tablespoons chopped garlic
⅔ cup reduced-sodium soy sauce
⅔ cup rice vinegar
1½ teaspoons cornstarch
2 teaspoons water

TO MAKE THE BRINE

Combine the water, sugar, and salt in a large saucepan and bring to a boil over high heat, stirring until the sugar and salt dissolve. Cool the brine completely.

TO BRINE THE CHICKEN

Combine the brine and chicken wings in a large bowl. Cover and refrigerate for 24 hours.

TO MAKE THE SAUCE

Combine the peppercorns, coriander seeds, annatto seeds, cumin seeds, and all-spice in a spice grinder or clean coffee grinder and grind to a powder. Mix the ground spices with the turmeric, cardamom, and curry powder in a small bowl to blend well.

Combine the honey and garlic in a heavy medium saucepan and cook over medium-high heat until the garlic is fragrant, about 3 minutes. Stir in the soy sauce and rice vinegar, reduce the heat to medium, and simmer until the liquid is reduced to about 1⅓ cups, about 18 minutes.

Stir the cornstarch and water in a small bowl to blend, then stir the cornstarch mixture into the sauce, bring the sauce to a boil, and simmer for 1 minute. The sauce should be just thick enough to lightly coat the fried chicken wings; continue to simmer the sauce if it is too thin, or add a bit of water to make it thinner if necessary. Add ¼ cup of the spice mixture, then set the sauce aside to cool. (Store the remaining spice mixture in a jar with a tight-fitting lid for future use.)

TO PREPARE THE CHICKEN SKIN CRUMBLE

Line a small baking sheet with parchment paper and lay the chicken skin flat on the paper. Freeze the skin until it is solid, about 2 hours.

Melt the lard in a Dutch oven over medium heat and heat it to 400°F. Working in batches, dredge the frozen chicken skin in the cornstarch to coat lightly and fry until golden brown and crisp, about 5 minutes. Using tongs, transfer the fried chicken skin to a plate lined with paper towels to drain. Cool the fried chicken skin completely, then chop. Reduce the heat slightly to bring the lard down to 350°F.

TO COOK THE CHICKEN WINGS

Drain the chicken wings and pat them dry; be sure they are thoroughly dry, or they will cause the lard to splatter too much while frying. Working in batches, fry the chicken wings until golden brown and cooked through, about 10 minutes. Using tongs, transfer the wings to a baking sheet lined with paper towels to drain.

TO SERVE

Toss the wings in a large bowl with the Jamaican sauce to coat. Transfer the wings to a platter, garnish with the chicken skin crumble, and serve immediately.

Yeah, you read that right. This is indeed a cold, savory fish-soup milk shake, served in a glass with a straw. It's one of those dishes that reminds you that you can't please everyone. Most customers slurped it down and immediately ordered another round, but some pushed it away after the first sip. A few, like Krissy, were so revolted by the notion of the shake that they never even tried it. New foods will do that—they can provoke an emotional response. Yet I suggest you take at least two sips before you come to a conclusion. Challenge yourself! You'll be surprised at how quickly your preconceived notions melt away.

bouillabaisse milk shake   SERVES 6

BOUILLABAISSE
2½ pounds rockfish, cleaned and scaled
2 tablespoons olive oil
1 fennel bulb, trimmed and diced
½ onion, diced
3 garlic cloves, chopped
2 Roma (plum) tomatoes, diced
2 teaspoons tomato paste
1¾ cups dry white wine
4¼ cups water
3 fresh thyme sprigs

1 small bay leaf
½ teaspoon saffron threads

SAVORY ANGLAISE
¾ cup heavy cream
¾ cup whole milk
4 large egg yolks
Kosher salt
Piment d'Espelette
Extra-virgin olive oil

TO MAKE BOUILLABAISSE

Rinse the rockfish under cold running water. Cut each fish into 2-inch pieces.

Heat the oil in a heavy large pot over medium-high heat. Add the fish, fennel, onion, and garlic and cook until the vegetables are tender, about 5 minutes. Stir in the tomatoes and tomato paste, then stir in the wine. Bring to a simmer and simmer until the wine is reduced by half, about 15 minutes.

Add the water, thyme, and bay leaf, bring to a simmer, and simmer, stirring occasionally, until the fish falls apart and the tomatoes are very soft, about 45 minutes. Stir in the saffron and simmer for about 10 minutes to infuse the flavor.

Strain the cooking liquid and set the fish and vegetables aside. Measure out 3 cups cooking liquid, and freeze the cooking liquid in six ½-cup portions until semi-frozen.

Meanwhile, pass the fish and vegetables through the coarse disk of a food mill into a bowl. The pressed mixture will look like a coarse puree; discard any solids that remain in the food mill. Measure out 1½ cups of the bouillabaisse puree, and freeze in six ¼-cup portions until semi-frozen.

TO MAKE THE SAVORY ANGLAISE

Combine the cream and milk in a heavy medium saucepan and bring just to simmer over medium heat.

Meanwhile, whisk the yolks in a medium bowl to blend. Gradually add the cream mixture, whisking constantly. Return the mixture to the saucepan and stir constantly over medium heat until the sauce thickens and an instant-read thermometer registers 165° to 170°F, about 2 minutes; do not boil. Strain the sauce through a fine-mesh sieve into a medium bowl. Set the bowl over a bowl of ice water and stir the sauce until it is cold.

Freeze the anglaise in six ¼-cup portions until semi-frozen.

TO MAKE THE MILK SHAKES AND SERVE

Blend a semi-frozen ¼ cup bouillabaisse puree, ½ cup bouillabaisse liquid, and ¼ cup anglaise in a blender until thick, creamy, and frothy. Season to taste with salt and piment d'Espelette.

Pour the milk shake into a small glass, drizzle extra-virgin olive oil over it, and sprinkle piment d'Espelette on top to garnish. Serve, and repeat to make the remaining milk shakes.

I can't just have a menu full of crazy concoctions like bouillabaisse milk shakes—I have to balance it with some less risky dishes. And ceviche is almost always a home run. Customers go gaga over its bright flavor, and the wide range of ceviches out there gives me the ability to play with flavors and textures, to do something different and exciting even though I'm playing it safe. I came up with this particular version in Redondo Beach when we were filming our TV show, *Ludo Bites America*. I marinate the fish very briefly, so the interior stays raw and melt-in-your-mouth tender, and spoon on vivid green cucumber water tarted up with vinegar. The crunch of pickled onion and the lemony succulence of purslane (what Mexicans call *verdolaga*) keeps every bite exciting.

dorade ceviche, cucumber water, purslane SERVES 6

CEVICHE
12 ounces skinless dorade fillets, very thinly sliced crosswise
1 cup fresh lemon juice

PICKLED RED ONION
1 red onion, cut into ⅛-inch-thick rings
½ cup sherry vinegar

CUCUMBER WATER
2 hothouse cucumbers, very coarsely chopped

3 tablespoons white balsamic vinegar
1 tablespoon champagne vinegar
Kosher salt and freshly ground white pepper
½ teaspoon xanthan gum

GARNISHES
2 small jalapeño chiles, cut into very thin rounds
⅔ cup loosely packed fresh cilantro leaves
1 cup loosely packed purslane sprigs
12 borage flowers
Fleur de sel

TO PREPARE THE CEVICHE

Gently toss the dorade with the lemon juice in a medium bowl. Set aside for 30 minutes, or until the fish is opaque. Drain off the lemon juice and refrigerate the dorade until cold.

TO MAKE THE PICKLED ONION

Blanch the red onion in a small saucepan of boiling water for 30 seconds, then drain and quickly submerge the onion in a bowl of ice water until cold. Drain the onion again and transfer to a small bowl. Add the vinegar and marinate the onion for 1 hour.

Drain the onion again, return to the bowl, cover, and refrigerate.

TO PREPARE THE CUCUMBER WATER

Blend the cucumbers in a high-powered blender until smooth. Strain the cucumber water through a fine-mesh sieve into a medium bowl; discard the solids. You should have about 2 cups green cucumber water.

Stir the balsamic vinegar and champagne vinegar into the cucumber water to blend. Season to taste with salt and white pepper, then whisk in the xanthan gum to thicken slightly. Refrigerate until cold.

TO SERVE

Arrange the fish slices in six shallow soup plates. Spoon about 5 tablespoons of cucumber water over the fish in each plate, then scatter the pickled red onion over the fish. Garnish with the jalapeño slices, cilantro leaves, purslane, and borage flowers. Season each with a pinch of fleur de sel and serve immediately.

Most of the time, my dishes begin with a flavor—that of a memorable meal, of a childhood treat, of an imagined combination that drives me to create. But here color served as the initial inspiration. I had visions of a striking plate, the stark contrast of white and black with a splash of color, maybe something bright, like orange. The colors appear in frenetic splotches and spatters, like a Jackson Pollock painting. Ah, but what ingredients could create such a thing? First I thought of the pearly whiteness of squid, then, aha, its midnight-black ink! Chorizo goes so well with squid, so I infused it into half-and-half to make my orange paint.

squid, black ash, chorizo cream

SERVES 4

CHORIZO CREAM

1 cup half-and-half

6 ounces hot Spanish chorizo (preferably Palacios brand), casing removed and chopped

ASH

Three ⅓-inch-thick slices country-style white bread

½ cup olive oil

2 shallots, thinly sliced

Kosher salt and freshly ground black pepper

1 tablespoon squid ink

SPRING ONIONS

½ cup grapeseed oil

2 ounces hot Spanish chorizo (preferably Palacios brand), casing removed and chopped

12 spring onions, trimmed

INK SAUCE

1 tablespoon grapeseed oil

¼ cup chopped onions

¼ cup chopped celery

¼ cup chopped peeled carrot

3 large garlic cloves, thinly sliced

2 fresh thyme sprigs

8 cleaned squid heads

⅔ cup dry white wine

3 cups water

1 cup heavy cream

2 teaspoons squid ink

Kosher salt and freshly ground black pepper

SQUID

16 cleaned squid bodies

8 to 12 nasturtium leaves for garnish

Combine the half-and-half and chorizo in a small saucepan and bring to a simmer over medium heat; do not allow the mixture to boil. Reduce the heat to medium-low and simmer very gently for 10 minutes. Remove the pan from the heat and set aside to infuse for 1 hour.

Strain the chorizo mixture through a fine-mesh sieve into a bowl, pressing hard to extract all the liquid. Chill the chorizo cream until it is cold (the orange-colored fat will rise to the top of the chorizo cream).

Using an immersion blender, blend the fat into the chorizo cream until smooth and creamy. Keep chilled until ready to use.

TO MAKE THE ASH

Preheat the oven to 350°F. Toast the bread on a small baking sheet in the oven, about 20 minutes. Set the toast aside to cool. Leave the oven on.

Meanwhile, heat the oil in a small saucepan over medium heat until it reaches 325°F. Add the shallots and fry until golden brown, about 5 minutes. Using a spider or wide-meshed spoon, remove the shallots from the oil, and transfer to a plate lined with paper towels to drain. Season with salt and pepper and cool completely.

Pulse the toasted bread to fine crumbs in a food processor. Add the squid ink and pulse until the crumbs turn black. Add the fried shallots and pulse until everything is black in color.

Spread the bread mixture on a baking sheet and toast in the oven, stirring once, for about 8 minutes, until the mixture is dry. Set aside to cool completely.

Pulse the crumbs again in the food processor until very fine.

TO PREPARE THE ONIONS

Combine the oil and chorizo in a heavy small saucepan and heat over medium heat for 10 minutes. Remove the pan from the heat and set aside to infuse for 1 hour. Strain the oil through a fine-mesh sieve into a small bowl, pressing hard to extract all the oil.

Bring a large saucepan of water to a boil over high heat. Add the spring onions, reduce the heat to medium, and simmer for 2 minutes or until the onions are al dente. Drain and transfer them to a bowl of ice water until cold.

Drain the onions again and pat dry. Cut lengthwise in half and toss them in a bowl with the chorizo oil. Let marinate for 30 minutes.

MEANWHILE, TO MAKE THE SAUCE

Heat the oil in a heavy medium saucepan over medium heat. Add the onions, celery, carrot, garlic, thyme, and squid and sauté until the onions are translucent, about 5 minutes. Add the wine and simmer until it has evaporated.

Add the water, bring to a simmer, and simmer for 45 minutes, or until the liquid is reduced to 2 cups.

Strain the liquid into a heavy small saucepan; discard the vegetables and squid heads. Simmer until the liquid is reduced to ⅔ cup, about 15 minutes.

Add the cream and simmer until it has reduced by half and is beginning to thicken, about 20 minutes.

Whisk in the squid ink; the sauce will be black. Season to taste with salt and pepper. Keep the sauce hot.

TO FINISH THE DISH

Heat a large nonstick sauté pan over medium-high heat. Lay the spring onions in the pan cut side down and cook until they are golden brown, about 3 minutes.

Meanwhile, heat another large nonstick sauté pan over medium-high heat. Lay the squid bodies in the (dry) pan and cook until they are opaque throughout, about 4 minutes.

TO SERVE

Arrange the spring onions on four large plates. Spoon the chorizo cream Jackson-Pollock-style over the onions and the plates. Cut each cooked squid body into 3 to 4 pieces and arrange on the plates. Drizzle the sauce, "JP"-style over the squid, then sprinkle the ash on top. Garnish with 2 or 3 nasturtium leaves.

I can't even count the number of times I've put a dish of cod and potatoes on one of my menus. Here the classic pairing is the launching pad for a completely unusual dish. It's essentially brandade, teased apart and chilled. I make a light potato-mousseline ice cream and perch it on top of salt-cod panna cotta. Traditionally when you work with salt cod, you first soak it in milk, then discard the milk. I thought, why not use the milk and serve the cod to my staff for family meal? I have to admit, though, as excited as I was about what I'd come up with, I was afraid to serve it. Even I thought "fish panna cotta with potato ice cream" sounded strange. A ten-year-old girl at LudoBites had the best reaction. After her first tentative bite, she winced. Then she said the cutest thing to the server: "I didn't like it at first, but then the flavors came together on my tongue and I did." What a grown-up thing to say! That's how we all are, I think: reluctant at first to try new things, but ultimately open to and excited by new experiences when we scale the initial hurdle.

salt-cod panna cotta, smoked tapioca, potato-mousseline ice cream

SERVES 8

PANNA COTTA

2 ounces salt cod

1½ cups whole milk

½ head garlic, separated into cloves, peeled, and crushed

2 fresh thyme sprigs

2 tablespoons minced peeled fresh ginger

1 stalk lemongrass, crushed

6 gelatin sheets

1¼ cups plain Greek yogurt

1¾ cups crème fraîche

SMOKED TAPIOCA

2¼ cups water

1 teaspoon honey

¾ teaspoon liquid smoke

½ cup large pearl tapioca

Kosher salt

Two ⅓-inch-thick slices of olive bread, crusts removed

2 tablespoons olive oil

About 1½ cups Potato-Mousseline Ice Cream (recipe follows)

½ cup olive oil

½ cup elderflowers

TO MAKE THE PANNA COTTA

Rinse the salt cod under cold running water to remove any surface salt. Put the cod in a medium bowl and add enough cold water to cover. Let the salt cod soak in the refrigerator, changing the water every 6 hours, until it softens, 12 to 24 hours.

Drain the salt cod and put it in a heavy medium saucepan. Add the milk, garlic, and thyme and bring just to a simmer over medium heat. Reduce the heat to medium-low and simmer very gently until the cod begins to flake, about 30 minutes.

Strain the cooking liquid into a small bowl and set the cod aside. Add the ginger and lemongrass to the cooking liquid, cover, and let infuse for 20 minutes.

Strain the infused milk. Combine the reserved salt cod and the milk in a blender and puree until smooth. Strain the milk through a fine-mesh sieve into a bowl. Reserve 1 cup of the cod milk; discard any remaining milk.

Soak the gelatin in a bowl of cold water to soften, about 5 minutes.

Meanwhile, stir the reserved cod milk, the yogurt, and crème fraîche in a heavy small saucepan over medium heat until the mixture is at a near simmer. Remove the softened gelatin from the water and whisk it into the hot cream mixture until dissolved.

Arrange eight 8- to 10-ounce ramekins on a baking sheet. Pour the cream mixture into the ramekins, dividing it equally. Cool slightly, then cover and refrigerate until the panna cottas are set, at least 8 hours.

TO PREPARE THE TAPIOCA

Combine the water, honey, and liquid smoke in a small saucepan and bring to a boil over high heat. Stir in the tapioca, reduce the heat to medium-low, and simmer,

stirring occasionally, until the mixture thickens and the tapioca is tender, about 30 minutes. Remove the saucepan from the heat and set aside to cool for 20 minutes, stirring occasionally.

Season the tapioca to taste with salt.

TO MAKE CROUTONS

Preheat oven to 400°F.

Cut the bread into ⅓-inch cubes and toss with the olive oil in a bowl. Spread the croutons on a baking sheet and bake until toasted and crunchy, about 12 minutes.

TO SERVE

Spoon a quenelle of the potato ice cream atop each panna cotta. Drizzle the oil over the panna cotta to create a thin layer on top of each one. Spoon a tablespoon of the smoked tapioca alongside the ice cream. Garnish each panna cotta with about 5 croutons and a tablespoon of elderflowers and serve.

potato-mousseline ice cream   MAKES ABOUT 2½ CUPS

10 ounces fingerling potatoes
⅔ cup whole milk
⅔ cup heavy cream

6 large egg yolks
Kosher salt and freshly ground
    white pepper

Cook the potatoes in a large pot of boiling salted water until tender, about 25 minutes; drain.

While the potatoes are still hot, peel them and press them through the finest disk of a food mill into a bowl. Set the potato puree aside.

Combine the milk and cream in a heavy medium saucepan and bring just to a simmer.

Meanwhile, whisk the egg yolks in a medium bowl to blend. Gradually whisk one-fourth of the hot milk mixture into the egg yolks. Return the milk-egg mixture to the saucepan with the remaining hot milk mixture. Using a silicone spatula, stir the mixture over medium-low heat, scraping the bottom of the saucepan and stirring in figure eights, until the custard thickens and coats the back of a spoon, about 10 minutes. Strain the custard through a fine-mesh sieve into a bowl and set the bowl in an ice bath. Set aside to cool completely, stirring often.

Whisk the potato puree into the custard. Strain the custard through a fine-mesh sieve into a bowl, cover, and refrigerate until very cold.

About 45 minutes before serving, season the potato custard to taste with salt and white pepper. Freeze the custard in an ice cream machine according to the manufacturer's instructions. Serve immediately.

In LudoBites after LudoBites, I served eggs precisely poached in an immersion circulator. Sometimes I took the egg to 63°C, sometimes two degrees higher. I love both results, but to be honest, anyone with a circulator could make these eggs. You press a few buttons, and *voilà.* I wanted to get back to my roots, to the days when I was a teenager, and the great chef Marc Meneau showed me how to turn something as elemental as scrambled eggs into something incredible. A pan, a whisk, eggs, and butter. I watched as he whisked eggs in a figure-eight pattern over surprisingly low heat, the eggs slowly morphing into a loose, creamy, nearly curdless marvel. They were unlike any scrambled eggs I'd ever had. The key is in the timing, the mastery of which only comes with practice. Once you get it right, the sky's the limit, as long as you keep the focus on the eggs. Here all I do is fold in custard-like lobes of sea urchin roe and garnish them with a boozy beurre blanc and caviar.

egg, sea urchin, caviar, champagne beurre blanc SERVES 4

BEURRE BLANC
3 cups Champagne
4 shallots, finely minced
6 tablespoons unsalted butter, at room temperature
Kosher salt and freshly ground white pepper

EGGS
6 tablespoons unsalted butter
¼ cup finely minced onion

8 large eggs, beaten to blend
8 lobes sea urchin roe (uni)
Kosher salt and freshly ground white pepper

GARNISHES
¼ cup hackleback caviar
8 chive flowers

TO MAKE THE BEURRE BLANC

Combine the Champagne and shallots in a heavy medium saucepan, bring to a simmer over medium heat, and simmer until the Champagne is reduced to ⅓ cup, about 15 minutes.

Gradually whisk in the butter to form a smooth, creamy sauce. Strain the sauce into a small saucepan and discard the shallots. Season the sauce to taste with salt and white pepper and keep warm in a water bath.

TO MAKE THE EGGS

Melt the butter in a heavy medium saucepan over medium-low heat. Add the onion and sauté until translucent, about 3 minutes. Whisk in the eggs and cook, whisking constantly and briskly, until the eggs just become creamy and thicken slightly (they should not be at all lumpy), about 5 minutes. Remove from the heat, whisk in the sea urchin roe, and season to taste with salt and white pepper.

TO SERVE

Spoon the eggs into four small bowls. Spoon about 1½ tablespoons of the beurre blanc over the eggs in each bowl. Spoon 1 tablespoon of the caviar on top of each, garnish with the chive flowers, and serve immediately.

There are so many tricks to making octopus tender, and they're all bullshit. People tell you to add vinegar or a cork to the water—or drive over the octopus with a car. I'm serious, I've actually heard this last one! When, after trying my octopus, customers ask for my secret, I tell them: cook it slowly until it's really tender. That's all. Sometimes that takes two hours, sometimes three. But forget about the time: just feel it, touch it, taste it. When it's done, it's done.

Ah, and then the fun begins, because all you have to do once it's tender is to sear it on a scorching-hot surface. I marinate it first in a spice mixture inspired by the one Indian cooks use for meats cooked in a tandoor oven. Then I finish it with some tangy yogurt, crunchy shavings of raw cauliflower, and tart grapefruit segments.

tandoori octopus, yogurt, cauliflower, grapefruit

SERVES 8

OCTOPUS

2 tablespoons grapeseed oil
1 onion, coarsely chopped
1 carrot, peeled and coarsely chopped
1 celery stalk, coarsely chopped
1 head garlic, halved horizontally
3 fresh thyme sprigs
8 cups water
4 cups dry white wine
2 large octopuses (about 2 pounds each), rinsed
2 tablespoons olive oil
Kosher salt and freshly ground white pepper

MARINADE

1¼ cups jarred tandoori paste
¼ cup tomato sauce
1½ tablespoons honey
1 tablespoon molasses
1 tablespoon sherry vinegar

YOGURT SAUCE

⅓ cup goat's-milk yogurt
⅓ cup Greek yogurt
Kosher salt

GARNISHES
1 large pink grapefruit, suprêmed
    (page 49)
¼ head cauliflower
Kosher salt and freshly ground white
    pepper

Olive oil
Fleur de sel

TO PREPARE THE OCTOPUS

Heat the grapeseed oil in a 6-quart pot over medium-high heat. Add the onion, carrot, celery, garlic, and thyme and sauté until the onion is translucent, about 5 minutes. Add the water and wine and bring to a simmer. Add the octopuses and bring the liquid to a near simmer, then reduce the heat to low, cover the octopuses with a small weight so that they are submerged, and simmer very gently for about 2 hours, or until a small knife glides easily through one of the octopus arms. (Never allow the water to boil or the skin will fall away; slow and gentle is the key.)

Remove the octopuses from the cooking liquid and let cool. (Discard the cooking liquid.) Cut each of the 8 octopus legs away from the head; discard the head.

TO MARINATE THE OCTOPUS

Mix all the marinade ingredients in a large bowl to blend. Add the octopus legs and toss them to coat completely. Refrigerate for 6 hours.

MEANWHILE, TO MAKE THE SAUCE

Mix the yogurts in a small bowl to blend. Season to taste with salt. Cover and refrigerate.

TO PREPARE THE GARNISHES

Cut the grapefruit segments into small dice; set aside.

Remove the stems from the cauliflower florets. Using a mandoline, cut the florets into 2-inch-thick slices.

Heat the olive oil in a large cast-iron skillet over high heat. Remove the octopus legs from the marinade and lightly shake off the excess marinade; the octopus should still be well coated. Add the octopus legs to the hot skillet and cook for about 3 minutes per side, or until almost black. Transfer to a cutting board.

Spoon about 1 tablespoon of the yogurt sauce into the center of each of eight plates. Mix the grapefruit and cauliflower in a bowl and season to taste with salt and white pepper. Place about 1 tablespoon of the grapefruit mixture on top of the yogurt on each plate. Cut each octopus leg into 3 pieces and arrange them on top of the grapefruit mixture. Lightly drizzle with olive oil, sprinkle lightly with fleur de sel, and serve immediately.

There's this amazing dish called *canard au sang* (literally "blood duck"), known here as pressed duck. At L'Espérance, I learned what it was. The waiters would present diners with a beautifully roasted duck and carve it tableside. Then they'd take the bones and put them into a giant gleaming press (made specifically for this purpose), and out came a bloodred liquid that they used to fortify a sauce. It's as if you put the duck in a juicer to extract every last bit of flavor! Oh my god, it's incredible. I *almost* decided to do this at LudoBites. I even found the press at Sur La Table, selling for $2,000. But Krissy would've killed me if I'd bought it. So instead, I decided on stand-ins for the deep-red color: summer cherries and beets. The sausage component (not made into links, don't worry!) was inspired by the duck on the lunch menu at Ssäm Bar, one of David Chang's New York City restaurants, where he served me an amazing roast bird with sausage tucked beneath the skin.

duck, cherry sauce, spicy saucisse, beets, radish

SERVES 6

CHERRY SAUCE
2½ pounds fresh Bing cherries, pitted
2 tablespoons red wine vinegar
6 tablespoons unsalted butter, diced
    and chilled
Kosher salt and freshly ground black
    pepper

SAUCISSE
12 ounces ground duck
1½ teaspoons crushed dried red chiles
Kosher salt

DUCK
6 boneless duck breasts, cleaned of
    silverskin and excess fat

Kosher salt and freshly ground black
    pepper

BEET GARNISH
4 baby beets (preferably assorted
    colors), scrubbed, sliced paper-thin
    on a mandoline
2 small black radishes, peeled, sliced
    paper-thin on a mandoline
1 tablespoon fresh lemon juice
2 tablespoons extra-virgin olive oil
Kosher salt and freshly ground white
    pepper

Juice the cherries. Pass the juice through a fine-mesh sieve; discard the pulp.

Bring the juice to a simmer in a small saucepan and simmer for 5 minutes.

Strain the sauce through a fine-mesh sieve, pressing on the solids to release all the liquid, and pour into another small saucepan. You should have about 1⅓ cups cherry juice.

Simmer the juice until it is reduced to ⅔ cup, about 5 minutes. Whisk in the vinegar, then gradually add the butter, whisking constantly. Season the sauce to taste with salt and pepper. Keep warm in a water bath.

MEANWHILE, TO PREPARE THE SAUCISSE

Mix the ground duck meat and chiles in a medium bowl to blend. Form the mixture into six 2-ounce patties.

TO COOK THE DUCK

Score the skin of each duck breast, then season the duck breasts on both sides with salt and pepper. Heat a heavy large skillet over medium heat. Put the duck breasts skin side down in the pan and cook for 8 to 10 minutes, or until the skin is golden brown and crisp. Turn the breasts over and cook for 3 minutes longer, or until cooked to medium-rare. Transfer the duck breasts to a cutting board and let rest for 5 minutes.

Meanwhile, return the skillet to medium heat. Season the saucisses with salt and cook them in the rendered duck fat for 3 minutes on each side until browned.

TO SERVE

Rinse the sliced beets and radishes and pat dry. Toss the sliced beets and radishes with the lemon juice and oil in a large bowl. Season to taste with salt and pepper.

Pour the warm sauce into six shallow soup plates. Cut each duck breast into 2 pieces and place them atop the sauce. Set a sausage patty alongside each breast. Top with the radishes and beets and serve immediately.

In France, of course, we often end dinner with a little cheese. But I feel bad charging customers triple for what they could get at a nice cheese shop, online, or even at Whole Foods. So I take my favorite cheese, the creamy, pungent Époisses of Burgundy, and fold it into risotto. To up the richness even more, I top each portion with an egg yolk, to be stirred in by the diner, and then, to counter that richness, I serve the risotto with a bright herb-heavy salad.

époisses cheese risotto, hazelnuts, egg yolk, herb salad

SERVES 8

RISOTTO
2 cups Arborio rice
2 tablespoons unsalted butter
¼ cup chopped shallots
1 cup dry white wine
4 ounces Époisses cheese
About ¾ cup heavy cream
Kosher salt and freshly ground white pepper

HERB SALAD
⅔ cup fresh chervil leaves
⅔ cup fresh flat-leaf parsley leaves
⅔ cup fresh tarragon leaves
⅔ cup micro sorrel leaves
1½ tablespoons fresh lemon juice
1½ tablespoons extra-virgin olive oil
Kosher salt and freshly ground black pepper

GARNISH
⅓ cup hazelnuts, toasted, skinned, and finely chopped
8 large fresh eggs

TO MAKE THE RISOTTO

Bring 4½ cups of water to a boil in a heavy small saucepan. Cover and keep warm over low heat.

Meanwhile, stir the rice in a dry large skillet over medium-high heat until toasted and golden, about 12 minutes. Set aside.

Melt the butter in a heavy large saucepan over medium heat. Add the shallots and sauté until tender, about 2 minutes. Stir in the rice, then add the wine and water. Bring the liquid to a boil, then reduce the heat to medium and cook, stirring constantly, until the rice is al dente, about 10 minutes. Remove the pan from the heat and stir in the Époisses. Stir in enough cream to create a thick, creamy consistency and season the risotto to taste with salt and white pepper. As the risotto sits, it will continue to thicken; add a bit more cream before serving if necessary.

TO PREPARE THE HERB SALAD

Toss all the herbs in a medium bowl with the lemon juice and olive oil to coat, then season to taste with salt and pepper.

TO SERVE

Spoon the risotto into eight shallow bowls. Sprinkle the hazelnuts over the risotto. Crack an egg into a cup, separate the yolk from the white, and place the yolk on top of a serving of risotto. Repeat with the remaining eggs (reserve the egg whites for another use, if desired). Scatter the herb salad over the risotto and serve immediately.

This treat is two desserts in one, a merging of Escoffier's famous creation for opera singer Nellie Melba and the French classic *vacherin*, which brings the chewy crunch of meringue. The addition of lavender was inspired by Alain Giraud, the chef before me at Bastide, who served a simple vacherin with vanilla ice cream and lavender that is among the finest desserts I've ever eaten.

peach melba vacherin, lavender chantilly cream

SERVES 8

MERINGUES

2 large egg whites
¼ cup granulated sugar
½ cup confectioners' sugar,
    sifted

PEACHES

2 cups sugar
1 cup water
4 white or yellow peaches

RASPBERRY COULIS

1¼ cups raspberry sorbet, melted
1¼ teaspoons granulated sugar
1¼ teaspoons red wine raspberry
    vinegar
¼ teaspoon xanthan gum

LAVENDER CHANTILLY CREAM

1½ cups heavy cream
3 tablespoons confectioners' sugar
1½ teaspoons ground dried edible
    lavender flowers

FOR SERVING

About 3 cups Vanilla Ice Cream
    (recipe follows)

GARNISHES

Confectioners' sugar
Ground dried edible lavender flowers
6 fresh edible lavender sprigs

Preheat the oven to 150°F. Line two heavy large baking sheets with parchment paper.

In the bowl of a stand mixer fitted with the whisk attachment, beat the egg whites and granulated sugar until very soft peaks form when the whisk is lifted. With the machine running on low, add the confectioners' sugar 1 tablespoon at a time, then beat on medium-high speed until firm peaks form when the whisk is lifted from the meringue.

Put the meringue in a pastry bag fitted with a plain tip. Pipe the meringue onto the prepared baking sheets, making 4-inch-long strips that are about ½ inch wide. Bake for 1½ hours, or until firm. Transfer the baking sheets to a rack and cool the meringues completely. (You'll have more meringues than needed; store the extras in a sealed container at room temperature.)

TO PREPARE THE PEACHES

Combine the sugar and water in a saucepan that's just large enough to hold the peaches in a single layer and bring to a boil over high heat, stirring to dissolve the sugar. Add the whole peaches and simmer over medium-low heat until they are just tender but not soft and mushy, about 7 minutes. Using a slotted spoon, transfer the peaches to a large bowl of ice water to cool completely, about 30 minutes; discard the poaching syrup.

Remove the peaches from the water and refrigerate.

TO MAKE THE COULIS

Whisk all the ingredients in a heavy small saucepan and bring to a boil over high heat, whisking often. Pour the coulis into a bowl and set the bowl in an ice bath to cool completely. Refrigerate until ready to use.

TO PREPARE THE CHANTILLY

Combine the cream, confectioners' sugar, and lavender in the bowl of the stand mixer, fitted with the clean whisk attachment, and beat just until firm peaks form

(you may also use a hand mixer); do not overwhip the cream, or it will curdle. Transfer the whipped cream to a pastry bag fitted with a large plain tip and refrigerate.

TO SERVE

Spoon the raspberry coulis into the center of eight soup plates. Tilt the plates to cover the bottoms with the coulis. Slice the peaches in half and remove the pits. Place 1 peach half, cut side up, in each soup plate. Spoon the ice cream atop the peaches. Top with the Chantilly cream, then dust with confectioners' sugar and ground dried lavender. Garnish each serving with a few meringues and the lavender sprigs and serve immediately.

vanilla ice cream

MAKES ABOUT 4 CUPS

2 cups whole milk
2 cups heavy cream
½ vanilla bean, split lengthwise

6 large egg yolks
⅓ cup granulated sugar

Combine the milk and cream in a heavy medium saucepan. Scrape the seeds from the vanilla bean and add to the milk mixture, along with the pod. Bring to a simmer over medium-high heat. Remove from the heat.

Meanwhile, whisk the egg yolks and sugar in a large bowl to blend. Gradually whisk in the hot milk mixture. Return the mixture to the saucepan and, using a silicone spatula, stir over low heat just until the custard thickens and leaves a path on the back of the spatula when you draw your finger across it, about 10 minutes; do not allow the custard to boil. Strain the custard through a fine-mesh strainer into a large bowl, set the bowl over another large bowl of ice water, and stir until the custard is cold. Cover and refrigerate for at least 2 hours.

Freeze the custard in an ice cream maker according to the manufacturer's instructions. Pack the ice cream into a freezer container, cover with plastic wrap and then the lid, and freeze until firm, at least 4 hours.

I love taking an iconic dish, breaking it apart, and putting it back together again—often upside down or inside out. Yet for this dish, I returned to my roots and set about faithfully re-creating the celebrated dessert from Saint-Tropez, brioche sandwiching cream. I barely put my spin on it. Nothing creative (except the lavender), nothing froufrou, and certainly nothing molecular. This is not intellectual food—it's just plain good.

SERVES 12

lavender tropézienne

DOUGH

¼ cup lukewarm whole milk (105° to 110°F)

1 tablespoon plus ½ teaspoon active dry yeast

1¾ cups all-purpose flour

2½ tablespoons granulated sugar

½ teaspoon kosher salt

2 large eggs

1 large egg yolk

6 tablespoons unsalted butter, cut into chunks, at room temperature

Nonstick cooking spray

CRUMBLE TOPPING

⅓ cup all-purpose flour

⅓ cup granulated sugar

2 tablespoons unsalted butter

Lavender Pastry Cream (recipe follows)

GARNISHES

Confectioners' sugar

12 fresh edible lavender sprigs

TO MAKE THE DOUGH

Stir the warm milk and yeast in a small bowl and let stand until the yeast dissolves, about 10 minutes.

In the bowl of a stand mixer fitted with the paddle attachment, mix the flour, sugar, and salt to blend well. Add the eggs, egg yolk, and yeast mixture, and beat on medium speed until the dough is smooth and elastic, about 2 minutes (the dough will be very sticky). With the machine running, gradually add the butter, beating until well blended.

Line a heavy large baking sheet with parchment paper. Transfer the dough to a pastry bag fitted with a large plain tip and pipe the dough into 12 mounds on the baking sheet, using about 2 tablespoons of dough for each mound and spacing the mounds evenly; since the dough is sticky, it's helpful to cut the dough with scissors after piping each mound. Alternatively, you can just drop the dough onto the baking sheet with a spoon.

Spray a large sheet of plastic wrap with nonstick cooking spray and cover the dough. Let the dough mounds rise in a warm, draft-free area until doubled in size, about 2 hours. Reshape any misshaped mounds if necessary.

MEANWHILE, TO MAKE THE CRUMBLE TOPPING

Using your fingers, mix the flour, sugar, and butter in a small bowl until little crumbs form.

Preheat the oven to 350°F.

TO BAKE THE TROPÉZIENNE

Sprinkle the crumble topping generously over the risen dough mounds. Bake until they are golden brown on the bottom and lightly browned on top, about 10 minutes.

TO SERVE

Cut each brioche horizontally in half. Set the bottom halves in the center of twelve plates. Spoon the pastry cream over the bottom halves, then cover with the brioche tops. Sift confectioners' sugar over the tropéziennes, garnish with the fresh lavender, and serve immediately.

lavender pastry cream

MAKES ABOUT 2½ CUPS

12 tablespoons (1½ sticks) unsalted
    butter, at room temperature
¾ cup granulated sugar
6 large egg yolks
3 cups whole milk

1½ vanilla beans, split lengthwise
½ cup all-purpose flour
¾ teaspoon ground dried edible
    lavender

In the bowl of a stand mixer fitted with the paddle attachment, beat the butter and ¼ cup of the sugar until well blended and pale yellow. Beat in 1 of the egg yolks and continue beating until well blended, smooth, and creamy. Set aside.

Put the milk in a heavy medium saucepan. Scrape the seeds from the vanilla beans into the milk, then add the pods. Bring the milk just to a simmer over medium-high heat. Meanwhile, beat the remaining 5 egg yolks, the remaining ½ cup of sugar, the flour, and lavender in a medium bowl to blend. Gradually whisk some of the hot milk into the egg mixture, then whisk the egg mixture back into the remaining milk in the saucepan. Add the butter mixture and whisk vigorously over medium heat for about 5 minutes, or until the mixture looks like a thick pudding and bubbles begin to break the surface.

Strain the pastry cream through a fine-mesh strainer into a bowl. Cover the surface of the pastry cream with plastic wrap and refrigerate for at least 3 hours before using.

BLOG LIST

To all of the writers and photographers who covered Ludobites on their blogs—thank you. Jonathan Gold wrote, "There are restaurants that food bloggers like. There are restaurants that food bloggers adore. And then there is LudoBites, a pop-up restaurant that sometimes seems as if it is run for the sole benefit of food bloggers, who cop scarce reservations online, tweet the wine, and photograph every course with the intensity of Annie Leibovitz cooped up with the Rolling Stones. If on a Thursday night there is a person in the house who doesn't sport at least a Twitter feed, I would be very surprised." Let us add: We adore you.

www.alli411.com/

www.kevineats.com

www.theglutster.com

www.twohungrypandas.com

www.eatsmeetswest.com

www.kungfoodpanda.com

www.rantsandcraves.com

www.gastronomyblog.com

www.gourmetpigs.blogspot.com

dianatakesabite.blogspot.com/

theactivefoodie.blogspot.com/

www.carolineoncrack.com

www.foodgps.com

www.darindines.com

www.laist.com

www.hungryhungryhanh.com

www.mattatouille.com

www.estarla.com

elizainhollywood.com

missionfruition.com

fooditude.wordpress.com

foodshethought.blogspot.com/

la-oc-foodie.blogspot.com/

theroamingbelly.blogspot.com/

www.nomsnotbombs.com/

www.savoryhunter.com

designnomad.blogspot.com

www.djjewelz.com/

theminty.com/

www.weezermonkey.com/

fforfood.blogspot.com/

gastronomnom.com/

www.theravenouscouple.com/

choisauce.wordpress.com/

www.foodjetaime.com/

www.oneforthetable.com

www.mylastbite.com

www.ladlesandjellyspoons.com/

tomostyle.wordpress.com/

www.freshmaninthekitchen.com

gastrophoria.blogspot.com

onemorebiteblog.blogspot.com

uncouthed.com/

www.mylifeasafoodie.com/

www.thisfoodieslife.com

lainstilettos.com

marisaleemiller.blogspot.com

lizziee.wordpress.com

www.thegourmetreview.com

www.savoryhunter.com

www.yoculinario.com

www.tastychronicles.com

www.rockmypalate.com

madhungrywoman.com

bryansander.com

www.danieleats.com

www.deependdining.com

www.inomthings.com

www.advancedhealing.com

www.brunelloshavemorefun.com

thesensualfoodie.com

www.southbayrantsnraves.com

www.thecattycritic.com

tangbro1.blogspot.com/

www.kat9lives.com

dishingupdelights.thedailymeal.com

damontucker.com

www.k1sworld.com

Docsconz.com

Vealcheeks.blogspot.com

www.chuckeats.com

www.opinionatedaboutdining.com

scentofgreenbananas.blogspot.com

epicuryan.com

fooddestination.blogspot.com

yutjangsah.blogspot.com

www.ladlesandjellyspoons.com

SUPPLIER LIST

Specialty Ingredients

TERRASPICE.COM You can find any specialty ingredient needed for modern cooking techniques (e.g., xanthan gum, agar-agar) under the heading "Industrial Ingredients."

Meat

Los Angeles: Lindy & Grundy—801 N. Fairfax, Los Angeles, CA 90046
New York: Dickinson's Farmstand Meats, www.dickinsfarmstand.com/store/
Chicago: The Butcher and Larder, www.thebutcherandthelarder.com
        Publican Qaulity Meats, www.publicanqualitymeats.com
Miami: Smitty's Old Fashioned Butcher Shop, www.smittysmeatandwine.com

The most important thing when buying meat is to make sure the cattle are hormone- and antibiotic-free. If you don't have a butcher in your hometown, you can always order online. I have visited the ranches of Little Red Barn in Nebraska and they raise some great cattle: www.littleredbarnbeef.com.

JIDORI CHICKEN *Jidori* is a Japanese term that means "chicken of the earth." True Jidori Chicken™ is a brand of chicken that is processed and sold by Mao Foods, Inc., in Los Angeles. This makes Jidori Chicken™ readily accessible to L.A. chefs, but not so accessible to the rest of the country. If you are unable to obtain Jidori Chicken™, you may substitute any cage-free, all-natural grain-fed, and hormone-free chicken, but if you can track some of the real stuff, it is worth it: www.Jidorichicken.com.

INDEX

Note: Page references in *italics* indicate photographs of completed recipes.

PHOTOGRAPH CREDITS

Page i: Colin Young-Wolff

Page v: Colin Young-Wolff

Page vi: Shayla Deluy

Page ix: Anne Fishbein

Page x: Colin Young-Wolff; painting by Matt Scofield

Page 5: *top,* Krissy Lefebvre; *bottom,* Eugene Lee

Page 8: Eugene Lee

Page 10: William Furniss

Page 13: Eugene Lee

Page 14: Eugene Lee

Page 15: *top,* Krissy Lefebvre; *bottom,* Eugene Lee

Page 17: William Furniss

Page 18 Anne Fishbein

Page 23: Wesley Wong

Page 24: Anne Fishbein

Page 26: Shayla Deluy

Page 29: *left,* Eugene Lee; *right,* Anne Fishbein

Page 33: Krissy Lefebvre

Page 40: Krissy Lefebvre

Page 43: *left,* Shayla Deluy; *right,* Krissy Lefebvre

Page 48: *left and right,* Shayla Deluy

Page 55: Shayla Deluy

Page 60: Shayla Deluy

Page 62: Krissy Lefebvre

Page 65: Shayla Deluy

Page 66: Anne Fishbein

Page 70: *top and bottom,* kevineats.com

Page 72: *left,* kevineats.com; *right,* Wesley Wong

Page 77: Krissy Lefebvre

Page 82: *left,* Krissy Lefebvre; *right,* Karina Santos

Page 87: Eugene Lee

Page 91: Krissy Lefebvre

Page 98: Eugene Lee

Page 102: Eugene Lee

Page 105: Shayla Deluy

Page 106: kevineats.com

Page 107: Eugene Lee

Page 109: *top,* gastronomyblog.com; *bottom,* kevineats.com

Page 110: weezermonkey.com

Page 122: Eugene Lee

Page 127: *left and right,* kevineats.com

Page 137: kevineats.com

Page 138: *left,* kevineats.com; *right,* Eugene Lee

Page 142: Wesley Wong/eatsmeetwes.com

Page 145: Wesley Wong/eatsmeetwes.com

Page 146: Eugene Lee

Page 147: *top and bottom,* Krissy Lefebvre

Page 149: *left and right,* Eugene Lee

Page 155: Shayla Deluy

Page 158: Wesley Wong/eatsmeetswes.com

Page 161: Wesley Wong/eatsmeetswes.com